Why Do Uzbeks have to be Muslims?

Exploring religiosity in the Ferghana Valley

In Uzbekistan, as everywhere in the former Soviet Union, religion was repressed under socialism. Irene Hilgers outlines the complex dynamics of religiosity in the new situation following independence, focusing on the tight relationship between being Uzbek and being Muslim. Knowledge of Islam declined under socialism, although some were able to reconcile their private faith with Soviet ideals of modernity. After independence, the evolved "lived religion" came under pressure from two sides. While the government reified local Islam as a key component of "tradition" in the new national ideology, conservative and Islamist forces condemned local practices for deviating from what was laid down in the sacred sources and urged a new universalism. In her analysis of the contemporary religious field, Hilgers draws attention to continuities with the socialist era in the way secular authorities undermine constitutional guarantees of freedom of conscience. A nominal pluralism is subverted by a surprising alliance between the state-sponsored muftiate and the Russian Orthodox Church. Both of these established religions have supported the government's measures to tighten the regulation of new religious movements that threaten their hegemony.

After describing these general developments and their specific constellation in Kokand, a city in the Ferghana Valley, Hilgers presents close-up accounts of individual "quests for spirituality". Her subjects exemplify general patterns in the renegotiation of religious selfhood. They include a "cultural Muslim" who remains imbued with the values of the Soviet intelligentsia; a former Communist Party member who was always privately committed to Islam and now engages with it more actively; a young man who has intensified his faith in the Islamist direction; and a woman who has become a born-again Christian. The author places their stories in the context of the "objectification of Islam" worldwide.

The latter chapters consist of a series of ethnographic studies. The first of these explores the discourses surrounding an "Islamic" wedding and explains why these new events are often evaluated critically in the local community. In the second case study, the author narrates a day she spent with a group of female pilgrims at the shrine of a female saint near Kokand. Hilgers shows that shrine veneration practices fuse sacred and profane elements into a satisfying unity for the participants, some of whom make innovative use of this "semi-public" space. In the final substantive chapter, Hilgers investigates a new congregation of Uzbek converts to Christianity, many of whom experience opprobrium within their communities and their families. The popular postulate of congruence between secular (Uzbek) and religious (Islamic) identifications reflects the novelty of this conceptual dichotomy in Central Asia in the postsocialist era. In some cases, however, prejudices could be overcome, and Protestant missionizing continues in spite of governmental repression.

Halle Studies in the Anthropology of Eurasia

General Editors:

Chris Hann, Thomas Hauschild, Richard Rottenburg, Burkhard Schnepel

Volume 22

LIT

Irene Hilgers

Why Do Uzbeks have to be Muslims?

Exploring religiosity in the Ferghana Valley

LIT

Cover Photo: Religious specialist (*Otin-Oyi*) at the shrine of Bibi Ubayda (May 2004) (Photo: Irene Hilgers).

∞

Gedruckt auf alterungsbeständigem Werkdruckpapier entsprechend
ANSI Z3948 DIN ISO 9706

Bibliographic information published by the Deutsche Nationalbibliothek
The Deutsche Nationalbibliothek lists this publication in the Deutsche Nationalbibliografie; detailed bibliographic data are available in the Internet at http://dnb.d-nb.de.

ISBN 978-3-643-10176-1

A catalogue record for this book is available from the British Library

Fresnostr. 2 D-48159 Münster
Tel. +49 (0) 2 51-620 320 Fax +49 (0) 2 51-922 60 99
e-Mail: lit@lit-verlag.de http://www.lit-verlag.de

Distribution:

In Germany: LIT Verlag Fresnostr. 2, D-48159 Münster
Tel. +49 (0) 2 51-620 32 22, Fax +49 (0) 2 51-922 60 99, e-Mail: vertrieb@lit-verlag.de

In Austria: Medienlogistik Pichler-ÖBZ, e-mail: mlo@medien-logistik.at

In Switzerland: B + M Buch- und Medienvertrieb, e-mail: order@buch-medien.ch

In the UK: Global Book Marketing, e-mail: mo@centralbooks.com

In North America by:

Transaction Publishers
New Brunswick (U.S.A.) and London (U.K.)

Transaction Publishers
Rutgers University
35 Berrue Circle
Piscataway, NJ 08854

Phone: +1 (732) 445 - 2280
Fax: + 1 (732) 445 - 3138
for orders (U. S. only):
toll free (888) 999 - 6778
e-mail: orders@transactionpub.com

Contents

List of Illustrations

Map

Plates

Preface

Irene Hilgers was born and raised in Kleve, a small town in West Germany, close to the Dutch border. She studied anthropology initially in Bonn and later in Cologne, where she first became interested in Central Asia. Her master's thesis, based on five months' research in Kyrgyzstan in 1999–2000, was titled "Private Household Economies in Transition". When the Max Planck Institute for Social Anthropology advertised scholarships for a new Focus Group to investigate the changing role of religion in postsocialist "civil society", Hilgers initially submitted a new project for Kyrgyzstan. For the sake of balance in our Central Asia cluster, she agreed to switch to Uzbekistan. She joined our Institute at the beginning of 2003 and, together with two postdoctoral colleagues, carried out fieldwork in Uzbekistan between summer 2003 and summer 2004. That fieldwork provided the empirical basis for this book.

During the writing-up phase back at the Institute, Irene was a creative and cooperative member of the Focus Group whose contributions were also much appreciated in our wider intellectual community in Halle. She made rapid progress on her dissertation, but she was not the sort of scholar who takes shortcuts by squeezing all her data into one safe paradigm. On the contrary, she was adventurous in her reading, always on the lookout for new sources of theoretical inspiration to complement her excellent knowledge of the Area Studies literature on Central Asia. She also returned to gather more data in Uzbekistan for several weeks in summer 2005. When her position at the Max Planck Institute expired, she was supported for a year by the newly established Graduate School at our neighbouring institution, the Martin Luther University. Despite the interdisciplinary temptations of this forum, she continued to focus on her dissertation.

Early in 2008 Irene sent me drafts of her main chapters, minus introduction and conclusion, just before setting off for a short private visit to Tashkent. She did not survive this trip. More than a year later, her death at the age of thirty-three remains unfathomable to us all.

Undoubtedly, this would have been a very different book if Irene had lived to complete her manuscript, defend her dissertation, and then (in the usual pattern with our students) execute a further round of changes before the definitive publication. She would certainly have expanded the opening chapter and written a concluding one. I drafted the present conclusion on the basis of her notes; the paragraphs on the back cover and the inside cover are my summaries, not hers.

Irene's main arguments, however, were sufficiently well developed for me to be able to work through the drafts in order to present the results of her work in book form in this series. Even if her arguments occasionally seem hesitant, uneven, or incomplete, each of the substantive chapters presents rich empirical material, much of which will be useful to other scholars, including those pursuing quite different theoretical agendas from hers. I have stuck close to the texts she sent me but have augmented them occasionally with materials from her personal files and her two published papers (Hilgers 2006, 2007). I have eliminated some repetition, translated occasional phrases from German, and edited for colloquial English, but my intention throughout has been to allow Irene Hilgers to express her own ideas in her own words. Scholars wishing to consult her original texts and data, which include extensive written and visual materials not incorporated into this publication, should apply to the archive of the Max Planck Institute for Social Anthropology.

Raw versions of most of these chapters were discussed in the writing-up seminar that I have convened for many years with Lale Yalçın-Heckmann. Irene benefited greatly from Lale's detailed comments, based on her comparative experience in other Muslim, Turkic, and postsocialist settings. I could not have completed this editorial task without additional help from numerous other colleagues more familiar with Central Asia than I, who have answered specific questions and in several cases cast a constructively critical eye over the entire manuscript. They include many who were regular members of that writing-up seminar, whose own work helped to shape Irene's ideas. Had she lived to prepare a list of acknowledgements, I am sure she would have wished to express her thanks to Ildikó Bellér-Hann, Jeanine Dağyeli, Paweł Jessa, Krisztina Kehl-Bodrogi, Kerstin Klenke, Julie McBrien, Patrick Neveling, Professor Jürgen Paul, Mathijs Pelkmans, Sebastien Peyrouse, Johan Rasanayagam, Paolo Sartori, and Manja Stephan. In Tashkent she would have wished to acknowledge the friendship and help extended by the Hakimjonov family, by her research assistant, who wishes to remain anonymous, and by the staff of the Institut Français d'Études sur l'Asie Centrale, especially Kirill Kuzmin and Ulug'bek Nurmukhamedov. In Kokand, her main field site, her debts were too numerous for me to begin to list them; some of the most important persons figure prominently in the substantive chapters, but names have been altered for the usual reasons.

In the final phase of preparing this book I have been grateful for the help of Jeanine Dağyeli, Kerstin Klenke, and Manja Stephan, friends of Irene whose combined expertise on Central Asia was indispensable in tracing references and quotations and resolving inconsistencies in multiple orthographic minefields. I also thank Berit Westwood and Katharina Wiechmann for their help in working through several versions of the manuscript, and Jane Kepp for her careful copyediting.

No one was closer to Irene Hilgers than Florian Mühlfried. I thank him for meticulously sifting through all of Irene's files, advising me on editorial decisions, making the final selection of illustrations from the many photographs Irene took in the field, and facilitating my work in countless ways. For him, for her family in Kleve, and for all who knew her, the memory of Irene Hilgers will always remain vivid. For everyone else, the following pages will have to suffice.

Chris Hann

Halle, June 2009

Chapter 1
Introduction[1]

Throughout my field research in Uzbekistan in 2003–2004 I noticed that when Uzbeks talked about Islam, they connected it to culture or tradition, *urf-odat*, which they considered to constitute the ultimate basis of their society. They implied that Islam had always been there and was unchanging. At the same time there seemed to be a great lack of consensus about what it meant to be a Muslim in the present and what it should mean for the future. There was much discussion of social conventions, of what should count as proper behaviour for an Uzbek, and of how exactly to locate religious practice both in the past – in the golden, pre-Soviet times – and in the modern age. In short, Islam was the subject of a discourse in which notions of tradition, "Uzbekness", and the modern nation were explicitly negotiated and made concrete.

The term *retraditionalization*, favoured by scholars such as Habiba Fathi (2007), creates the impression that religion and tradition vanished during Soviet times, only to be revived after Uzbek independence. My approach in this study is more complex. I see Islam as subject to continuous and as yet unresolved tensions between "modernization", "traditionalization", and "indigenization". These processes can be traced back in history, and as I show in chapter 2, decisive changes were accomplished in the early decades of the Soviet Union. For this reason it is inadequate to focus on the short period of "post-Soviet transformation"; many of the processes had already been under way for generations (see Abramson 1998). As in the Georgian case analyzed recently by Mathijs Pelkmans (2006), I see the greater salience of Islam in Uzbekistan's Ferghana Valley in recent years as

---

[1] Editor's note: The Introduction and Conclusion were the most fragmentary of all the chapters Irene Hilgers had begun work on at the time of her death. Parts of this Introduction existed in note form only and the final structure was not yet worked out. The author was still immersing herself in the relevant theoretical literature and would undoubtedly have expanded this section considerably. Her outline indicates that she also intended to add a section previewing the arguments of the following chapters. The version offered here draws on additional materials in her files and on Hilgers (2006).

a religious phenomenon not in the narrower sense but in the context of wider struggles within the postsocialist environment that involve the contestation and redefinition of worldviews at multiple levels, from the familial to the national and transnational. As in any other part of the Muslim world, to understand processes of religious change and the nature of the Muslim self, one must supplement micro-level observation with analysis of the larger-scale forces that constrain individual agency (see, e.g. Meneley 1996, 2007, for the case of Yemen).

What are the main distinguishing features of Islam in postsocialist Central Asia? In spite of the differences in their history and environment, much of what Bruce Privratsky has written about Kazakhs applies equally well to their Uzbek neighbours. To identify as a Muslim has little to do with knowledge of dogma:

> Even when our informants could not list the Five Pillars of Islam, they still spoke comfortably and consistently of their "Muslimness", the Muslim way, the experience of Islam that feels like it has always been with them on the Kazak steppe. I thank Kazaks for the distinction between Islam and "Muslimness", which, of course, is already evident in Arabic but becomes very striking in Kazak usage. As I learned the Kazak language, I realized I wanted to study "Muslimness" rather than Islam *per se*. In the West we may yet overcome our stereotypes of Islam if we look more intently at Muslims (Privratsky 2001: 243).[2]

This is exactly the aim of this study: to reveal the processual dynamics that lie behind the image of a static, unchanging Islam held by many locals and Western observers alike.

Main Research Questions: Theoretical and Intellectual Context

My central theoretical question pertains to modernity, not so much as defined in economic or macro-sociological terms but as the subjectively perceived condition of being modern. Such perceptions, as Shalini Randeria

[2] Similar views have been expressed more recently by scholars such as Lukas Werth (2002), Maria Louw (2006, 2007), and Johan Rasanayagam (2007). Louw (2006: 321) makes the point as follows: "I do not find it illuminating to view Central Asian Islam in the Soviet Union as a quasi-primordial defence against modernization. Similarly, I do not subscribe to the argument commonly found in post-Soviet studies which compares how Islam is understood and practiced in the region to some kind of orthodox, 'pure' Islam, concluding that an eradication of knowledge about Islam took place during the Soviet years. While a Muslim believer or Islamic theologian might argue in these terms, I find it much more interesting to bracket questions concerning the status of people's ideas and beliefs relative to some idealised Islamic canon, and instead focus on the ways in which Islam is lived and experienced in practice".

(2004) has shown, are always informed by a variety of regimes of knowledge. I am not interested in locating Uzbeks at a certain point along a teleological trajectory from traditional to modern, but rather in how they themselves make use of such terms, along with others such as *authenticity*, in making sense of who they are in the world. This is the position taken by Talal Asad (1996b: 1): "I think that one needs to recognize that when one talks about tradition, one should be talking about, in a sense, a dimension of social life and not a stage of social development. In an important sense, tradition and modernity are not really two mutually exclusive states of a culture or society but different aspects of historicity".

The literature on modernity is tightly connected to that on secularization. My analysis casts doubt on this often taken-for-granted linkage. Modernity in the Ferghana Valley involves a redefinition of traditional understandings of Muslimness such that the religious identity is fused with the national identity, Uzbek. But this in turn raises the question of what happens when an Uzbek seeks to change his religion? In trying to answer this question, I looked at the wider religious context, paying particular attention to recent conversions to Christianity (see also Hilgers 2007).

We still know very little about how Muslims were affected by Soviet propaganda of scientific atheism and the extent to which they responded by developing an oppositionist consciousness. Much of the Anglophone literature is marred by the bias of what Devin DeWeese has termed "Sovietological Islamology". He defines this as "an approach to Islam in the Soviet context informed more by scholarly expertise in the Soviet system, and in the twentieth-century development of the Soviet-defined 'nations' into which the Muslim communities of the USSR were grouped, than by training in the history or religious culture of the regions of 'Soviet' Islam, let alone of the broader Islamic world" (DeWeese 2002: 298). An influential example of work in this genre is Alexandre Bennigsen and Marie Broxup's book *The Islamic Threat to the Soviet State* (1982).

There is a curious convergence between the "Sovietological" genre and some of the Soviet ethnographic literature on Islam in Soviet Central Asia, which also highlighted a sharp opposition between "survivals" of religion and Soviet modernization (Poliakov 1992). Both sides, the Soviet and the Sovietological, postulated a static notion of "the Muslim community". Both took it for granted that one could not be a full-fledged Soviet citizen – loyal to the Soviet state, integrated socially and culturally into Soviet life – and a believing Muslim at the same time. Rural populations in particular were depicted as immune to the influence of Soviet modernity, their responses shaped by pre-revolutionary values and aspirations. These claims are no more convincing than are contrasting assertions to the effect that Central Asian Muslims were fully divested of their religious identity by the end of the Soviet era (for more balanced summaries of the Soviet legacy, see Shahrani 1995, 2006).

The entire literature on the "anthropology of Islam" (El-Zein 1977; see also Asad 1996a) was long riddled with distorting dichotomies, among which the most enduring has been that between popular (or folk) and high (or orthodox) Islam. This was a variation on the older opposition between the little and great religious traditions, according to which the former was characterized by ecstatic, magical, and mystical practices, the veneration of saints, and a fascination with the miraculous, and the latter was based on scriptural learning and sober performance of canonical duties. Ernest Gellner's well-known model of Muslim society (1981) is a radical version of this dichotomy. The history of the Muslim world, according to this model, consisted of cycles in which high and popular Islam were dominant in turn, until modernization began eroding the social foundations of popular Islam and ushered in an inexorable and irreversible shift towards urban-based, scripturalist, permanently reformed Islam. In a later essay, Gellner (1992) attempted to account for the Islamic resurgence of the 1980s in the light of this model and to explain Islamic scripturalism as a functional equivalent of the secularization that had accompanied modernization in western Europe. The model has been heavily criticized, but its underlying dichotomy, and with it the assumption that popular practices are bound to disappear in the course of modernization, remains highly influential. I, too, am critical, and I do not find Gellner's view helpful in accounting for contemporary beliefs and practices in the Ferghana Valley.

It is also necessary to take into account recent influences from the West and from various parts of the Muslim world and to locate religious globalization (Heelas, Lash, and Morris 1995; Eade and Sallnow 2000) in the wider context of global flows of people, goods, information, and images (Robertson 1992; Lash and Urry 1994; Featherstone, Lash, and Robertson 1995; Waters 1995; Castells 1996; Albrow 1997; Tomlinson 1999). Rather than viewing globalization as accelerating de-traditionalization, in the Uzbek case we must recognize that many actors are trying hard to identify new criteria by which to specify tradition. It is too simple to speak of retraditionalization, for there can be no question of a return to pre-Soviet practices and understandings. We must acknowledge a certain process of individualization, but this is subject to strict constraints. The individual whose religiosity is considered to be "un-Uzbek" is likely to face formal sanctions at the political-ideological level and to be informally ostracized from the community for having affronted its common-sense understanding of "our tradition".

The issue of modernity and secularization in post-Soviet Uzbekistan can be explored through three related questions. How has Islam been used, or instrumentalized, by the state in the course of nation-building? How has ethnic identification become tied to religious affiliation? And how has the religious self changed? In answering the last question, one needs to consider new patterns of individualization, but also the countering factors that constrain individual agency in Uzbek society. The cultivation of a new religious self may bring a new sense of stability and independence when the older system of social existence seems to be falling apart. As my data on conversion reveal, however, Uzbek society provides little opportunity for the development of substantively different identifications. Decisions concerning religiosity are individual, but de facto they are "de-privatized" – not in the sense in which José Casanova (1994) has argued that religious institutions have made inroads into the public sphere, but in the sense that individuals' decisions are treated as a matter of public concern at all levels, from the immediate family to the nation.

The Development of Religious Pluralism in Uzbekistan[3]

In pre-Islamic times, Manichaeism, Zoroastrianism, Nestorian Christianity, and Buddhism were the main religions in Central Asia, existing in parallel with animism. Jewish communities appeared in the region in the first century CE, and significant numbers of Jews settled later in Bukhara and Samarqand. The disunity of political and religious life in the region was a precondition for the Arab invasion and the Islamization of the local population, which began in the seventh century. At first rejected by the local people, Islam became in the eighth century the main religious doctrine in the territory of present-day Uzbekistan and the spiritual-ideological and legislative foundation of the region.

On the initiative of the Russian empress Catherine the Great (r. 1762–1796), a wave of settlers from Germany and the Baltic moved into the historic region of Turkistan. The majority of the settlers were German Lutherans, Mennonites, and Baptists. In the second part of the nineteenth century, Christianity spread in the region, due to the expanding power of the Russian monarchy there. In 1871 the eparchy of the Russian Orthodox Church and the Central Asian bishopric were established in Tashkent. Around that time, members of the Baha'i faith, persecuted in Persia, sought refuge in Turkistan and established their first small communities. The first Armenian Apostolic church was inaugurated in 1903. Tsarist rule in Turkistan interfered little

[3] Editor's note: This section and the following two have been taken with only minimal changes from Hilgers (2006). More historical detail is provided in the following chapter.

with the religious practices of local Muslims (Bacon 1966: 111), but the religious contest manifested itself in a political power struggle between the Muslim Central Asian khanate and Orthodox tsarist Russia, and religion became important in Central Asian–Russian affairs of state (Allworth 1999: 3). The era of Russian colonialism in Turkistan was marked in its final decades by an emerging schism among Muslim intellectuals – between conservative "traditionalists", the so-called *qadimchilar*, or Qadimis (from Arab. *qadīm*, old), and local Muslim reformers, the so-called Jadids (from Arab. *ǧadīd*, new) (see Abduvakhitov 1996).[4]

The situation in the religious sphere changed dramatically after the October Revolution in 1917 and the Bolsheviks' rise to power. Anti-religious policies and the propagation of atheism were launched in the mid-1920s, and religious life was increasingly banned from the public sphere (Northrop 2004). Although atheism was the norm, the Soviet government made minor concessions to "indigenous faiths", which included Russian Orthodoxy, mainstream Islam, Judaism, and Buddhism. All other denominations, such as the charismatic Protestant denominations, Pentecostalists, Hare Krishnas, Jehovah's Witnesses, Baha'is, and certain Islamic movements or associations, were treated as "sects" or "cults". These terms always had strong negative connotations, implying the cult-like, "possessed" behaviour of believers and their blind obedience to religious doctrine. Both leaders and followers of such communities experienced discrimination and persecution by state authorities (Anderson 2002: 182; Peyrouse 2003; for the case of Ukraine, cf. Wanner 2003: 284).

Because of anti-religious propaganda and repression by the Soviet regime, some religious groups, such as the Baha'is, completely ceased their corporate religious activities, and their religious knowledge came to be transferred only at the individual level. Other congregations continued practising as underground churches or even openly in their old church build-

---

[4] The Jadids, whose ideas spread to Central Asia from the Russian Empire in the late nineteenth century, sought to reform teaching in the Islamic elementary religious schools (*maktabs*) by introducing new teaching methods and new subjects such as geography and mathematics. Jadidism is commonly defined as a manifestation of Islamic reformism, but it is more accurate to see it as a form of Islamic modernism (see Khalid 1998; Frank 2001). The key figure was Ismail Gasprinskiy (1851–1914), a Crimean Tatar intellectual, politician, publisher, and one of the founders of the Union of Muslims (İttifaq-i Müslümanlar) in 1907. The union's aim was to unite the intelligentsia of the Muslim Turkic peoples of the Russian Empire. Gasprinskiy called for solidarity among Turkic peoples and advocated their modernization through Europeanization. With the coming to power of the Bolsheviks, some Jadids initially supported communist ideals. In the Great Purge, the Bolsheviks targeted the Jadids as enemies of the state. Most of them were killed, imprisoned, or sent to labour camps (see Carrère d'Encausse 1981; Khalid 1998; Bergne 2003). The schism between the Jadids and the traditionalists is discussed further in chapter 3.

ings, if those were not destroyed or transformed into workshops or storehouses.

The Soviet government's anti-religion policies led to a weakening of the structures of religious institutions but could not erase religious practices and community life completely. On the contrary, the deportations and labour migrations under Stalin and Khrushchev in the 1950s and 1960s brought increasing religious diversity to the Soviet Republic of Uzbekistan. The first adherents of charismatic Protestant movements such as the Full Gospel Church, Pentecostal churches, Seventh-Day Adventists, and Jehovah's Witnesses came into the region during those decades (Peyrouse 2004a). Religious life and the transmission of knowledge were restricted under Soviet policy largely to the levels of families and religious communities. Especially for members of ethnic minorities, closed religious communities based on ethnicity were vehicles for maintaining knowledge about culture and language, transmitting that knowledge to the next generation, and avoiding the loss of ethnic characteristics (Peyrouse 2004b).

The first liberalizations in the sphere of religion were introduced in the Soviet Union by the reforms of perestroika in the mid-1980s. The community lives of religious groups were revived, and people could once again enact their beliefs in public. In addition to the internal restructuring of local religious community life, faith communities from abroad began to support their Central Asian co-religionists with financial and material help and sent representatives to the ex-Soviet countries to help establish new congregations. New foreign-based faith communities opened centres in the country as well, among them the International Society for Krishna Consciousness (ISKCON), the Mormons, and various charismatic and Pentecostal Christians. After Uzbekistan declared independence in 1991, this trend towards diversification in its religious landscape increased rapidly. Soon afterwards, foreign-based religious communities such as the American Baptist and Jewish associations began encouraging their believers in postsocialist countries to migrate to the United States or Israel.[5]

These developments in the religious sector intensified further with the adoption of Uzbekistan's new law on religion in 1992. Largely modelled on the last version of the Soviet law (Anderson 2002: 184), it guaranteed freedom of religion and the right to establish religious organizations. The newly independent Republic of Uzbekistan defined itself as a secular state with no official state religion, but it retained control over the religious sector. Religious groups and organizations were allowed to operate provided their objectives and doctrines did not run contrary to the legislation, did not

[5] Personal communication with Baptists and Jews in Tashkent, Kokand, and Bukhara, 2003.

threaten security, and would not provoke ethnic, social, or inter-confessional conflicts.[6] In response to the increasing activities of radical Islamic groups, government authorities undertook a major clampdown on political and "unofficial" Islam, including a wave of mosque closures and arrests of individual believers accused of being "Wahhabis".[7] In May 1998 the parliament revised the 1992 Law on Freedom of Conscience and Religious Organizations to impose new restrictions on religious groups, as I describe in chapter 2.

The government's stated reason for increasing its control over and restrictions on religious groups was that these measures were necessary to fight terrorism and radical Islamic movements. But the measures were also aimed at limiting the missionary activities of religious groups within the local Uzbek population. When I asked about the reasons for such laws, the chief expert in the Department of Confessions of the State Committee of Religious Affairs explained that the original concern was that religious conversions might lead to tensions within Uzbek society:

> So among the ordinary Uzbek people there is absolutely no idea about Christianity. No one knows what a church is like on the street, and if someone says that there are Uzbeks in it, they will ask why. It might bring bad consequences. In order to prevent this, explanatory work is to be implemented. The church itself possesses no bad characteristics – it also calls to the unity with God, makes people believe in religion, leads to goodness. But in some places, some representatives of the local population become members of churches, and instead of helping that church, they render more harm to it. If an Uzbek becomes a member of a church, he will promote it to other Uzbeks with the claim that nothing bad happened to him after his conversion. And an opposite reaction will be caused by the other people: those people will say that this person went astray and is trying to drag others from Islam to his way of belief, and people will say that the church is bad. So the missionary activity is the worst characteristic of such churches. Once you have accepted religion, you should not propagate it to others; it is your personal thing, which should remain with you. [Otherwise] bad events might happen. This is the same with Wahhabism, which is one of the branches of Islam,

[6] Articles 4 and 5 of the Constitution of the Republic of Uzbekistan, version 1998.

[7] The term Wahhabi is used loosely in Uzbekistan to denote any "religious extremists" of whom the state disapproves. There is no direct link to the movement of this name that originated in Saudi Arabia. Rasanayagam (2006a) describes in detail how the term Wahhabi, on the one hand, is associated with fear of state sanctions while, on the other, it can be a tool in personal conflicts. See also the chapters by McBrien and Stephan in the same volume.

> or the basic religion of Saudi Arabia. It is not bad, but the actions of some of the representatives of this branch led to accusations against the whole religion. …
>
> After seventy years of atheism, a lot of people suffered from irreligiosity and stood in hesitation, and then the pastors started to come, and no one could distinguish whether these were good religions or not. Those missionaries were using the moment of material and spiritual difficulties [for their own purposes].

The chief expert's concern about foreign-based religious communities that were abusing the current situation of social and economic insecurity represented a broader concern in society about the tensions that might result from a growing number of conversions away from Islam.

Defining the Uzbek Muslim

Although Uzbekistan is a secular state, it grants Islam a special role in nation-building. As part of its ideology for legitimating and consolidating the Uzbek nation-state, the government stresses the region's Islamic history and heritage and the Hanafi school of Sunni Islam as the foundation of Uzbek culture and tradition. Islam is framed as an important marker for Uzbek national identity, something that shapes the nation's social organization and gives it a moral and ethical framework.

Islam Karimov, who became president of Uzbekistan in 1990, when it was still a republic of the Soviet Union, and was elected as first president of the independent state in December 1991, promotes a "cultural" or "civil" Islam, emphasizing the tradition of religious tolerance, which is presented as a special characteristic of the local interpretation of Islam (State Committee of Religious Affairs 2004). This view refers back to the region's multi-religious, pre-Soviet past and is legitimated by the writing of a specifically national history, the rehabilitation of Islamic intellectuals and the Islamic tradition, and the elimination of most vestiges of the Russian colonial and Soviet religious eras (see Melvin 2000; March 2002).[8] Local practices such as shrine veneration and Sufism are integral parts of the official definition of a nationalized, "Uzbek" Islam.

In defining and propagating a so-called enlightened and peaceful Islam, the government aims to counter radical Islamist notions and to consolidate a collective national Uzbek identity by emphasizing the common good (State Committee of Religious Affairs 2004). Through public speeches, the

[8] March (2002: 379) described this manipulation of Uzbek history to favour the legitimation of the independent Uzbek nation-state as "Uzbekifying Islamic history and Islamifying Karimovism".

state-controlled media, slogans on billboards, and the teaching of subjects such as "spirituality and enlightenment" in schools, the government spreads its view of what constitutes "Uzbekness" (*o'zbekchilik*) and "Muslimness" (*musulmonchilik*). By clearly communicating its concepts of Uzbek tradition and culture, the "typical Uzbek mentality", and proper Uzbek religious practice, the government defines what is acceptable and creates the parameters of legitimate behaviour. Religious behaviour that transgresses this framework is deemed a threat to the stability and democracy of the country and therefore, in Karimov's rhetoric, must be regulated and controlled (see Karimov 1997).

Even without the government's presentation of Islam as an inevitable product of Uzbek history and cultural life, the notion that Islam forms an important part of people's sense of community and culture appears to be deeply internalized. Ethnic Uzbeks and non-Uzbeks alike often told me that "Uzbeks have to be Muslims" or "Uzbeks are Muslims". Among Uzbek Muslims, leaving Islam is one of the worst sins an Uzbek can commit – not only in terms of religious doctrine but also as a sin committed against the Uzbek nation, traditions, and culture. Uzbeks who convert to other religions are accused of having betrayed their nation and their ancestors, and their decision often comes with high social costs. The majority of Uzbek converts I met had experienced rejection by their families, friends, and neighbours after confessing their new belief, and many had experienced persecution by the Uzbek National Security Service (known as the SNB, the acronym of its Russian name, Sluzhba Natsional'noy Bezopasnosti). Uzbek society exerts tight social control, and individual behaviour perceived as "not Uzbek" is socially penalized.

Such social penalties apply not only to Uzbeks who turn away from Islam but also to those who orient themselves towards scriptural interpretations of Islam. Uzbek Muslims who reject and criticize local Islamic practices and dress codes as being "not Islamic" risk being stigmatized as Wahhabi or extremist (see Babadjanov 1999). The term Wahhabi, usually understood as referring to a group of orthodox Sunnis that is dominant in Saudi Arabia, was used in the Soviet period as shorthand for Islamic fundamentalism. Its meaning has been broadened in the official usage of the government of independent Uzbekistan to refer to religious expression or behaviour that departs from official government definitions or is perceived by Uzbek Muslims as inappropriate. The label is applied to members of radical Islamic movements and to devoted individual believers, as well as to believers in proselytizing religious movements such as the Full Gospel and Jehovah's Witnesses.

Traditional versus Non-traditional Religion

In introducing measures to limit the activities of religious organizations in Uzbekistan, the government was also reacting to pressure from so-called traditional religions. The overwhelming majority of citizens in Uzbekistan, 92.46 per cent, are Muslims. The Russian Orthodox Church, with 4.89 per cent of the citizenry, follows as the second largest faith.[9] Islam and Russian Orthodoxy claim supremacy on the religious scene in Uzbekistan and claim themselves to be the traditional religions of the country. They legitimate this claim in terms of their long-standing roots in the territory and their large numbers of adherents of specific ethnicity, among whom religious affiliation is automatically passed on to the next generation.

Because of their large numbers of adherents – both active and nominal believers – and their power and authority in the region, Islam and the Russian Orthodox Church are becoming political players in Uzbekistan, calling for the promotion of their interests by the government. In October 1995 the Muslim Board of Uzbekistan (O'zbekiston Musulmonlari Idorasi) and the metropolitan of Tashkent jointly demanded, during a conference, that the government implement measures to constrain and control the activities of religious movements declared illegitimate for not being traditional in the region (see Peyrouse 2004b). The initial reason for their demand was the decline in membership the Russian Orthodox Church was experiencing because of the growing number of conversions from Orthodoxy to new, non-traditional religions, especially to the charismatic branches of Protestantism. The Muslim authorities shared this concern, even though the number of conversions from Islam to other religions was much smaller. Their greater concern was the potential attraction of Muslims to politically motivated Islamic movements such as Hizb ut-Tahrir and the Islamic Movement of Uzbekistan.

Although the main players in pressuring the government for stricter regulation and control were the ulema (Uzb., *ulamo*), or scholars of Islam, and the clergy of the Russian Orthodox Church, other deeply rooted groups in the country claiming to be traditional religions, such as the Roman Catholic Church, the German Lutherans, the Armenian Church, and the Jews, joined in urging the government to take measures against the "sects". At a conference on inter-confessional tolerance organized by the Tashkent Islamic University and the State Committee of Religious Affairs in November 2003, representatives of the traditional churches emphasized that they considered it obligatory to respect and tolerate different religious beliefs. They

---

[9] Statistics on the religious affiliations of the population of Uzbekistan were provided by the Council for Religious Affairs, Tashkent, 2003.

took exception to the missionary activity of other faiths because they saw it as a violation of such respect and tolerance.

Differentiating between legitimate and illegitimate religions and labelling non-traditional religious organizations "sects" and "cults" in a strongly negative sense is common in the rhetoric of representatives of traditional religions in Uzbekistan. Most members of the religious elite subscribe to this view and openly propagate it in their preaching, at conferences, and in the media. The muftiate of Tashkent, together with government institutions, issues spots on state-controlled television in which Muslims are reminded of their duty to attend to the religious education of their children. These spots show pictures of "Islamic extremists" – sinister-looking people wearing beards who seduce young people with their ideology and money – but they are also directed against the new, foreign-based religious organizations.

The traditional religions in Uzbekistan, motivated by the desire to maintain their supremacy and prevent losses of their adherents, have served as potent allies to the government, which is motivated by its desire to consolidate its legitimacy and keep the influence of international organizations weak. Together they have supported laws intended to control and restrict the activities of non-traditional religions. Yet when individual believers or religious communities experience limits on their religious freedom, they do not accuse the state directly as the agent of the limitation. Instead, they typically refer to individual bureaucrats who use their executive power to restrict or reshape religious practices or adherents they perceive as wrong. And indeed, when the laws themselves are unclear, administrators can easily claim to have legal grounds for expressing their personal opinions and stances on certain issues.[10] They act not on the basis of individual interests alone but within a larger socio-economic matrix. Officials supposed to represent the state discourse are in practice entangled in social (or, as believers, in religious) norms and values and are always under informal pressure to fulfil social obligations and expectations.

The Region and the Field Methods

With nearly 28 million people, Uzbekistan has by far the largest population of the post-Soviet Central Asian republics. All religious organizations and the religious institutions of the state are based in Tashkent, the capital, and my exploratory work there, together with shorter trips to Samarqand and

---

[10] This observation was confirmed in conversations throughout my fieldwork with local lawyers, journalists, and specialists from international organizations such as the Organization for Security and Co-operation in Europe (OSCE), Human Rights Watch, and UNESCO. For further details, see Human Rights Watch 2004.

Bukhara, gave me useful insights into rural-urban differences and the country's considerable regional diversity. It is widely acknowledged that religiosity is much more salient in Ferghana, an administrative subdivision in eastern Uzbekistan (as well as a valley and a city), than at the opposite end of the country, in the administrative subdivision of Khorezm (Kleinmichel 2001, vol. 1; Kehl-Bodrogi 2008).

After an initial stay in Tashkent, I moved to the city of Kokand in the Ferghana Valley for the bulk of my fieldwork. Kokand had a population of approximately 200,000 persons at the time of my work, of whom the overwhelming majority were Uzbek. Each neighbourhood, or *mahalla* (the smallest administrative unit), typically possessed its own small mosque and a range of religious specialists and healers. I found, however, that many urban residents in both of my main field sites practised their religion in multiple locations, inside and outside their immediate neighbourhoods. My study thus proceeded at the level of the whole city rather than of a particular *mahalla*.

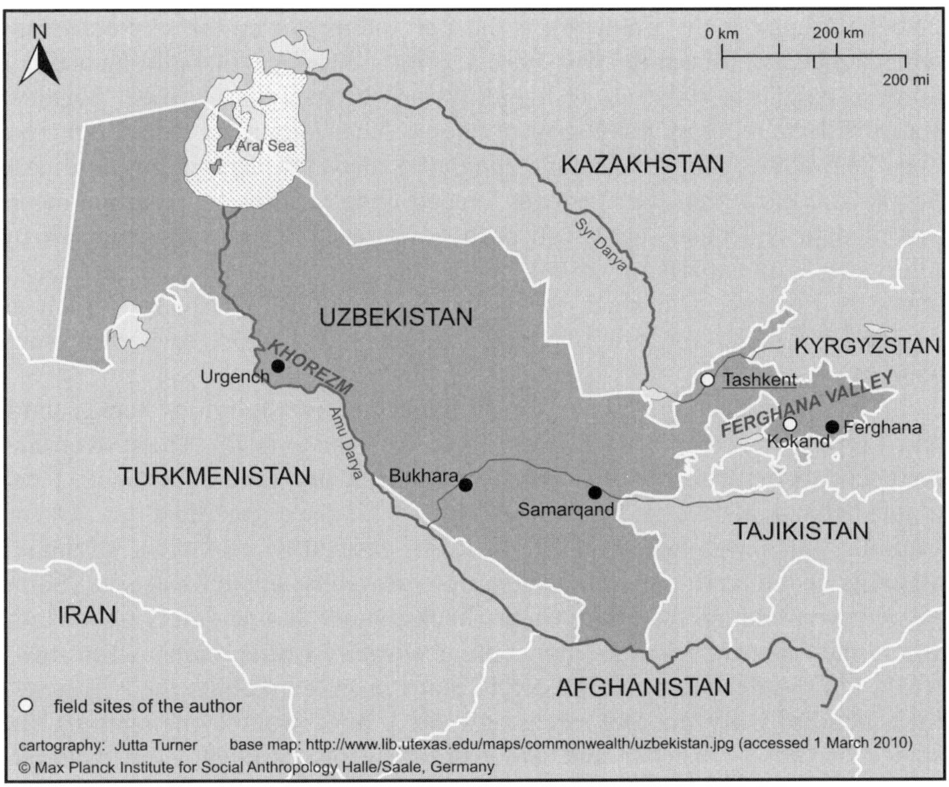

Map 1. The research area.

Aided in both Tashkent and Kokand by a research assistant, I had little difficulty in gaining access to people and establishing social networks. I was well aware of the sensitivity of my topic, but to my surprise, I encountered no problems in moving between the different religious groups. When I explained that I was interested in Uzbek customs and what it meant to be an Uzbek, people responded readily by giving their own views about *o'zbekchilik* and *musulmonchilik*. They were also willing to comment on radical religion, although many were uncertain how the government distinguished between extremist and normal manifestations of Islam. People talked about religion all the time – on the streets, in shared taxis, and at all kinds of festive gatherings. This talk, however, was strongly inflected by the government's propaganda, and when conducting interviews I sometimes had the feeling I was being fed official policy rather than what the person really thought.

Thanks to my prior knowledge of Kyrgyz and to intensive language training in Uzbek after my arrival in Tashkent, I was able to communicate in Uzbek throughout my fieldwork (I used an interpreter on the rare occasions when I needed Russian). This was a great advantage in building trust. I allowed people to elaborate at length on any themes they wished, however statistically unrepresentative their opinions. A questionnaire would not have been helpful and might well have generated suspicion, among both ordinary people and the authorities. Instead, I relied upon informal, qualitative methods of data collection, above all participant observation, supplemented by interviews with experts in various fields. Access to archival materials was in any case difficult, and since the accuracy of published materials such as newspaper articles often left much to be desired, I chose to neglect such sources.

Many Uzbeks were keen to ask about my own religious background, and a few followed up with attempts to convert me to Islam. These overtures were not difficult to handle. When pressed on my religious stance, I explained that I had been "socialized" as a Christian, specifically a Roman Catholic, but I was not an active believer. Instead of provoking strenuous attempts to convert me, this confession generally elicited respect. Some people even told me that, with such a background, I could surely understand where they themselves stood concerning religion. I often emphasized that I was a PhD student, genuinely keen to learn from them about their lives and their beliefs. Only on rare occasions did I have trouble maintaining the stance of passive listener and concealing my own values – for example, when a girl told me in all seriousness that her neighbour was the devil incarnate, and when listening to discussions of homosexuality. Contrary to some pervasive stereotypes, I experienced no difficulties with Uzbek men.

Different communities perceived me in different ways. If most Muslim interlocutors saw me as a "cultural" Christian, the equivalent of a cultural Muslim, then Christians could interact with me as one of them, since I had been baptized and had a Christian background. The smaller Baha'i and Krishna communities perhaps hoped that the more I learned about their religion, the more likely I would be to adopt it; but they never attempted active proselytizing. For a few people, the mere fact that I was interested in religion was enough to lead to suspicion of concealed missionary ambitions on my part. I did indeed have contact with Christian missionaries, but I was careful never to allow myself to be instrumentalized by these foreigners.

Finally, some readers may be surprised by one glaring omission in this study. Sufism has a great tradition in Uzbekistan in general, and in Kokand in particular. Although it influences many rituals, such as the saint veneration that I discuss in chapter 6, I do not address Sufism directly. I simply did not come into much contact with members of Sufi orders (*tariqa*s) in Uzbekistan, and Sufism was scarcely mentioned by the people with whom I did interact. It follows that the emphasis of this study is not on the mystical side of Islam. This should not be taken to mean that I underestimate the significance of the mystical and the spiritual in religious experience. Again, Privratsky's conclusion concerning the superficially very different case of the Kazakhs is relevant:

> If the Kazak case demonstrates one thing about religion, it is that Muslims are energized as much by a longing to touch the world of spirit (*ruh*) as by a need for the social way of religious law (*din*). For this reason, I have not limited myself to the political economy of religion, which turns Islam into a social process without residue. At every turn I have looked as squarely as I could at religious experience, risking the twin objections that as an ethnographer I cannot claim access to the experience of the other, and that as a Christian I cannot possibly know the experience of a Muslim. There was, however, no alternative, because no one had yet described in a Western language the Muslim spirituality that Kazaks had been assumed to lack. Kazak religion had been denied its integrity (Privratsky 2001: 260).

Chapter 2
Ideology and Policy towards Religion: An Historical Overview

> We aim to live according to our sacred religion and national identity, while modernizing our country on the basis of the principles of democracy and the achievements of science and technology.
>
> – Islam Karimov, *Alloh qalbimizda, yuragimizda*

It is impossible to write about Islam in Central Asia without taking careful account of its historical background. In this chapter I describe the ideological and legislative frames surrounding the attempts of both Soviet and post-Soviet governments to define the role of religion in Uzbek society. Socialism and its associated ideals of progress, education, and civilization unquestionably left strong imprints on people's worldviews and their perceptions of traditions, rituals, and what it means to be religious. During my fieldwork I found that people often invoked the Soviet period, with its policies and ideology, as a point of reference when trying to explain the particularities of religious life in present-day Uzbek society. Although scholars still dispute the extent to which socialist ideology penetrated everyday life, socialist institutions and regulations designed to promote a consciousness of "Soviet man" and eradicate the "survivals of a feudal past" shaped the conditions of possibility within which people could express their faith (DeWeese 2002).

Much the same can be said about the independent state of Uzbekistan, which replaced the former ideological framework with a new one focused on the idea of an Uzbek nation-state. The extensive comparative literature on national identity is highly relevant here. In constructing a new national identity, the Uzbek state reactivated pre-socialist symbols and values, among which locally "authentic" religion came to be central to the imagination of a unified statehood (see Kaschuba 2001). The new identity had to be created by elites through historical myths of ethnic descent and community, in the propagation of which a common religion was a most powerful resource for the putative nation (Smith 2000).

Between Fear and Favour: Soviet Policies towards Islam, 1917–1985

Soon after taking power in Russia after the 1917 Revolution, Lenin openly demonstrated his hostility to the church by passing the "Decree on the Separation of the Church from the State and the School from the Church". The Bolsheviks targeted the Russian Orthodox Church as a pillar of tsarist Russia (Bourdeaux and Popescu 2006). Secularization was a basic tenet of their political program from the beginning (see Powell 1977). They employed the power of the Soviet state to realize their revolutionary objectives and implement Marxist-Leninist ideology. The ultimate objective was to free the new Soviet society of negative traits such as individualism, bourgeois nationalism, chauvinism, indolence, religious prejudices, and superstition. The ideal citizen of the new era, "Homo Sovieticus", was supposed to be infused with proletarian internationalism, collectivism, socialist patriotism, love of labour, and militant atheism. Religion was deemed to be a "spiritual creed", "a hangover from the pre-socialist past", and a "mere survival doomed to disappear" (Powell 1977: 137). It was incompatible with Marxism-Leninism and therefore had to be overcome (Erşahin 2005: 4).

Although Marx's slogan declaring religion to be the "opiate of the people" was always upheld ideologically, and the active promotion of scientific atheism was never abjured, in practice policies were less consistent than the official program pretended. Soviet policies oscillated between "fear and favour" (Shahrani 1995: 277; see also Bennigsen and Lemercier-Quelquejay 1967; Krämer 2002, Khalid 1998, 2003). Although all religions were targeted, Islam was from the beginning of the incorporation of Muslim Turkistan into the Soviet Union represented as the most conservative, reactionary, and least "social" of all religions, for it was thought to imbue its followers with values of fanaticism, intolerance, and xenophobia. Muslim morals were seen as contradicting communist morals; the latter propounded a vision of friendship between different peoples of the Soviet Union, whereas Islam asserted a fundamental divide between believers and infidels. Moreover, Islam was perceived to be the basis of a feudal, backward, and even primitive society with no potential to evolve and progress, and therefore no place in an advanced Soviet socialist society (Erşahin 2005: 4). It was necessary to overcome these feudal structures by instigating a class struggle in the Muslim societies. The Soviet powerholders aimed at the systematic destruction of Islam and traditional Muslim social institutions and political culture in Central Asia, replacing them with the new Soviet socialist ideology and political culture (Simon 1986: 113; Shahrani 1995: 277).

The anti-Islamic propaganda of the first years of Soviet rule had to be reconciled with the Communist Party's promise that "non-Russian cultures should flower". It was "very important that anti-religious workers find some way to show that one could be a good Marxist-Leninist and still enjoy nonreligious national customs and pride" (Keller 2001a: 326). The twelfth congress of the All-Union Communist Party (Bolshevik), in 1923, decided to implement a form of anti-religious propaganda based on patient, long-term educational strategies to convince the Soviet people of the lies and contradictions inherent in all religions (Keller 2001a). But early Soviet efforts to eradicate Islam without attacking ethno-national identity were a failure. The Soviets simply did not appreciate the extent to which Islam in Central Asian was intertwined with the total collective identifications of the Muslim Turkic populations, precluding any easy separation between sacred and secular or between religious and national (see Keller 2001a, 2001b; Sengupta 2003: 190).

By 1927 the party had recognized that patient propaganda alone was not working and mounted an open assault against Islam (Shahrani 1995; Khalid 1998, 2003; Keller 2001a, 2001b). Even before this, the revenues of the pious foundations (*waqf*) were diverted to the commissariat for education, and numerous elementary religious schools (*maktab*s) and advanced religious schools (madrasas) had been closed (Krämer 2002: 58ff.; Khalid 2003: 577). The measures taken against Islam reached a first peak at the end of the decade after Stalin eliminated his rivals in Moscow. Members of the ulema were killed or sent to labour camps, the nationalization of religious foundations continued, and mosques and madrasas were closed. The buildings, if they were not destroyed, were adapted for other purposes, becoming warehouses, stables, and workshops. Only the historically most important edifices were preserved as "architectural monuments" (Zarcone 2002: 136; Khalid 2003: 577). Soviet Muslims' links to the wider Muslim world were cut off, a rupture that was reinforced linguistically by the alphabet reform. The replacement of Arabic script with the Cyrillic alphabet denied future generations access to Islamic literary traditions (Shahrani 1995: 278).

The principal symbol of the aggressive new policy towards Islam was the *hujum* – the "storming" or "assault". Launched in 1927, this campaign targeted all traditional social practices deemed to oppress women, such as arranged marriages of underage girls, brideprice, and, of course, the most visible symbol, the veil. By liberating women from patriarchal structures, the Soviets attempted to rescue women from the seclusion (*purdah*) of the household and to integrate them into the labour market and the party (Roy 2000: 79; Keller 2001b; Northrop 2004). Although neighbouring Muslim countries were also affected, the *hujum* was carried out principally in Uzbekistan, the republic that held the traditional centres of Islam in the region and had the largest population.

This assault by the Communist Party proved to be counterproductive. The Muslim population perceived it as an attack on their local traditions and way of life, and the customs attacked became highly valued markers of local identity. The campaign may even have led to an increased identification with Islamic symbols and practices.[11] Laws drafted to ban practices such as polygamy, the payment of brideprice, and the marriage of underage girls proved ineffective; people could easily find ways to circumvent them, often supported indirectly by the "ignorance" of local government administrators and judges (Rasanayagam 2006a). For instance, the *paranji,* the enveloping garment worn by Uzbek women, covering the face, was viewed as an element of local custom, and many women continued to wear it in public.[12] Legally, all public expressions of religion, including prayers, religious education, and ritual performances, were prohibited until the end of World War II. Of course religious practices did not disappear completely overnight, but this legislation gave the authorities the power to arrest, try, and sentence people for "crimes of custom" (Shahrani 1995: 277).

The entry of the Soviet Union into World War II in 1941 led to a further turn in Soviet policies towards Islam and religion in general. The stance became more accommodating in order to gain popular support for the war effort. Concessions were made to gain the support of the local ulema. In 1943, the Spiritual Directorate of the Muslims of Central Asia (SADUM) was established in Tashkent, along with two other regional boards, one in Baku, for the Caucasus, and the other in Ufa, for Inner Russia and Siberia. The Muslim spiritual boards, formally independent and self-governing organizations, were placed in charge of the registration of mosques and imams, the training of imams, and matters of religious dogma within their jurisdictions.

In the postwar decades, SADUM became the most important Islamic institution in the USSR and the only one endowed with its own publishing facilities. After the reopening of the Mir-i Arab madrasa in Bukhara in 1946, the muftiate of Tashkent became (alongside the muftiate of Kazan) the

---

[11] For overviews, see Khalid (1998: 576); Northrop (2004); Saroyan (1997a, 1997b). The literature on the *hujum* in Uzbekistan and its implications for women is large; see also Kamp (1998); Keller (2001a, 2001b); Massell (1974). For a study of the dynamics of national and religious awareness among Uzbek elites as a reaction to the Soviet policies of this period, see Alimova (2004).

[12] Veiling was prohibited by law in Uzbekistan only in 1951, after which it could be punished with fines and even prison. Until 1951 women could still wear the *paranji* in public, especially in rural areas, without risking serious consequences, depending on the attitude taken by local government officials.

leading centre for Islamic education in the USSR. The Soviet government viewed the mufti of Tashkent as the principal channel for propagating its views among all the Sunni Muslims of Soviet Central Asia, who made up more than 75 per cent of the entire Muslim population of the Soviet Union. The mufti was also called upon to represent Soviet Islam to the outside Muslim world (Roy 2000: 79; Erşahin 2005).[13] With the creation of these "religious administrations", which divided Islam geographically and created a politically docile and loyal Muslim establishment, the Soviet government aspired to control the activities of radical-conservative and anti-Soviet elements more effectively (Saroyan 1997a; Erşahin 2005: 3).

The general approach to Islam in the postwar era emphasized the idea of enlightenment: through processes of social modernization and education, people would realize the backwardness of religion and become good socialist citizens (Rorlich 1991; Akiner 1996; Krämer 2002). Soviet schools and the mass media were the main channels for disseminating anti-religious propaganda and Marxist-Leninist dogma (Powell 1977; Keller 2001a, 2001b). This period of mild accommodation was interrupted by a further bout of repression under Khrushchev, culminating in the early 1960s. The new hard line towards Islam must be seen in the context of rising nationalism in the Soviet republics (Krämer 2002: 62).

In the Brezhnev era (1964–1982), although the ideology remained in place and manifestations of religious life beyond the parameters set by the state could lead to sanctions, a more moderate stance was practised once again, and further concessions were made (Anderson 2002). The journal *Muslims of the Soviet East,* founded in 1968 and published in Russian, English, French, Arabic, and Uzbek, explored issues pertaining to "Soviet Islam" throughout the USSR. The Imam al-Bukhari Islamic Institute, an institution of higher Islamic studies, was opened in Tashkent in 1971, underlining the privileged position of Uzbekistan within the Soviet Union as a centre for Islamic education. Although nominally independent like the Muslim spiritual boards, the institute found its activities strictly monitored by the communist authorities.

The combined effect of the rise of Islamic movements in the Middle East, the Iranian revolution of 1979, and the Afghanistan war of 1979–1989 was to make the Soviet government aware that Islam might potentially evolve into an internal security problem for the USSR (Rashid 2003). Even before the last two of these events, the new Constitution of 1977 introduced a shift from "anti-religious" to "atheistic" propaganda. This policy looked

[13] Traditionally, the authority of a mufti, a Muslim scholar able to issue legal opinions, derived from his reputation for learning and piety. In modern times, states have often turned the office of mufti into a formal post, as Uzbekistan has done.

forward to an elimination of both religion and (regional) nationalism, and it marked the beginning of a further crackdown on Islam. For example, female religious specialists (*otin-oyi*) were presented on television and mocked for the backwardness of their practices (Krämer 2002: 65). Observation by the KGB, media denunciations, the detention of Muslims, and the welter of atheistic propaganda combined to frighten people and to displace religious practices into clandestine spaces. This marginalization of religion, however, led to a heightened awareness of ethno-national identifications (Rorlich 1991).

Despite these fluctuations in religious policies, the dominant trend in the later decades of the USSR can be summarized as co-option. With the progressive transformation of Central Asia's Muslim society, Soviet power-holders sought increasingly to collaborate with influential religious figures (Sartori 2007). Thus an Islamic judicial institution was placed under the control of local leaders, a typically colonial measure. Although short-lived, this collaboration nonetheless had long-term consequences in that it allowed the ulema to exercise religious authority in a cultural environment that was increasingly threatened by the spread of militant atheism.

While conceding a certain scope for the active continuation of religious life, Soviet rulers severely constrained the diversity of the ulema and the "conditions of possibility" of Islam in general by introducing the dichotomy of "official" versus "unofficial" ulema. The former consisted of state-approved mullahs and imams, who had graduated from the Soviet institutions of Islamic education and were considered loyal to the Soviet state. The latter were Islamic specialists who had not received their religious education from a state institution and had no legal status. Unofficial Islam became a catchall for all the negative aspects ascribed to Islam in Soviet rhetoric, including the attributes of being backward, superstitious, pre-modern, incapable of progress, and even anti-Soviet and extremist (Saroyan 1997c: 104). Official mullahs and imams were instrumentalized to support and legitimate the policies of the USSR and to guard against the dangers of theological revivalism or any reformist currents that might threaten state controls (Roy 2000: 53). It was of course known that the activities of the unofficial Islamic specialists continued.[14] But the official ulema were expected to present the

[14] In addition to unregistered mullahs and imams, I include in this category female Islamic specialists such as *otin-oyi*s, shrine custodians, and *eshons* (Sufi masters or members of religious families whose genealogies refer to a local saint, the Prophet's family, or a follower of the Prophet). Most of these obtained their knowledge in pre-Soviet times or, during the Soviet era, by self-study or under the clandestine supervision of other religious specialists. See the studies of Fathi (2004) and Krämer (2002) on female religious specialists for examples of the way religious knowledge was passed down to the next generations outside the state-controlled institutions.

USSR to the outside world as a showcase of communist economic achievements in which Islam, too, was prospering through the creation of a distinctively Soviet Muslim (Erşahin 2005: 3). In this way the USSR was portrayed as a partner to the Muslim world.

To preserve Islam under the conditions of "infidel" rule, the Soviet ulema developed a liberal and even progressive intellectuality. They promoted an intellectual revival among Soviet Muslims by arguing that Islam was the highest and most progressive culture, a religion well adapted to the construction of real socialism. The mufti of Tashkent, Ishan Babakhan, who held that office between 1943 and 1957, exemplified the way members of the Soviet ulema reconciled their religion with Marxist-Leninist dogma. In its ideal form, socialism could even be presented as a fulfilment of Islam (Erşahin 2005: 4ff.). Numerous similarities between communist ideology and Qur'anic values were identified, including the equality of nations and sexes, freedom of religion, and the dignity of labour (see Saroyan 1997a).

The reforms of perestroika and glasnost, introduced under Mikhail Gorbachev in the mid-1980s, introduced a new, conciliatory attitude towards religion. Restrictions on religious practice were loosened (Peyrouse 2003: 369). The new policy was provoked partly by the systemic crisis of the economy, but also by the need to manage the nascent internal "Islamic threat" and to counter the effects of "fundamentalist" movements based in Iran and Afghanistan (Rashid 1995, 2003; Khalid 2003). In an attempt to improve the general moral climate, Gorbachev's government (re)discovered the potential influence of religious leaders. This was to be achieved by propagating a "Central Asian Islam" that would emphasize the traditions and specificities of the practice and teachings of Islam in the region while minimizing foreign influences (Akiner 2003). Religious and spiritual issues now received more media attention, and the ethical values of Islam were presented in a more positive light.

This conciliatory policy can of course be interpreted as a continuation of the instrumentalization of Islam by political elites. Thus mufti Mukhammad Sodiq supported perestroika publicly and endorsed the government's line when ethnic tensions surfaced in the Ferghana Valley in 1989 (Anderson 2002: 182). By the end of the 1980s, however, the shift in official policies towards religion began to have a visible effect (Anderson 2002: 182). While celebrations of the millennium of Christianity in Russia in 1988 highlighted the link between Orthodoxy and Russian culture, Muslim shrines remained subject to tight controls because of concerns over the Islamic threat (Rorlich 1991: 203–204). But gradually, obstacles to the building of mosques and restrictions on foreign travel were lifted. The numbers of pilgrims to Mecca and students going abroad for religious education increased rapidly.[15] To meet the shortage of imams for the many new mosques that were constructed, many mullahs who had hitherto been unofficial were now granted official registration and integrated into the state's structures (Saroyan 1997a; Northrop 2004). Young mullahs, irrespective of whether they had been trained in Soviet madrasas or in religious institutions abroad, were appointed to leading positions in the official Muslim institutions. This new generation of Uzbek ulema was seen by the government as loyal to the state's interpretation of Islam (Akiner 2003).[16]

Continuities and Changes: Religion in the Ideology of National Independence

With the dissolution of the Soviet Union, the Central Asian republics declared their sovereignty as nation-states within boundaries that had been fixed in 1924.[17] In its attempts to legitimate and consolidate an Uzbek nation-state, the Uzbek government, led by President Islam Karimov, declared the "restoration of national tradition" to be a cornerstone of state policy (see Koroteyeva and Makarova 1998; Fumagalli 2003). Especially in the early years of independence, the Uzbek leadership pushed radically to eradicate the Soviet legacy and, more specifically, "Russian cultural heritage" (Djumaev 2002). In the process of "Uzbekization", Uzbek was declared the official state language as early as 1989. After independence, ethnic Uzbeks received rapid promotion in the state bureaucracy and in the security forces; they quickly came to dominate the key positions in both politics and economics (Khalid 2003: 587).

---

[15] In the early 1990s, many Muslim charitable organizations offered financial support to Uzbek Muslims. They also financed the education of imams and mullahs abroad. These organizations were expelled from the country after the introduction of the new religion law in 1998, the exception being the Committee of Muslims of Asia, established in 1989 by the Kuwait-based, international Islamic Charitable Organization, which remained active for many years after that date (see Corley and Rotar 2006).

[16] In fact, as I show in the next chapter, the Uzbek *ulema* were not as loyal to the state as had been hoped. According to Muminov (2007), at least some of the new imams and mullahs promoted a "purist" Islam aimed at the cleansing of superstition and all the syncretic accretions characteristic of local Islamic practice.

[17] The "National Delimitation" plan implemented in 1924–1925 had aimed to shape new national identities on the basis of language and territory. The Soviet Constitution further solidified the new national frameworks in 1936 by granting the republics of Turkmenistan, Uzbekistan, Kazakhstan, Kyrgyzstan, and Tajikistan the status of Union republics. These collective identities had their top-down origins in the second half of the nineteenth century but were widely disseminated only in the course of the establishment of Soviet controls (Perrin-Wagner 1999).

Like the other successor states of the Soviet Union, Uzbekistan had to develop a new set of shared values to replace Soviet ideology and to give a profile to the national character of the new state. President Karimov asserted that his ideology of national independence was "authentic" (1999, cited in March 2003: 311) and in every sense a full replacement of the Marxist-Leninist ideology of the Soviet era (March 2003: 308). The explicit goal was to promote the national traits of Uzbek society (Karimov 1997) and to anchor the sovereignty of the new republic in Uzbek statehood and nationalism. Karimov sought in this way to justify his authoritarianism, proclaiming a pre-political consensus on the basis of the higher, common goals of the unity and authenticity of a multi-national population (March 2003: 373). On the official website of the Uzbek press agency, the national independence ideology was outlined as follows:

> The national ideology must lean on primordial tradition, customs, language, religion and the spirit of the nation. It must not belong to the government and turn into government work. Our ancestors raised, developed Islam and made it available to people. They left an immortal scientific-philosophical inheritance. ... the ideology of national independence must be based on these values (PAPU 2004).

The slogans of the national independence ideology were soon omnipresent in everyday life. Billboards with slogans were displayed along streets, on official buildings, and even at religious sites. Uzbek citizens were constantly reminded of their historical and religious national heritage, upon which the future of the Uzbek state depended. Karimov (1997) defined the Uzbek nation as tolerant, hospitable, humane, and benevolent. His teachings were made mandatory at all levels of education, starting with kindergarten; knowledge of them was a prerequisite for entrance into institutions of higher education.[18] The mass media and other state-controlled institutions, including religious organizations, all had to propagate Karimov's views. University professors were sent out to villages on "agitation" tours.

---

[18] Applicants for places at university have to pass an entrance exam in which, in the history section, they may well have to answer multiple-choice tests on Karimov's publications. Questions about Karimov's works constitute one-third of the questions posed in the entrance examinations for the Tashkent Islamic University and Islamic Institute. The final, most difficult hurdle for students applying for scholarships from the UMID foundation to study abroad is a test based on "spirituality and enlightenment" according to Karimov's precepts. In all institutions of higher education the curriculum includes subjects such as national ideology and "spirituality and enlightenment". The corresponding textbooks have titles such as *National Independence Ideology: Main Concepts and Principles* (published by the Science and Techniques State Committee of Uzbekistan, the Ministry of Higher and Special [Middle] Education of the Republic, and the National Society of Philosophers of Uzbekistan).

Plate 1. "What is YOUR contribution to national independence?" – Slogans of the national ideology are omnipresent in everyday life, as this oversized road sign in Kokand city testifies.

The Council for Spirituality and Enlightenment (Ma'naviyat va ma'rifat jamoatchilik markazi) was established by presidential decree in April 1994 to "create leading ideas that define the rich spiritual and cultural legacy of the Uzbek people on the basis of universal eastern values".[19] The council supports the government's emphasis on the national ancestry of distinguished theologians rather than on the religious content of their work (Ilkhamov 2001: 45). Islam Karimov himself, in his book *Uzbekistan on the Threshold of the 21st Century* (1997: 86ff.), summed up the importance of national history and memory in a chapter entitled "The Revival of Spiritual Values and National Self-awareness". He wrote: "Historical memory, the restoration of an objective and truthful history of the nation and its territory, is given an extremely important place in the revival and growth of the national self-consciousness and becomes a source of moral education and imitation. The history of Central Asia reveals many outstanding personalities

[19] "Presidential Decree on the Establishment of the Council for Spirituality and Enlightenment", 23 April 1994. According to the head of the Department for the Scientific Propagation of the National Independence Ideology of the Council for Spirituality and Enlightenment, eastern values are to be understood in this context as "the customs and traditions of the region of today's Uzbekistan" (personal communication, Tashkent, August 2004).

who had political wisdom, moral values, and a religious perception of the world".

The writing and rewriting of a specifically national history involves presenting the region as an ancient civilization, on a par with others along the Silk Road. In this Uzbekified history, the tenth and eleventh centuries are highlighted as the genesis of the Uzbek nation.[20] Amir Timur (1336–1406) is presented as the key cultural hero (see Melvin 2000; Ilkhamov 2002; Finke 2006). By contrast, more than seventy years of recent Soviet history have been eradicated from the textbooks: "During the Soviet era, history as well as the national history of the Soviet republics was written by Russian historians and partly changed to favour Soviet ideology. Now we have the possibility to show our version of Uzbek history, to write and actively create it", said a history professor whom I interviewed in Tashkent in October 2006.

Soviet heroes and other historical figures celebrated during Soviet times are now replaced by new heroes, especially Amir Timur. Historical figures such as Abu Rayhon al-Biruniy, Alisher Navoiy, and Ibn Sino have been retained, but whereas in Soviet times they were acclaimed as major intellectuals and scientists, they are now represented as exclusively Uzbek, even if their Uzbek roots are in fact questionable (Finke 2006).

From the beginning of the independent Uzbek state, the new national ideology was made visible in public symbolism, notably in the renaming of streets, squares, official buildings, and cooperative farms. Statues of Lenin were exchanged for monuments of Amir Timur. Muslim holidays, notably *ramazon*, or *ro'za,hayiti* (the festival of fastbreaking at the end of Ramadan), *qurbon hayiti* (the Sacrifice Festival, also called *qurbon bayrami*), and the spring solstice festival, *navro'z*, were officially re-established. September first was declared National Independence Day and is celebrated lavishly every year with the new national symbols (Adams 1998). Other former Soviet holidays, such as International Women's Day (8 March), Victory Day (9 May), marking the defeat of Nazi Germany, and Teachers' Day (1 October), have been retained, but given a new Uzbek focus.

---

[20] This nationalist historiography is highly contested. See, for instance, Alisher Ilkhamov's article "Archeology of Uzbek Identity" (2006a) and his edited *Ethnic Atlas of Uzbekistan* (2002), which was funded by the Soros Foundation. The controversial debate over Ilkhamov's publications is documented in *Uzbek Identity Debate,* the Spring 2006 special issue of the *Journal for Anthropology and Archaeology of Eurasia.* Whereas Ilkhamov and other national and international scholars see 1924 as the turning point in the creation of a modern, political Uzbek identity, supporters of the ethnogenic approach reject this view, claiming that the modern Uzbeks had already come into existence as early as the eleventh century.

Plate 2. Performing the official celebrations to mark *navro'z*, the traditional spring festival in Central Asia and an Uzbek national holiday, in Tashkent.

When Karimov was inaugurated in January 1992, he took the presidential oath with one hand on the new Constitution and the other on the Qur'an. Two years later he made the pilgrimage to Mecca, a gesture noted with surprise by many people who remembered him as an apparatchik under the Soviet government. This sort of shift from communism towards Islam could also be observed in the neighbouring Central Asian republics. It represented not only a distancing from the anti-religious policies of the USSR but also a new positioning towards the Muslim world, with secular (economic) as well as religious implications.

Constitutionally, Uzbekistan, like its neighbours, upholds the separation of religion and state. Article 31 of its Constitution declares: "Freedom of conscience is guaranteed to all. Everyone shall have the right to profess or not to profess any religion. Any compulsory imposition of religion shall be impermissible".[21] Besides including the right to exercise religious freedom and to establish religious organizations (Article 4), the Constitution provides for the official rehabilitation of religions, which has facilitated the reopening

[21] The text of the Constitution in English can be found at www.gov.uz/en/constitution/#s268.

and construction of mosques, madrasas, churches, and holy places and the acknowledgement of religious associations.

Recognizing the importance of Islam for the cultural and religious identification of the majority of Uzbekistan's population, Karimov and his intellectual advisers allocated it – despite the legal separation of religion and state – a special role in nation-building. Islam acquired a status akin to that of a state ideology.[22] Upon the achievement of independence from the Soviet Union, campaigns were set in motion to emphasize the role of Islam as an integral component of the national heritage, one that would provide the ethical and moral foundation of the state (Akiner 2003: 75ff.). In the new national independence ideology, religion – which in practice always meant Islam – was seen as offering a moral framework with which to fill the spiritual vacuum that officials feared would follow the abandonment of Marxist-Leninist dogma and that could lead to the destabilization of society. Islam became a marker of Uzbek identity that transcended regional, linguistic, and clan affiliations (see Schoeberlein-Engel 1994; Finke 2006). The government sought to adapt the ethno-religious correlation between being Turkic and being Muslim as the unifying element in creating a national Uzbek identity. Islam was the traditional religion of the Uzbek people because it had been the dominant faith in the territory of Uzbekistan for so long, not to speak of its importance for science and culture.[23]

Two statements exemplify President Karimov's understanding of the position and function of Islam in Uzbek society and politics:

> The revival of the spiritual-religious foundation of our society, the Islamic culture that contains the centuries-old experience of the moral consolidation of our people, is an important step on the path to self-identification and the restitution of historical memory and cultural-historical integrity. Old mosques are being reconstructed and new ones are built; education centres are being expanded; religious literature is being published. However, the process of the revival of the national traditions of Islam and culture has been a vindication of the decision not to "import" Islam from outside, not to politicize Islam, and not to Islamize our politics (Karimov 1997: 89).

> Islam is our parents' religion, and we shouldn't forget that for us it is both belief, behaviour, conscious[ness] and enlightenment. It is not

[22] Islam has been subject to similar instrumentalization in other postsocialist cases, as well as in quite different contexts such as Malaysia (McDonell 1990).

[23] The principle of privileging the dominant religion of the titular nation as a traditional religion was also observed in the case of the Russian Orthodox Church in Russia after the collapse of the USSR (Bourdeaux and Popescu 2006).

> [a] simple collection of convictions. Our people willingly accept such education. They try to be honest, respectful to each other, modest, [and to] obey [the] rule of good citizenship (Karimov, cited in Husniddinov 2002: 96).

Karimov's notion of Uzbek-Muslim synthesis is analogous to that which developed towards the end of the twentieth century in Kemalist Turkey: to be a Muslim is an important unifying marker of national identity (cf. Hann 1997: 32). The state attempts to monopolize the answers to the questions of what it means to be a Muslim and what conduct is acceptable for both Muslims and members of other religions.

In Uzbekistan's national independence ideology, Karimov's "Uzbek Islam" is the legitimate religion of the Uzbek ancestors, the ultimate expression of Uzbek national values or moralities – in a word, of *o'zbekchilik* (Uzbekness) (see Louw 2004). Karimov sees the revival or restoration of a proper conception of Islam and Muslimness in terms of a recovery of the national memory (Louw 2004: 75). Uzbek Islam is said to build upon or encompass pre-Islamic faiths and to be tolerant towards other faiths as a result of the multi-religious past. Thus, practices such as shrine veneration, considered heterodox by followers of a rigid, scriptural interpretation of Islam, can be seen as integral parts of Uzbek Islamic culture (see chapter 6). Sufi orders can be considered integral parts of the local Islamic universe (see Akiner 2003: 79; Papas 2005: 39; Rotar 2006). So, too, can the Jadids, the reformers of the early twentieth century. Important Sufi masters such as Bahauddin Naqshband, the founder of the Naqshbandiya order, were claimed for the national pantheon, and shrines were reopened and restored at the behest of President Karimov himself. Sufi masters, who were already seen as part of the cultural heritage of the region in Soviet times, were now represented as sources of a uniquely Uzbek spiritual heritage. Some of them were put on a par in the government's discourse with Western philosophers such as Kant, Hegel, and Feuerbach, writers previously condemned by the Soviet orthodoxy (Papas 2005: 38).[24]

This emphasis on the distinctive local character of Uzbek Islamic practices was designed both to cement a greater identification of the Uzbek Muslim population with the ideals of the new government and to counter radical notions of Islam, summed up in the official discourse as "Wahhabism". In his definition of Uzbek Islam, Karimov clearly favours an

---

[24] While granting Sufism an important role in the religious and spiritual life of Uzbekistan, the government hesitated to approve of the formation of Sufi brotherhoods, which traditionally have been political hotbeds, difficult to control because of their semi-clandestine character (see Forum 18 News Service [n.d.], www.forum18.org/Archive.php?article_id=441; Meixler 2000).

Islam that bases its teachings on the Sunni Islam of the Hanafi school of jurisprudence. Proper Uzbek Muslimness is grounded in internalized faith in the private sphere. Religious practices form part of the cultural package, but they are not to intrude into politics, and there is no question of introducing elements of sharia (Uzb., *shariat*), the Islamic legal and moral code, into the legal framework of the state. Altogether, the path for the legitimate expression of Islamic belief and practice sketched by the government in its ideology, and backed up by decrees and laws, is a narrow one. Deviations are considered a threat to the democracy and stability of Uzbek society.

Plate 3. The burial site near Bukhara of the great Sufi master and founder of the Naqshbandiya order, Bahauddin Naqshband, is both a popular pilgrimage site and an officially recognized heritage site, representative of what the government sees as authentic "Uzbek Islam".

Defining the "Other"

Although the definition of a legitimate Uzbek Islam is given clearly, the definition of the significant "other" remains broad and vague (Khalid 2003: 588). The government adjusts it constantly in order to further its control over religious life. While hailing Islam's contribution to the rebirth of an independent, just, and progressive Uzbekistan, Karimov also maintains that amongst the numerous Islamic organizations active in Uzbekistan, certain militant groups are undermining the synthesis of nation and Islam and threatening both state and society. He has repeatedly condemned international terrorism, religious extremism, and fundamentalism, declared these to be the greatest threats to Uzbek sovereignty, and attributed them to the difficult socio-economic situation of a country in transition:

> Religion, as a component of social life, is linked inextricably with other spheres of social pressures. It is not accidental that most of the religious systems existing today were formed during periods of social, economic and political revolution and crisis. This shows that religion has, throughout human history, been employed to a greater or lesser degree to achieve political goals which were not always noble.
>
> Unfortunately, the history of mankind has many examples of people's faith, a component of religious consciousness, being used not as a constructive power, but as a destructive force, as fanaticism, which is characterized by such features or manifestations as a passionate conviction in the veracity of only one confession and an accompanying intolerance towards all others.
>
> Precisely those people or groups of people who are guilty of fanaticism are capable of generating the greatest destabilization in society because, by painting such movements as "people's actions", they enable the population to relinquish feelings of personal responsibility for individual actions (Karimov 1997: 21).

This "stability" argument is grounded in immediate political contexts (March 2003). It follows that the government's rhetoric makes frequent reference to the transitional character of the society, the difficult socio-economic situation, and the ideological vacuum left by the demise of the USSR.

In addition to public moral exhortations, Karimov's government interprets its constitutional powers in a way that restricts unauthorized religious activities in the name of constitutional safeguards protecting individual rights. The right to profess or not to profess any religion, clearly stated in Article 31 of the Constitution, has been consistently undermined. One significant early factor was the outbreak of civil war in Tajikistan in May 1992, when pro-democracy activists and advocates of an Islamic state joined forces in opposition to a Tajik government dominated by ex-communists. Arguably, it was this war that led Karimov and his advisors to fear domestic opposition in general and Islamic opposition in particular (Human Rights Watch 2004: 20). To reduce political threats, the government has banned opposition political parties, including the Erk (Freedom) Democratic Party, the Birlik (Unity) Party, the Adolat (Justice) Party, and the Islamic Renaissance Party. To defend the ostensibly secular state, the government has banned unregistered mosques and Islamic organizations. The primary targets are the followers of "Wahhabism". The groups subsumed under this pejorative label include the Army of Islam, the Islamic Movement of Uzbekistan (IMU), and the Hizb ut-Tahrir (Liberation Party). These and similar Islamic organizations are characterized as conservative or fundamentalist.[25] Their teachings are said to conflict with the ethos of toleration and pluralism found in all decent societies (Rasanayagam 2006a).

The increasing activity of such movements prompted repressive measures in the mid-1990s, with a wave of mosque closures and arrests of suspected Wahhabis (Human Rights Watch 2004). As a result of the perceived Islamic threat to stability and peace, the 1992 Freedom of Conscience Law was amended in 1998. Although freedom of worship was upheld, the new law on "Freedom of Conscience and Religious Organizations" was considerably more restrictive than its predecessor, which was itself modelled largely on the old Soviet law and hardly liberal. In order to control the activities of religious organizations more effectively, existing state recognition was withdrawn. All religious communities had to acquire new legal status by registering with the Ministry of Justice and the State Committee of Religious Affairs. The main requirements for obtaining this registration were evidence that a minimum of 100 adults of Uzbek citizenship were members; the religious leader's verification of his position by means of a diploma issued by a state-approved religious institution; and the organization's ownership of a suitable building complying with official safety and hygiene standards.[26] Henceforth, new religious buildings, associations, and courses in theology would all require official permission.

According to Articles 4 and 5 of the 1998 law, religious communities were allowed to operate in Uzbekistan only if their objectives and doctrines were consistent with the legislation and not threatening to internal security by virtue of being likely to provoke ethnic, social, or inter-confessional conflicts. The law also imposed restrictions on religious practice. Article 14 prohibited religious activities and the wearing of religious clothing in public spaces on the part of anyone other than religious leaders. The dissemination of religious ideas and the freedom to assemble for religious purposes were proscribed, measures that affected many private religious study circles that were not part of a state-registered religious institution. Both imported reli-

---

[25] In the following discussion, I prefer to avoid the contested term Wahhabi and instead to use *Islamist* to denote Muslims whose declared political aim is the establishment of an Islamic state on the basis of the Qur'an and the Sunna.

[26] As I show in the following chapter, many of the smaller religious organizations and neighbourhood mosques could not fulfil these requirements. Some of them had to close, and others continued their activities illegally, often dependent on the goodwill of government officials.

gious literature and materials printed in Uzbekistan had to be authorized by the state censors.

The increasing activity of new religious groups labelled "non-traditional", and their success in instigating conversions from the traditional religions, led to a coalition between the patriarchate of the Russian Orthodox Church of Uzbekistan and the Muslim Board of Uzbekistan to counter what they deemed to be sects and cults. The government was responsive to demands from the traditional religions, because the pluralization of existing ethno-religious affiliations was perceived to threaten the stability of Uzbek society.[27] Thus, foreign-based religious organizations were assimilated into the pre-existing category "bad Islam". To limit the influence of religious ideas "alien to Uzbeks", Karimov prohibited proselytizing. Any missionary activity directed towards individuals or members of other faiths was punished with heavy fines and even imprisonment.

Local and international critics of the 1998 law, including human rights activists I met during my fieldwork, alleged that the Uzbek government was de facto anti-religious and that the numerous amendments to the law in the form of presidential decrees and orders constituted violations of international standards that, formally speaking, the state had ratified.[28] The lack of precise definitions of key terms such as *proselytize* and *missionary activity* exposed people to arbitrary implementation of the law by officials. The same was true concerning the distinction of the "religious" from the "cultural".[29]

These changes in the law pertaining to religion in no way modified the quasi-state structure developed to control religious institutions, which was taken over by the Uzbek government from the Soviet legacy with only minor changes. When the USSR disintegrated in the early 1990s, the overarching Spiritual Directorate of the Muslims of Central Asia (SADUM) was split into separate national administrations, each headed by its own mufti. The clergy of the resulting Muslim Board of Uzbekistan (MBU) were able, as in

---

[27] Committee for Religious Affairs, Tashkent, Uzbekistan, personal communication, July 2004.

[28] Personal communications with Alison Gill, director of the Human Rights Watch department in Tashkent, and Igor Rotar, a member of the National Centre for Human Rights, a correspondent of Forum 18 news service, and a lawyer who regularly defended the rights of a charismatic Christian church in Uzbekistan.

[29] One example often given is the definition of "religious clothing", the wearing of which is prohibited by Article 14 of the religion law. Human rights organizations frequently report that Muslim men wearing beards and clothes that are traditional to Muslim countries, and women who wear headscarves that completely cover the hair and neck, are subject to discrimination and are charged by government officials with violating Article 14 (Rotar 2006). A representative of the Baha'i faith in Uzbekistan was personally approached by agents of the Uzbek National Security Service and told that his organization was free to approach Russians, Tatars, and Koreans but should keep clear of ethnic Uzbeks (personal communication, May 2003).

Soviet days, to exercise certain forms of religious and even state authority, but they were not considered to represent the community of Muslim believers (Rasanayagam 2006a). In short, the MBU, like its predecessor, SADUM, represented only official Islam. It was responsible for the registration of mosques and madrasas, the appointment and dismissal of imams, the contents of sermons, and the formal examination and registration of all Muslim clerics. The MBU was expected to promote its vision of Uzbek Islam, in opposition to radical Islamic movements.[30]

As under the Soviet government, acceptable Muslim practice was limited to that which took place within the framework of state-sponsored religious institutions, supervised by religious teachers and imams appointed by the MBU but ultimately controlled by the State Committee of Religious Affairs. This is a state body created by a presidential decree in 1992, ostensibly to monitor the constitutional guarantee of the right of freedom of conscience. The 1998 law empowered the committee to liaise more generally between religious organizations and state agencies (Human Rights Watch 2004: 43). It carries out a wide range of functions, including the supply of advice to the government and the general control of information pertaining to religion. The committee is responsible for supervising all religious educational institutions and for censoring religious literature. It has its own publishing house, and its books are sold in bookshops all over the country. They are used as textbooks in schools and universities, consistently promoting the government's views not only on religion but also on associated topics such as tolerance and terrorism.[31] The committee coordinates all research carried out on religious topics by official religious and secular institutions of education and science. It cooperates closely with the MBU, which gives every large mosque a topic for the Friday sermon. After the sermon, a report has to be submitted to both the committee and the muftiate. If Uzbekistan is invited to send a senior representative to an international Islamic forum, the MBU has first to consult the committee, which has the final say in the matter.

---

[30] The muftiate's lack of independence is illustrated by the case of Muhammad Sodiq, who became the country's chief mufti in 1991. Only two years later he was forced to resign his post and leave the country under pressure from the authorities, who charged him with collaborating with the Islamic opposition in Tajikistan. Muhammad Sodiq had criticized the government's brutal methods in fighting religious extremism (see Polat 2000). He was replaced as chief mufti in 1997 by Abdurashid Bakhramov, who was known for his loyalty to Karimov.

[31] The committee's expertise is also made available to law enforcement agencies. Literature with religious content found by border control agencies or confiscated from persons suspected of religious fundamentalism and terrorism is sent to the committee for an opinion. This procedure is set out in the Criminal Process Law, which stipulates the use of such expert opinions in the courts. In practice such literature often provides the main evidence that the accused has been involved in banned organizations, whereas formally it was supposed to constitute only supplementary evidence.

Plate 4. Encountering history: Framed by old Islamic and Soviet architecture, the new design of the main Friday mosque in Tashkent is meant to convey the government's idea of a "national Islam".

Conclusion

In Uzbekistan, as in other successor states of the USSR, the collapse of one political system and ideology was accompanied by the birth of another, in which the vehicles for propagating the government's viewpoint remained largely the same. But while the form remained, the content changed from the promotion of internationalism and a unifying Soviet identity to ethno-national symbolism. This is better understood not as an "invention of tradition" in the sense of Hobsbawm and Ranger (1983) but as a transformation of the nation that already existed. In Uzbekistan, the political elites have sought to legitimate the newly sovereign nation-state by, on the one hand, reactivating values and traditions that are presented as characteristic of Uzbek people in the pre-Soviet era while, on the other hand, transforming those Soviet symbols still seen as valuable for society.

Islam occupies a special position in this process. First, it is the "social glue" that binds together the Turkic-speaking people who live in this territory, and it is the principal element in their cultural-historical legacy. Second, Islam is also a significant "other", a force that can threaten the stability and peace of Uzbek society. This dual role of Islam in nation-building has allowed the government of Islam Karimov to maintain strict control over what constitutes legitimate religious belief and practice and to take any measures it considers necessary against "subversive" notions. The rhetoric of stability and social security has dominated official discourse and is always invoked by officials when they explain why all religious organizations in the country have to be carefully controlled. Although the Constitution proclaims religious freedom, in fact the authorities have continued to equate ethno-national affiliation with a particular "local" Islam, a congruence partially shaped during the Soviet period. In thus nationalizing Islam and at the same time contrasting the "good", characteristically Uzbek model with the "bad" Islam that threatens from outside, the government provides a frame that citizens transgress at their peril. The religious affiliation and practice of ethnic Uzbeks is a public issue in the sense that this concept of Uzbek Islam is elaborated as a common good, too important to the polity to be left in the realm of the private (see McGlinchey 2007: 306).

Chapter 3
Contested Space: The Religious Field in Kokand

> After the fall of the USSR the borders were opened, the wind of all faiths and beliefs started blowing, a division occurred here between the denominations. Some were very much involved in those teachings coming from abroad and split up. New forms of worship and service not observed before appeared in the now independent state.
>
> – Protestant pastor, Kokand

In his catalogue for a Silk Road excursion, a typical Uzbek tour operator offers a one-day stop in Kokand. The city is advertised as one of the three main centres of traditional Islamic scholarship and the capital of the famed Kokand khanate. Besides the Khudoyar Khan palace, the seat of the last khan of Kokand, who reigned between 1845 and 1872, the G'ishtlik mosque, the Jome' mosque and minaret, the Kamol Qozi mosque, the Mulkobod mosque, the Miyen-Hazrat madrasa, the Dahman Shohon necropolis, and the Modarikhon mausoleum are the prime places of interest.[32]

The dominance of Muslim buildings in the cityscape of Kokand and its reputation as a great centre of Islamic scholarship and arts – the hometown of such influential intellectuals as Muqimi, Furqat, and Hamza Hakimzoda Niyaziy – leave the impression that little space in the city can be left for other religions. Only upon getting to know Kokand intimately does one discover a multi-religious dimension behind this visually dominant layer of Islam. Leaving the main streets, one finds the Russian Orthodox church close to the Khudoyar Khan palace, almost hidden in a *mahalla*, or neighbourhood. Also in the vicinity of the church, with its golden onion domes, a sign reading "Yangi Hayot" (Uzb., "new life") marks the prayer house of an Evangelical community. But these two buildings are exceptional: the great majority of non-Muslim religious communities in Kokand remain invisible to the uninitiated visitor. The Baptist church and the prayer

[32] The example given here comes from the website of the Sindbad Travel and Tourism Company, http://travel.albatros.uz/eng_kokand.html.

house of the Pentecostals are situated in typical Russian-style houses that give no hint from the outside that they house religious communities. Five minutes' walk from the Yangi Hayot prayer house and the Russian Orthodox church, in the district still known as the Jewish *mahalla*, stands the city's last remaining synagogue (there once were six), hidden behind a gate with a bell but bearing no inscription to reveal its identity.

The liberal reforms of the late Gorbachev era, followed by the proclamation of full religious freedom in the wake of the collapse of the USSR, created new opportunities for all religious organizations. Communities and streams of theological thought previously unknown in the region sent their representatives to stake the claims of their particular faith.[33] The religious landscape of Uzbekistan had been diverse in the past, but the developments that culminated after independence created a new situation, challenging the status quo of the established religious groups by introducing competing ideas about theological interpretation and religious practice.

In the previous chapter I showed how religious developments in Uzbekistan have been actively shaped and controlled by the government at all levels through its laws and ideology. But it is not only the government that has an interest in maintaining stability in the religious sphere. The religious organizations, especially the long-established ones, also strive to maintain their positions within the evolved religious landscape. How can religious pluralism be consolidated in a socio-political environment that is subject to such vested interests? More concretely, what strategies can religious actors devise to consolidate their local positions?

Bourdieu's concept of the "religious field" (2000) is helpful in illuminating the competition for power and legitimacy in a complex setting like this. The religious field is an arena in which competing agents contest the right to monopolize the exercise of power. Drawing on Max Weber's description of the opposition between priests and prophets, Bourdieu depicted the contest in terms of those who defend orthodoxy versus those who advocate heresy. The orthodox-heterodox opposition generates an ongoing struggle for a monopoly over religious legitimacy. The right to confer or withhold this "consecration" is contested on the basis of two fundamentally opposed

---

[33] At the time of my fieldwork, sixteen religious organizations were officially registered in Uzbekistan. Only 0.69 per cent of the population of Uzbekistan belonged to religions other than Islam and Russian Orthodox Christianity, among them Roman Catholics, Baptists, adherents of Hare Krishna Consciousness (ISCKON), Jehovah's Witnesses, Baha'is, Jews, Buddhists, and a wide range of Protestant congregants (charismatic and Pentecostal) who had managed to obtain registration with the Ministry of Justice. These numbers, taken from the official statistics of the State Committee of Religious Affairs for 2004, represent only the religious organizations registered with the committee and the Ministry of Justice.

principles: the personal authority called for by the creator, and the institutional authority favoured by the teacher (Bourdieu 2000).

In the religious field of Uzbekistan, the most powerful resource in the establishment of religious dominance is the appeal to tradition. This concept tends everywhere to be subtle and elastic (Eickelman and Piscatori 1996). It can refer to the unwritten, shared understandings of a small group, passed on from generation to generation, or to the main dogmas of the major world religions. "All these senses of tradition," wrote Eickelman and Piscatori (1996: 37), "are subject to considerable flexibility as they are sustained and re-created in various social and historical contexts, ranging from the intimacies of family life to the conduct of state affairs". Before looking at the way the concept of tradition is deployed in the contemporary multi-religious field in Kokand, I provide some background on the economy and politics of the city under tsarist and Soviet rule.

The Religious Landscape in Kokand before Perestroika

Kokand's multi-religious landscape today embodies the consequences of complex political processes and socio-economic changes that began under the tsarist colonial regime. In his account of his journey through Russia and Turkistan in 1865, more than a decade before the city's incorporation into the Russian Empire in 1876, Eugene Schuyler drew a picture of Kokand as a modern city of trade and Islamic scholarship:[34]

> Kokand is a modern town, not more than a hundred years old, and therefore has wider streets, and is more spacious than most Asiatic towns. ... In a large square open place at the edge of the bazaar, where fruit is sold all day long, are two large *medressés*, well built of burned brick picked out at times with blue tiles, and surmounted by domes and small blue turrets. One is called *Ali* and was built by Mussulman Kul. The other which is not yet finished was begun by Sultan Murad Bek, the brother of the Khan, in fulfilment of some vow. Near the bridge ... is the spacious *medressé* Khan, built by Madali Khan, containing rooms for 200 Mullahs. It was, however, never completed according to the original design. In the eastern part of the city is the *medressé* Mir, built by Narbuta Bii about eighty years ago, and close by is a large cemetery, with a primary school connected with its mosque (Schuyler 1966: 177–178).

[34] At the time of his journey, Eugene Schuyler (1840–1890) was the American consul in St. Petersburg. The purpose of the journey was to acquaint himself with the way of life of the Muslim peoples inhabiting the region and to see how they were coping under Russian rule.

The capital of the khanate of Kokand (1709–1876) was also the gateway to the Ferghana Valley and the major centre for Islamic scholarship in the region. Estimates of the number of madrasas in the city in the nineteenth century range from thirty-eight (Arslanzoda 2004) to fifty-two (Abduqodirov 2004). The number of mosques lay between 200 and 382 (Bergne 2003).[35] The annexation of the Kokand khanate by the Turkistan governorship in 1876 brought not only an influx of administrators and military personnel but also an economic boom and rapid demographic expansion.[36] In the course of urban development, large sections of the residential neighbourhoods of the local Uzbek population were destroyed and replaced by a grid of streets in the Russian style, with shops, administrative buildings, and eleven banks, all of which testified to the city's new international character (Abramson 1998: 87; Bergne 2003). The German sewing machine manufacturer Singer was one notable foreign investor; its sign can still be found on a house on the main street, now called Independence Street (Istiqlol ko'chasi). With the connection of the city to the railroad system and the further extension of infrastructure and new means of communication into the valley, regional and international trade supplanted the old handicraft industries. By the time the Bolsheviks seized power in Turkistan, Kokand was one of the most important financial and commercial-industrial centres of Central Asia. Under Soviet rule, it became a centre for the manufacture of fertilizers, chemicals, and machinery and of the cotton processing industry. Labour migration and the settlement policies of the Soviets ensured that growth continued.

Ethnic diversification under tsarist rule and in Soviet times was accompanied by growing religious plurality. Immigrants included Russian and Armenian Orthodox Christians, Baptists, and Russian Jews. However, Bolshevik repression of the Muslims began with a crackdown on Kokand's autonomy in 1917. The background to this event was the internal changes the Muslim community had been experiencing because of the effects of Jadidism, the local movement for Islamic reform. The term *jadid* ("new") was translated locally as *taraqqiyparvarlar* ("progressives") or simply *yoshlar* ("youth"). The Jadids relied heavily on the print media to spread their message. In Kokand they published the newspaper *Sadoyi Farg'ona*

---

[35] The figure 200 comes from Mr. Turdaliev, director of the Hamza Museum in Kokand, personal communication, December 2003.

[36] In 1897, Sven Anders Hedin counted "11,600 houses, nine cotton mills, 35 medressé, and three Jewish schools with 60 pupils" in Kokand (Hedin 1898: 78). The number of inhabitants increased from an estimated 35,000 in 1880 to 120,000 in 1915. Since 1979 the city's population has grown by more than 3,000 persons annually (Abramson 2001).

and the journal *Yurt* between 1917 and 1930.[37] To reach the illiterate, they performed didactic plays intended to promote moral behaviour.[38]

The Jadids criticized the conservative ulema, not only concerning modernization of the educational system but also with respect to entrepreneurship, the public health system, and the emancipation of women. While the traditionalists, or Qadimis, stood for the status quo, the Jadids wanted both modernization and a Turkistan nation-state free from Russian rule (Khalid 1998; Roy 2000). Their imagined model of Central Asian statehood was the ancient Turan, which embraced all the sedentary Muslims of Central Asia (Khalid 2003: 575–576).[39] The traditional term *millat* was redefined in the sense of "nation-state".[40] This ideal was embodied in the 1917 proclamation of "Turkistan autonomy" or "Kokand autonomy", which led promptly to a military conflict with the Bolsheviks. In the course of three days of violence and looting, large parts of the city were burned down and 14,000 Muslims killed (Nahaylo and Swoboda 1990: 37ff.; Swoboda 1992: 766; Sartori 2006). Despite this setback, the Jadids remained active in Kokand until the 1930s, when most of them fell victim to Stalin's successive waves of repression. During the following half-century, Muslims and all other religious communities were subject to the vagaries of Soviet power as outlined in the previous chapter.[41]

The Islamic Boom (mid-1980s–1990s)

David Abramson, in a dissertation with the telling title "From Soviet to *Mahalla*", pointed out that in the perception of Kokand residents, their city was a "microcosm of a larger 'cosmopolitanism' that was allowed to flourish in the Soviet Union" (Abramson 1998: 91). One day in Kokand, as I walked to the bazaar with Feruza, the daughter-in-law of my Uzbek host family, she told me that she missed the multicultural atmosphere of the city, which in

---

[37] Mr. Turdaliev, Hamza Museum, personal communication, December 2003.

[38] One of their most prominent members was the writer and theatre director Hamza Hakimzoda Niyaziy (1889–1929), whose controversial plays critiquing the ulema were frequently performed in Kokand (Olcott 2007: 5).

[39] Turan is the ancient Persian name for Central Asia, and Turanism was a political movement for the unification of all the Altaic peoples.

[40] The concept of *millat* (Turk. *millet*) referred in the Ottoman Empire to a community defined in religious rather than ethno-national terms. This definition altered in the nineteenth century with the rise of nationalist movements. Nowadays the word is synonymous with "national" throughout the Turkic-Persian area (Roy 2000).

[41] Editor's note: At this point in her manuscript, Hilgers indicated that she intended to revise this section, correct the oversimplified impression of an explicit political struggle between the Jadids and the Qadimis, and work in a reference to Keller (2007), which evidently she read only after completing her draft of this chapter.

her view had vanished with Uzbekistan's independence.[42] "Before, you could see all kinds of different people and different faces on the streets, but look around now. Most of the people you see now are Uzbeks. I used to have many school friends from different nations. My best friend was Greek. But after all that happened here since the late 1980s, most of them left the town and the country. The city changed, this multi-nationality was lost, and the city became Uzbek."

Mass emigration by non-Uzbek minorities began in 1989 following a series of violent interethnic clashes in the Ferghana Valley, which were accompanied by increasing public expression of Uzbek nationalism. The conflict between Uzbeks and Meshketian Turks, which began in Ferghana, soon spread to Kokand and other cities of the valley. For three days in June 1989, Uzbeks attacked and burned down the houses of Meshketian Turks. Several people were killed, hundreds were injured, and many local businesses and municipal buildings were destroyed (Abduvakhitov 1993: 92–93; Abramson 1998, 2001).[43] On the basis of official statistics, Abramson (2001: 16) estimated that about 13,000 people left the city between 1989 and 1991, most of them non-indigenous Central Asians (i.e. neither Turkic nor Tajik).[44] Feruza's account of vanishing multicultural flair therefore had a solid demographic basis. I heard many other, similar accounts during my fieldwork, sometimes linked to complaints that Uzbek domination had become excessive, Islam too public, and fashion more conservative. Only a few Turks remained in Kokand. Russians, Tatars, Koreans, Ukrainians, Greeks, and Germans also took the exit option in the 1990s. The "Ferghana events" became a symbol of the demise of Soviet cosmopolitanism. Throughout all vicissitudes, the region had somehow maintained its historical reputation as a bulwark of Islam, and this was now given fresh emphasis.[45]

When showing me around the city during the first week of my stay, one of my guides, a teacher of history and political science at the Pedagogi-

---

[42] Except when quoting people holding official positions, who would expect to be acknowledged by their actual names, I use pseudonyms for all those I worked with.

[43] Abramson (2001: 93) reported between five and twelve civilian fatalities and nearly 100 people hospitalized in Kokand. A series of trials lasted until February 1991, as a result of which 194 people were sentenced. Two of them received the death penalty, and the others received prison terms, suspended sentences, or stints of correctional labour. See also "Uzbekistan Muslims Demonstrate against Communist Leadership", Russian Television 1700 GMT, 22 September 1991, BBC Summary of World Broadcasts, 24 September 1991, available at LexisNexis.

[44] The 1989 Soviet census recorded Kokand's population at 182,000. The non-indigenous Central Asian population made up an estimated 30 to 40 per cent of the total (GosKom Stat 1988: 16, cited in Abramson 2001: 95).

[45] Editor's note: The author indicated in a note that at this point she intended to insert more material concerning contemporary regional identity in the Ferghana Valley.

cal Institute in Kokand, pointed to some street stalls opposite the Jome' mosque and commented, "Islamic kitsch". The stalls were selling all kinds of items for Muslims, including white skullcaps, prayer beads, the Qur'an printed in Uzbek, Russian, and even Arabic, tapes of celebrated sermons, posters depicting motives of Mecca in bright colours with Arabic inscriptions, amulets for automobiles, prayer rugs, "Muslim" perfumes, and a wide selection of printed matter about Islam. Such stalls, my companions explained, had mushroomed throughout the city in the first years after independence. Whereas before perestroika, religious literature had circulated in the format of *samizdat* (Rus., self-published underground literature), now it was available in public next to mosques all over Uzbekistan.

Plate 5. Market in Kokand: In front of mosques and madrasas, as well as in bazaars, street vendors offer materials for Islamic worship as well as a variety of texts.

At first books were printed in Russian and Uzbek by publishing houses based in foreign Muslim countries, but local publishers soon rose to the challenge. Apart from the Qur'an and Hadith collections, strong demand was experienced for secondary literature covering topics such as instructions for ritual ablutions, for performing *namoz* (the ritual prayers performed five times a day), for being a "good" bride (*kelin*) or groom (*kuyov*), and for conducting oneself during a pilgrimage. In addition to audio- and videotapes of sermons by well-known imams, it was possible to purchase recitations of the Qur'an in Uzbek and Arabic. Courses in Arabic were advertised by the reopened madrasas as well as by private teachers. The textbooks and dictionaries used in these courses were available in public bookshops and from street vendors.

One of my guides, a professor of political science who presented himself as an academic in the Soviet tradition and hence a rather unreligious person, pointed out that one trader in front of the Jome' mosque was wearing a white skullcap and a long white shirt over his white, ankle-length trousers. "This is a new fashion here," he said, "coming from Saudi Arabia. Now these pious people think that wearing a white skullcap is more chic than our traditional *do'ppi*.[46] ... That kind of Muslim fashion got imported here increasingly after independence, but somehow it does not belong here. People think that a Muslim has to look like that after seeing pictures from other Muslim countries or returning from *hajj*" (pilgrimage to Mecca).

The late 1980s and early 1990s are generally remembered in Kokand as times of unlimited freedom in terms of religiosity (see also chapter 4). They were years marked by a pioneering spirit, with new organizations and doctrines appearing (and disappearing) from one day to the next. As in other parts of Uzbekistan, numerous mosques and madrasas reopened in Kokand and new ones were built, financed by local donors or by foreign Islamic organizations. When I asked approximately how many mosques had opened during this period, the mullah of a small *mahalla* mosque explained that it was impossible to keep track of what was going on in the neighbourhoods at that time. He preferred to indicate the current number of officially registered mosques in the city, which in 2003–2004 was twelve, compared with only one during Soviet times.[47] My interlocutor estimated the number of unregistered *mahalla* mosques at about eighty, but he added that the number was constantly changing. With the demise of the USSR, Qur'anic study groups in mosques and private homes became popular in Kokand, and, as in the whole of the Ferghana Valley, a number of Islamist groups appeared on the scene and became increasingly active.

The story of Sevara, a local Uzbek in her early sixties at the time of our meeting and the head of a non-governmental organization (NGO), is typical of people's experiences with "new ideas of Islam" during this period. From the end of the 1980s, she told me, Muslim missionaries came into the

---

[46] A *do'ppi* is a skullcap worn by Uzbek (and by Uighur and Tajik) men. It is generally dark and often embroidered with patterns of flowers.

[47] Munawwarow (1999) estimated the number of mosques restored or newly built in Uzbekistan by the beginning of 1992 at about 3,000. Polonskaya and Malashenko (1994: 115) suggested the same number. Human Rights Watch (2004: 19) estimated an increase from 80 during Soviet times to as many as 4,000 at the beginning of the 1990s.

region. She perceived them as “fundamentalist” and “orthodox”, promoting “wrong and ignorant” interpretations of Islam that were incompatible with Uzbek Islam, which was allegedly rooted in a tradition of tolerance derived from the region’s multi-religious history. According to Sevara, Kokand was among the first places in Uzbekistan where those *ekstremistlar*, as she called them, publicly propagated their religious and political agendas.

At that time Sevara was working as an official in the town hall (GorKom). In 1989 her department received a request from an Islamic organization for permission to organize a public meeting. She and her colleagues felt themselves to be in a dilemma and did not know how to handle the request. Uzbekistan was still a socialist republic, and religious activities in public were not allowed; yet the reforms of perestroika had granted a larger public space to religion, and from that point of view the Islamic organization’s request was legitimate. The head of the GorKom passed the request on to the local office of the Communist Party, which decided to approve the meeting.

As a Muslim who did not see her faith as incompatible with her work or her membership in the party, Sevara remembered that she felt enthusiastic about the liberalization of the religious sphere. She had been one of the supporters of the meeting question. Despite her sympathy, when the meeting took place she felt uneasy about it and was unable to shake off the feeling that this public manifestation of religion was somehow illegal and dangerous. It was strange for her to see so many men wearing what she called “religious clothing” and praying openly, and it was difficult to get used to the idea that such “backward” attire was now legal. Many people attended the meeting, and much discussion focused on the “right” way of Islam.

After the meeting, Sevara took a critical distance. She recalled being taken aback by the aggressive and fanatical rhetoric as well as the political message propagated by people whom she perceived as dangerous and antidemocratic. In the days and weeks that followed, this meeting was a hot topic in the city, and Sevara recalled highly ambiguous reactions and ensuing tensions. While some criticized the program of this organization for mixing religion and politics, others sympathized with the goal of purifying the faith of so-called non-Islamic elements and approved of the introduction of sharia. Sevara depicted the latter persons as “Wahhabis”, who tried to coerce men to go to mosque and insulted or spat at women who did not wear headscarves or were otherwise improperly clad.

Of course this account, related to me more than a decade after the event, was informed by later incidents and public discourse. Yet I think it mirrors people’s ambivalent feelings during this period, which ranged from enthusiasm for and fascination with new notions of Islam to fear and insecurity. From this point onwards, the struggle for doctrinal hegemony among Muslim elites became increasingly a physical experience for "ordinary" Muslim believers in their everyday lives, and national identity was the clinching trope. "Musulmonmisiz? O'zbekmisiz?"– Are you a Muslim? Are you an Uzbek? The subtext was, "If so, then why don't you go to mosque as an Uzbek should?" As in other cities of the valley, in the early 1990s militants belonging to Islamist organizations such as Adolat (Justice) and Odamiylik va Insonparvarlik (Humanity and Mercy) patrolled the streets of Kokand, assuming all the functions of law enforcement agencies. There were sporadic attempts to implement sharia law.

The fragmentation of the local Muslim community in Kokand, particularly the opposition between those who identified with local interpretations and practices and those who pursued a stricter Islamist agenda, reached its peak in 1992 with open fighting between the followers of two competing Friday mosques. The mullah of the mosque in the *mahalla* where I lived gave me his version of the events:

> It is true what you have heard. After independence nearly all people went to a mosque or joined Qur'anic courses. But then a mistake was made and people were misusing the situation. The directors of groups from Iran and Pakistan entered the country, donated large amounts of money, giving dollars, appointing imams, and giving them instructions what to do, supporting them, building mosques. We found out about it much later. Those imams went outside Islam. People split up into two or three groups; some practised properly, others worshipped outside Islam, the Wahhabi groups. Illiterate people did not know what to do; some went to one mosque, and some went to another. Those who followed the right sharia told them not to do so. But Wahhabis said that their direction is the right one. Each group claimed to be right. Finally it came to a conflict. In Kokand, imams even fought each other using their fists, and when people saw this, disappointment set in. Around 50 per cent of the population stepped back, away from their imams altogether, due to this disillusionment. So they formed the third group, eventually.

The opposition between being "inside" – that is, performing what the local ulema perceived as "traditional Hanafi" religious practices – and being "outside", referring to a new, foreign, politicized form of Islam, was subjectively experienced by local people as a schism (Babadjanov and Kamilov 2001). The Wahhabi current was seen not as a legitimate diversification but as an external threat to the authenticity and customs of the local, "good" Islam. When the government closed Kokand's Jome' mosque in 1992, it became a symbol of this felt split.[48] The official statement released by the government cited the use of inflammatory language and civil disobedience by the mosque's leadership (Abramson 1998: 202). Before this intervention, two imams had been struggling to dominate: Mukhammad Rajab was the radical who had become head imam (*imom-khotib*), whereas Ismail qori Kokandi identified with the traditional Hanafi orientation. The latter was temporarily taken captive by the so-called Wahhabis, and open fighting between rival supporters became commonplace after Friday prayers (Olcott 2007: 12). Mukhammad Rajab was arrested in 1994 and sentenced to fourteen years' imprisonment, with confiscation of property for narcotics possession.[49]

Plate 6. The Jome' mosque in Kokand.

[48] The Jome' mosque was reopened in 1998. The muftiate appointed an imam, who has the reputation of following the state's discourse for the position of head imam.

[49] Editor's note: In notes at the end of this draft chapter, Hilgers indicated her intention to explore further the political tensions of the early 1990s. Specifically, she cited McGlinchey (2007) concerning the fate of another cleric, who was forced to leave the country, apparently because he posed a threat to the corrupt, cross-regional "patronage politics" of President Karimov. In September 1991, thousands of protestors took to the streets of Kokand to demand Karimov's resignation and his replacement by the Islamic scholar and head mufti of Central Asia, Muhammad Sodiq Muhammad Yusuf. That the Karimov government pressured the popular mufti to flee Uzbekistan in 1993 is an indication that the Uzbek leader may indeed see in Islam a real threat to his authority (McGlinchey 2007: 309).

The Tension between "Hanafi Traditionalists" and "Wahhabis"

Even in the times of the iron curtain in the 1970s, Islam in Uzbekistan was never completely isolated from larger currents in the Islamic world. In their survey of Islamic movements and schools of thought among the Uzbek ulema since the 1970s, Babadjanov and Kamilov (2001) described the shaping of the religious field between the two poles they labelled "Hanafi traditionalism" and "Wahhabism".[50] This usage of the term Wahhabi is arguably reductionist and does not reflect the diversity of ways in which the radical camp gives priority to scripturalist interpretation.

In a sense, the tension between Hanafi traditionalism and fundamentalist scriptural interpretation is a rerun of that which divided the Jadids from the traditionalists in the 1920s, before the Soviet crackdown. The rise of Islamic political parties in various parts of the world after 1945 did not influence the Soviet Central Asian republics directly, but international controversies among Muslim elites nonetheless filtered through to the Soviet ulema (Babadjanov 2002). Discord simmered, and the religious establishment was criticized for its lack of purity (Babadjanov and Kamilov 2001; Olcott 2007). Criticism also came from adepts of the Sufi orders (Babadjanov and Kamilov 1999: 5; cf. Abduvakhitov 1993). Babadjanov and Kamilov (2001) traced the roots of contemporary contestations within the Uzbek ulema back to the 1970s, when a new generation of Muslim theologians appeared, many of whom had experienced some form of underground education in unstructured circles (*davra*s) (see also Abduvakhitov 1993; Rashid 2002). Although illegal, these circles were popular in the Ferghana Valley. For most participants they were a means of disseminating religious knowledge and reading the Qur'an, but for a minority they functioned as revolutionary cells.

Such clandestine groups formed around two Uzbek Muslim scholars, Muhammadjan Hindustani and Hakimjon qori, who were both critics of the Soviet religious establishment (Babadjanov and Kamilov 2001; Olcott 2007: 10). The former stood for Hanafi traditionalism.[51] He provided the first exposure to Islamic teachings for some who later became prominent figures in the radical camp (Olcott 2007: 12), but the majority of the ulema trained by Hindustani continued to exemplify Central Asia's Hanafi tradition and sought to extend it rather than call it into question (Olcott 2007: 12). Ismail

---

[50] Similar cleavages between reformists or modernists, on the one hand, and traditionalists, on the other, have been identified in other parts of the Muslim world. See, for example, Bowen (1998) on Indonesia, Horvatich (1994) on the Philippines, Eickelman (1992) on Morocco, and Schiffauer (1991, 2000) on Turkish migrants in Germany.

[51] For an in-depth account of Muhammadjan Hindustani's life and works, see Babadjanov and Kamilov (2001).

qori Kokandi, the opponent of the Wahhabis in the early 1990s, was a pupil of Hindustani.

Hakimjon qori was a first-generation student of Hindustani who later broke with his teacher and shifted towards a more politicized Islam. Rahmatullah-alloma and Abduhvali qori, who established their own influential groups in the 1970s, and Said Abdullah Nuri, the leader of the Islamic Renaissance Party of Tajikistan, were among the students of Hindustani's who shifted their loyalty to Hakimjon qori (Abduvakhitov 1993; Olcott 1995, 2007; Babadjanov and Kamilov 1999). By the late 1970s, some of Hakimjon qori's students were criticizing their teacher for not being political enough and for shying away from direct confrontation with the Soviet authorities. Rahmatullah-alloma and Abduhvali qori went their own ways. They are said to have been influenced by the writings of Maududi, which were studied in underground circles in the Ferghana Valley in the late 1970s, and by two commentaries on the Qur'an, *Kitab-at-Tawhid,* by Abd Al-Wahhab, the founding figure of the Wahhabi movement in the Arabian peninsula, and *Fi Zilal al-Qur'an,* by Sayyid Qutb, a leading member of the Muslim Brotherhood from Egypt (Olcott 2007: 14). Mukhammad Rajab, the radical imam of the Jome' mosque when the tensions peaked, was among the later generation of students of Hakimjon qoris. His name became a synonym for Wahhabism throughout the city.

It seems safe to assume that the term Wahhabi was first used in the 1970s by Hindustani to label those of his students who advocated a more politicized form of Islam and more purified Islamic practices than Hindustani himself countenanced (Babadjanov and Kamilov 2001; Olcott 2007). Neither Abduhvali qori nor Rahmatullah-alloma ever used the term Wahhabi as a self-ascription, nor did either describe the direction of Islam they advocated as Wahhabiya. Nonetheless, these terms were widely taken up in elite discussions (see Akiner 2003). When the government of independent Uzbekistan began to deploy the term Wahhabi in 1992, it added a second meaning to Hindustani's by making direct reference to the eighteenth-century conservative reform movement of Sunni Islam known as Wahhabiya. Thanks to the government's propaganda, the term became known to a much wider public.

In this propaganda, Wahhabi denotes anyone who is perceived to stand outside the paradigm of the imagined Hanafi traditionalism promoted by the government and the state-sponsored ulema (Rashid 2003: 46). The term Wahhabi is used differently in Yemen (Meneley 2007) and Georgia (Sanikidze 2007), but throughout postsocialist Central Asia government leaders and government-aligned ulema use it to condemn "Islamic fundamentalism", "extremism", and "militant Islam". It is often deployed as a slur, implying foreign sectarianism (Human Rights Watch 2004: 47), with strong political implications and even connotations of crime and terrorism.[52] The government's control of the mass media enabled it to generalize this dichotomizing usage. Not to be a Wahhabi meant that one preferred the local, "tolerant Uzbek Islam", including canonically suspect practices such as saint veneration (Ilkhamov 2001; Rasanayagam 2006a). Anyone whose religious practices were considered exaggerated, such as certain Christians and Baha'is, was liable to be called a Wahhabi in popular parlance.

As Martha Brill Olcott (2007) has shown, the majority of those branded Wahhabis in Uzbekistan had little in common with the revivalist movement of Wahhabiya, a branch of the Hanbali school of law, apart from advocating a purification of local Islamic practices they viewed as polytheistic and heretical (they were sometimes also known as *mujaddidiya,* or "renewers"). Many Islamist reformists in Uzbekistan wanted merely to promote an orthopraxy that adhered more closely to the scriptures of Islam, and in this they shared common ground with Hanafi traditionalists, at least some of whom were similarly critical of certain local practices (Polat 2000: 40; Olcott 2007). Despite this common ground, Wahhabi came to be a blanket term for the Islamic "other".

The "great schism" (Babadjanov and Kamilov 2001) of the early 1990s did not put an end to the tension between Hanafi traditionalists and Wahhabis. In the following years, numerous Islamic activists remained influential in the Ferghana Valley, among them Tahir Yuldashev (later the head of the Islamic Movement of Uzbekistan), Juma Namangani, Badulahad Banrayev, Abdurauf-khon Gafurov, and Dowud-khon, all of whom lived in Namangan (Olcott 2007). The teachings of Rahmatullah-alloma and Abduhvali qori, who combined their puritanical religiosity with calls for a more politicized Islam, became increasingly popular, as demonstrated in the numbers of their respective associated religious teachers, or *domla*s (Olcott 2007: 17ff.). The early 1990s also saw the establishment of several new militant Islamic groups, among them Adolat (Justice), Islom Lashkarlari (Warriors of Islam), Tavba (Regret), and Odamiylik va Insonparvarlik (Philantropy and Humanism). Adolat was formed in Namangan in 1991, ostensibly to maintain public order, combat corruption, and promote social justice. It cooperated with the local authorities as well as with local imams. Its meetings were often held in mosques, and some members received the

---

[52] Bobrovnikov (2006) observed a similar usage of the term Wahhabism in the North Caucasus, and Sanikidze (2007) gave an example from the Kists of the Pankisi Gorge in Georgia. Rasanayagam (2006a) gave a detailed analysis of the effects of the government's interventions to regulate Muslim orthodoxy in Uzbekistan by using the term as a political category. For further critique, see Corcoran-Nantes (2005).

status of police volunteer assistants (Polonskaya and Malashenko 1994: 133; Polat 2000; Ilkhamov 2001; Olcott 2007). After Adolat became popular in Namangan, thanks to its success in reducing the crime rate, it expanded into other cities of the valley, including Kokand. Its patrols were supposed to monitor the observation of sharia by local Muslims.

Alarmed by the increasing activity of Islamic groups, and following clashes in Namangan, Kokand, and other cities in the valley, the government cracked down on this embryonic opposition (Human Rights Watch 2004: 21). Mosques and madrasas thought to be meeting points for cells of militant Islamists were closed, and imams suspected of militant sympathies were replaced by imams known to be loyal to the state. Adolat was banned, and its leaders and numerous members were arrested (Babadjanov 1999; Human Rights Watch 2004). More generally, anyone who visited a mosque more than once a week, who dressed "Islamic" (*islomiy*), or who otherwise deviated from traditional Hanafi norms was liable to be arrested.

In the second half of the 1990s, the radical Islamic movements were either forced underground or driven out of Uzbekistan (Olcott 2007: 28). A few preachers, however, continued subversive activities such as the distribution of leaflets. Influential extremist groups of the late 1990s included Tavba (Repentance), Hezbollah (the Party of Allah), and Hizb ut-Tahrir.[53] In 1998, former members of Adolat joined other, similar groups united around Juma Namangani and Tahir Yuldashev to form the Islamic Movement of Uzbekistan (IMU), which in 1999 claimed responsibility for a series of explosions in Tashkent and organized armed raids and the seizing of hostages (Rashid 2002; Naumkin 2005). The IMU was formed to create an Islamist state in the territory of the former Turkistan. According to Olcott (2007: 28), its structure was little suited to ideological innovation, and it lacked the intellectual or doctrinal substance of the Muslim intellectual groupings of earlier years.[54]

---

[53] Hizb ut-Tahrir al-Islami (Islamic Party of Liberation) is a radical movement that advocates doctrinal practice and the establishment of a borderless, Islamic caliphate throughout Central Asia and the entire Muslim world (Rashid 2002).

[54] Editor's note: At this point the author indicated in a series of notes that she was not yet satisfied with her arguments in this section. Instead of relying heavily on the accounts of the "great schism" between so-called Hanafi traditionalists and Wahhabis presented by several contemporary historians, she intended to probe further into the origins and dissemination of this metaphor and then to convey more of the complexity of what her informants had to say about these events. The disputes among the elites were at the time by no means as clear as they seem to be in retrospective expert accounts. Hilgers wanted to bring out the way the confusion was experienced on the ground as different groups each claimed to be pointing to the unique truth. Individual decision-taking was inevitably influenced by many contingencies. At the same time, she did not wish to depict those with whom she was working as merely "naive" or as "victims".

Non-Muslim Religious Communities in Kokand

As in other parts of the Soviet Union, religious diversity in Kokand until the mid-1980s coincided largely with ethnic diversity and was the result of complex historical migration processes, including the deportations under Stalin (Barker 1997: 37). Armenians and Russians established communities in Kokand at the end of the nineteenth century.[55] A small Baptist community was founded in 1912 by Russian immigrants, who initially met for prayers in private houses. In 1948 they were given a house in a Russian *mahalla,* and in 1950 it was transformed into a church.

Russian Jews found an existing community of Bukharan Jews, who had been present in the Kokand khanate since around 1840 and had been expanding rapidly (concentrated in specific districts) since the annexation of the khanate by Russia in 1876.[56] During the 1920s and 1930s, many Jews fled the repressions of the Soviets, and only one synagogue out of six in Kokand continued to function as such. Although previously they worshipped in separate synagogues, Russian and Bukharan Jews nowadays conduct their services jointly. The current rabbi indicated that as many as 100 people attended the synagogue regularly in Soviet times. Because of emigration to Israel, the United States, and Germany, the community of Jews is still continuously shrinking. By the time of my research in 2004, the rabbi estimated the regular participants in his services to be fewer than fifteen, most of them elderly.

The former building of the Armenian Orthodox church in Kokand was erected in 1905 by the first wave of Armenian immigrants (Abramson 1998: 83).[57] After its confiscation by the Soviets, it served as a youth club and a textile store before being transformed into a prayer house by the Russian Orthodox church in 1946. Elena, the daughter of Father Vladimir, head of the Russian Orthodox church in Kokand since 1956, was the chief administrator of the church at the time of my fieldwork. She explained to me that the building was gradually converted into a proper church again in the 1960s, when those who gathered there to pray started to buy candles. Some icons were donated by a parish in Kazan, Tatarstan, and others were painted by

---

[55] See Peyrouse (2003) for more detailed information about Christianity in Central Asia.

[56] The settlement of Bukharan Jews in the towns of the former Kokand khanate was a consequence of tsarist policy. The Kokand authorities had allowed them to settle in the khanate as silk dyers, but at the time of the annexation the number of Bukharan Jews was reported to be only six. By 1887, 200 were reported in the documents (Poujol 1993: 552).

[57] Abramson (1998) mentioned an Armenian church built just before the 1917 Revolution. According to the current head administrator of the Russian Orthodox church in Kokand, this Armenian church was constructed in 1905. It is possible that Abramson was referring to another church – that is, there might have been more than one in the city in pre-Soviet times.

local artists. In 1992 the onion domes of the church were finally gilded, completing the transformation of an edifice originally built in the Armenian tradition. Elena, who was in her early forties when we spoke, recalled the large congregations of the 1970s: "There used to be up to 200 believers attending the Sunday services regularly, and I can remember that on special holidays such as Easter and Christmas the number was even higher. Today, the attendance at the Sunday service is a mere 10 per cent of what it used to be, and at the major holy days of the year there are about sixty people attending. It is mostly the old people who come to church".

Looking back on the same era, the pastor of the Baptist church and his wife recalled that in the early 1970s, when they joined the congregation, about sixty active members participated regularly in Sunday services. Despite the hardship caused by an environment hostile to religion, the pastor proudly pointed out that, unlike other religious communities that gave in to the pressure, the Baptists, as "upright", "faithful", and "brave" committed believers, had managed to survive.

Other narratives of Christian religious communities active in Kokand in Soviet times follow a similar pattern. Founded by an ethnic minority in colonial times, in a setting dominated by Muslims, they were then persecuted by the atheist regime (Peyrouse 2004b) but managed to define their position in the religious landscape as minority communities with an ethno-national character. Over time, these communities evolved into formal parishes, each with a church or at least a small prayer house, though because of Soviet anti-religious policies, such parishes were sometimes pushed into semi-clandestine existence. Christian minorities in Central Asia expressed their collective identity during socialism by emphasizing their "cultural" aspects (Peyrouse 2004b). The church was a place in which to profess religiosity, but it also played an important role as a vehicle for practising the national culture (Peyrouse 2004b: 653).

People did not necessarily view "believer" and "Soviet citizen" as mutually exclusive categories. All faith communities, Islam and Russian Orthodoxy included, followed an unwritten rule of non-interference in the internal affairs of other such communities. Conversion was not unknown, as is shown by the case of the Baptist pastor and his wife, both ethnic Russians who converted from Russian Orthodoxy in the early 1970s, but the general attitude was to respect the given boundaries, whether they had an ethnic overlay (as was considered to be the case not only with the Armenian Church and Turkic Muslims but also with Jews) or whether they demarcated simply a "faith minority" (Baptists and Russian Orthodox). According to the religious leaders I spoke to, Muslim and non-Muslim alike, it was rare in Soviet times for people to visit the religious buildings of a community other than their own. An Uzbek Muslim woman told me that once, when she was a teenager, she wanted to see a Russian service out of curiosity. As soon as she entered the church, some people asked her to leave, because as an Uzbek Muslim she was not supposed to visit a Russian Orthodox church. The Russian Orthodox Church continues to defend the idea of the "Russianness" of its faith, and this identity is upheld not only by active believers but also by many outsiders (Peyrouse 2004b: 669; cf. Barker 1997). Throughout the Soviet Union, government repression rendered the religious organizations of minorities largely passive in social and political terms; yet in a way the persecution helped to shape communities and maintain denominational boundaries (Kazmina and Filippova 2005: 1056). Restricted scopes of operation, limited access to information and religious literature, and discrimination and anti-religious propaganda created a religious landscape in which the character of religious communities became more ethnicized. Their public, physical invisibility assured a certain stability and continuity of membership.

In Uzbekistan this equilibrium was disturbed towards the end of the 1980s by ethnic tensions, growing Uzbek nationalism, economic decline, and external assistance for certain minorities, particularly Jews, who were helped to leave the country by American and Israeli Jewish associations as well as by the Federal Republic of Germany.[58] As elsewhere in the Soviet Union in the 1980s, American Baptists assisted their co-religionists in migrating to the United States, not only in terms of administrative procedures but also financially.[59] These foreign encounters, together with the arrival of some new religious groups in Uzbekistan, changed the religious landscape and the collective memory (Davie 1999: 80).[60] Most of the newcomers belonged to charismatic Protestant congregations. Pentecostals were especially active in their proselytizing.[61]

---

[58] For a detailed ethnographic study of German immigration policy as it shaped the biographies of Russian Jews, see Becker (2001).

[59] The pastor of the Pentecostal community in Kokand and his wife, both ethnic Koreans, told me they had converted to Baptism for rational reasons: "In 1992 missionaries came here. During this time American Baptists helped [local Baptists] to move to the US. So I said to my wife, 'Let's become Baptists and then we can go to America!'" They bought a Bible, began studying the teachings of Christianity, and were baptized into the Baptist church. By the time they were eligible to apply to the American Baptist organization for assistance, however, they had both become born-again Christians and now saw it as their mission to stay and help their home country improve in spiritual terms.

[60] As Peyrouse (2004b) has shown, when parishes receive foreign assistance, they often find themselves criticized because their liturgical practices are considered unorthodox. Foreigner-led "modernization" could lead to protest and resistance in the local congregation (cf. Wanner 2004: 744ff.).

[61] The degree to which foreigners are equated with missionaries became clear to me when I learned from a Jewish family I often visited during my fieldwork that the wife of the rabbi had

Among the established congregations, the Baptist parish suffered the most, losing members to both emigration and conversion. Knowledge of alternative directions within Baptism led to a breach as "modernizers", mainly younger parishioners, criticized familiar modes of praying and the organization of the service and demanded a more charismatic approach. When they failed to gain support from the majority of the parishioners and the pastor, this group separated and continued to meet in private. In April 2004 the pastor explained the split as follows:

> There are these new Baptists [*novyye baptisty*] … that's a difficult issue. … People are paid money, that's one reason. Foreign missionaries are coming offering a "new way" to the people – of course, their way. They get new recruits only by paying money to make people follow their way and to become adherents of their direction: "Kto platit, tot i zakazyvayet muzyku" [Rus., he who pays the piper calls the tune]. A second reason for this split was that young people often do not like to follow rules and restrictions. Instead of obeying, they demand something new and to change the given order, such as the way of praying. The new direction of Baptism was brought here by foreign missionaries after independence. … It must have started here three or four years ago.

In the first years after independence, this pastor had organized screenings at the local cinema of films of Billy Graham, the American Baptist preacher and one of the founders of the Evangelical movement. Later, increasing government restrictions – prompted not by problems with the Protestants but by the problem of radical public Islam, as indicated earlier in the story of Sevara – precluded such public initiatives.

The case of the Baptist community shows the ambiguity of change as it was experienced by the established congregations. Opportunities to take up a more active public life were welcomed, but only if they did not threaten the established character of the local community. A similar concern with protecting an imagined church tradition can be found in the Russian Orthodox church in Kokand, where Father Vladimir rejected innovations and played on tradition as a weapon to hold onto the souls and minds of the Orthodox parishioners. Thus, while the parish in Ferghana city decided to postpone celebrations of feasts falling on workdays until the following Sunday, Father Vladimir continued to celebrate them on the calendrically correct day. According to Elena, his daughter, this conservatism was highly valued and had led believers from parishes such as Ferghana city to join the services in Kokand. According to this strategy, changes should be introduced only

---

warned them that, since I was a German Christian, my true intention in conducting this research must be to convert Jews.

gradually and by means of consensus, so as not to challenge the status quo of the community.

The first entirely new Christian denominations in the city were established on the initiative of South Korean missionaries of charismatic Protestant movements, whose initial prime target group was the local ethnic Korean population.[62] The missionaries organized gatherings in Korean cultural centres to spread the Christian gospel among people who had previously identified as nominal Buddhists or as atheists. Ilya, an ethnic Korean whose family was second generation in Kokand, explained: "You know, we are ethnic Koreans, but yet we are not … we are Russian Koreans. We do not speak Korean, but Russian. Our religion is Buddhism, but we have no idea about it".

Although he himself had not converted, Ilya had attended such a meeting of the Korean missionaries and observed their initial consolidation. A prayer house was financed by the South Korean mother church. At about the same time, another charismatic Protestant prayer house opened near the Russian Orthodox church. This Evangelical community was, by the time of my fieldwork, the largest Christian congregation in Kokand, and it was still expanding. Its pastor quit in 2000, taking a group of members with him to found a new Pentecostal congregation, but they remained on amicable terms with the older community. By the time of my research, these Pentecostalists consisted of about twenty members of various nationalities. They were unregistered and therefore formally an illegal religious organization, but in practice the local officials tolerated them.

Some years after the departure of this pastor, the Evangelical church experienced a second split when a group of Uzbek members began to conduct Bible studies in the Uzbek language instead of Russian and proceeded to found their own "Church of Uzbek Christians", with membership open only to ethnic Uzbeks (see chapter 7). Like the Pentecostal and Baptist splinter groups, these Uzbek Christians met in private houses and had no official registration, because they had fewer than the 100 members required by law.

One further "community in the making" was being initiated at the time of my fieldwork by a young Ukrainian couple, graduates of a Christian

---

[62] These Koreans were the descendants of migrants who had fled famine and Japanese political repression in Korea at the end of the eighteenth and beginning of the nineteenth century. Under Stalin, large numbers of ethnic Koreans were accused of espionage for the Japanese and resettled in the Kazakh and Uzbek republics in 1937. The number of Koreans still residing in Uzbekistan is about 200,000 (Kim 2005; Oh 2006: 114). Korean churches have the status of "national churches" in Uzbekistan, although they do not limit themselves exclusively to Koreans but proselytize actively among the Turkic and Slavic populations as well (Kim 2005).

institute in Ukraine. They worked with drug addicts and their families, and their base was a rehabilitation centre in an industrial city close to Tashkent.[63] Alongside this charitable work, their goal was to form a new Christian community called Loza. The husband, Sasha, described the couple's vision as follows: "My wife is from a different church than I. I belong more to that old conservative direction, my wife to the new charismatic one. Now we want to create a new kind of church, which we have adapted from the two extremes to the middle. We let people remain themselves". At the time of my stay, this community consisted of a loose network of about seven families, both Uzbeks and Slavs, all of whom were engaged in the rehabilitation program.

On Alliances and Boundaries

The Russian Orthodox Church has reacted to the "threat" posed by new religious organizations in post-Soviet Central Asia by seeking to polarize the religious spectrum around an Orthodoxy-Islam axis (Peyrouse 2004a: 49). The conversation I had with Father Sergej, pro-rector of the Russian Orthodox seminary in Tashkent, in 2003 drew out opinions similar to those I heard from other priests, as well as from members of the ulema:

> *Hilgers*: What is a traditional church?
>
> *Father Sergej*: Traditional religious establishments and institutions, first, have a centuries-old history. Second, they are traditional for a specific territorial area, that is, a region. Third, they exhibit some definite stable norms of worshipping and so on. And … the other difference is that they co-exist peacefully with other religious and public associations, do not cause any harm or get into conflict with anyone. A traditional religion does not start a conflict with other religions and organizations. More often, traditional religions form the culture of the nation where they exist. Non-traditional religious associations have totally contradictory features.
>
> *Hilgers*: What are your relations with other denominations?
>
> *Father Sergej*: We have close and good neighbourly relations with Islam; we are friends and we at the same time teach our believers to assist each other and to be friends.
>
> *Hilgers*: Why Islam?

[63] In working with drug addicts, this centre followed a holistic approach including a twelve-step program based on the Bible and involving regular prayers and collective worship. Treatment of the addicts involved living with them and their families for several months; the family had to be integrated into the therapy during and after the patient's detoxification. The program's headquarters was in the Netherlands.

Father Sergej: It is interesting to begin mutual study with the ancient cultures. Islam, too, has got some divisions or schools, and we accept only those propagating peace and accord. …
Hilgers: What is your relation to the new religious groups in Uzbekistan?
Father Sergej: Emphatically negative. …
Hilgers: Why?
Father Sergej: Because most of them, psychologically, break the person, sometimes making zombies out of people … taking them out of their usual way of life. … Families and the basis of the state are destroyed. … Quite often money is the aim … they are working only for money. … Cults have commercial characteristics … there is no discussion about saving the soul … nor about internal perfection.

Father Sergej's opinions conformed to the official dichotomy between traditional and non-traditional religions, a major element in the government's ideology. Many Orthodox priests see an indissoluble tie between Russianness and Orthodoxy, and for them, to be a Muslim means, similarly, to belong to a national rather than a universal religion. Members of the official ulema and the Orthodox clergy issued a joint declaration in 1995 that included the words, "We speak out for our common interest in strengthening the Islamic spirit of the Muslim people, as well as the Christian spirit of the Slavic population of Central Asia, because the two religions are the holy heritage of our ancestors".[64] Archbishop Vladimir, of the Orthodox Diocese of Bishkek and All Central Asia, traces the historic friendship and mutual respect between Islam and Russian Christianity back to the Middle Ages. Their alliance was strengthened by the common fight against militant atheism under the Soviet regime, and it is strengthened today by the necessity of combating foreign influences from both Christian sects and Wahhabism (Archbishop Vladimir 2000).

Islam is not classified officially as a national religion, but it is the basis of all tradition in the government's ideology, where it is routinely equated with "native" in a cultural sense.[65] This status empowers the state-sponsored Islamic elites, represented by the muftiate (the Muslim Board of Uzbekistan, or MBU), and the Russian Orthodox clergy, represented by the metropolitan of Tashkent, to become key players in shaping the regulative framework for

[64] See www.bahaindex.com/en/news/1-general-news/1161-not-losing-their-religion.
[65] This usage derives from the Soviet discourse concerning indigenous or ethnic tradition. As Koroteyeva and Makarova noted (1998: 580), "native" was loaded with a double meaning: it referred to the purely cultural and was also an evaluative term in which tradition meant backwardness, in opposition to modern Soviet civilization.

all religious activity.[66] The Russian Orthodox Church and the MBU undertook an effective lobbying campaign to change the 1992 law on religion, which in their view was too favourable to the development of religious pluralism. The 1998 revised law, described earlier, met most of their demands by opting (as had Russia itself by this time) for a rather vaguely defined category of "traditional religious communities" (Anderson 2002; see also Richardson 1997; Shterin 2003; Wanner 2004). The state-approved Muslim religious authorities and the Russian Orthodox Church were the most self-evidently traditional religions. Minorities such as Baptists, Armenian Orthodox Christians, and Lutherans perceived themselves as having historic roots in the region, but even when officially acknowledged to have such roots, they were still not granted the same privileges as the two dominant religions. Occasionally, however, they, too, were mobilized against the new religious movements – for example, by being invited to conferences aimed at fostering "inter-religious dialogue". The Russian Orthodox Church tends to be hostile to all the minority faiths, degrading them under the category of non-traditional.

In Kokand, the Russian Orthodox priest and the *imom-khotib* of the Jome' mosque both refer to the newcomer groups as threats to the stability of society, even though they may have friendly personal relations with some of their leaders, with whom they interact at ecumenical conferences. All the Christian communities in Kokand apart from that of the Russian Orthodox Church (and including the pastors who have previously initiated fission) cooperate closely and insist that they do not see themselves as being in competition. These congregations invite each other to their services, celebrate festivals together, and organize recreational activities such as picnics, sporting events, excursions, and holiday camps. They help each other out when necessary.[67] At Easter 2004 they watched the recently released movie *The Passion of Christ* together in the Evangelical church.[68]

Towards the end of my fieldwork, the pastors were discussing how to break down the boundaries between their communities in the city and join

---

66 The general pattern according to which dominant religions in the former Soviet Union became effective political players has been noted by Wanner (2004: 754). The developments in Uzbekistan are distinctive because of the close alliance of the Russian Orthodox Church with the official Muslim ulema, although some similarities can be seen in Kyrgyzstan and Kazakhstan (see Peyrouse 2004; Pelkmans 2006).

67 During my stay in Kokand, the pastors told me they were sharing the responsibility for an Uzbek Muslim woman who had been possessed by an evil spirit (*jin*) and were conducting the exorcism jointly.

68 This movie, dramatizing the last twelve hours of the life of Jesus Christ, is considered controversial because of its violent scenes, and Jews have accused it of promoting anti-Semitism.

forces on the basis of Christian universalism. It was clear, however, that this universalism would not include what they called “traditional religions”, including Russian Orthodoxy and Roman Catholicism. Criticism of these churches was a constant theme of sermons and study groups. The Evangelical pastor caricatured Muslims and Russian Orthodox Christians as “robots who perform their program of prayers automatically … a mere form and soulless sequence of movements for fulfilling obligations, lacking real belief and contact with God”. Those religions were alleged to be bound to material goods and to traditions that included the lavish robes of the leaders, the veneration of icons, saints, and ritual objects, and a highly ritualized liturgy.[69] The new Protestant congregations understood their own faith to be “modern”. In theory there was no place for denominational boundaries, because all who professed faith in Jesus Christ belonged to the universal category of Christian believers. The boundary separating them from the dominant groups was still there, but in optimistic moments even this might be overcome. The Pentecostal pastor gave me the following view of the tensions in the religious field:

> *Hilgers*: What is your relation to the Russian Orthodox church in this city?
> *Pastor*: Bad!
> *Hilgers*: Why?
> *Pastor*: Because for the Orthodox all these movements are sects.
> *Hilgers*: And why is that?
> *Pastor*: Because Orthodoxy is built on traditions. We don’t have icons and big temples and we don’t worship these dead bodies and the things the saints used to possess, and our service is conducted differently. But the Orthodox Church is also changing now. I think that in the end all denominations will come to unity. I don’t think that all will become Orthodox or Baptists, but the secondary things will just disappear. Because Jesus is coming to take his body and not denominations, that’s why.

Assertions that such congregations belong to the universal community of Christian believers, outside not only formal, ritualized, and institutionalized religions but also outside ethno-religious boundaries, can be understood as a way of responding to accusations from members of the local ulema and the Russian Orthodox priest that all the new Protestant congregations are merely sectarian. Yet the new communities see themselves as national in the sense that they, too, are concerned with the moral and spiritual condition of the country. Prayers for the future of the nation and for President Karimov

[69] This scepticism and critique is shared by some Muslims with regard to the established ulema, as I show in chapter 4.

are regular features of the Sunday services and study groups of the new Christian congregations in town. The Evangelical church organized a special weekly meeting specifically to pray for the prosperity of the nation and its leaders.

Conclusion

Catherine Wanner (2004: 755), writing about Protestant congregations in Ukraine, emphasized their non-national aspects: "These localized and transnational communities challenge traditional ties that link a particular religion to a certain group, social hierarchy, territory, or state. In return, they provide new social capital that links individuals to communities in another form by creating new cultural values and practices that simultaneously separate nations that have been politically united … and reattach these groups to a far greater social field inhabited by a global community of believers".

In the case of Uzbekistan, Wanner's analysis seems more readily applicable to alternative interpretations of Islam – that is, to the new currents critical of the traditional Uzbek Hanafi orthodoxy – than to the new Christian communities. Ideally, Islam is sharply opposed to any notion of distinctive local communities; in Islam, "the confessional group, or *umma,* was to displace the nation, and the Arabic language of its revelation was to transcend its ethnic origins and have a supra-national status" (Peel 2000: 281). The critics of Karimov's Uzbek Islam transgress its prescribed boundaries when they argue with reference solely to the Qur'an and Hadith and condemn notions of tradition in terms of local customs and practices transmitted over the generations, which can represent only the local rather than the universal (see Muminov 2005).

Fragmentation on the basis of diverging tendencies – one towards a scriptural, universal reading of Islam and the other towards a localized version – is common in the contemporary Muslim world, in which the ulema no longer have a monopoly over sacred authority and in which broader access to information and doctrinal knowledge has empowered "ordinary" Muslims (Eickelman and Piscatori 1996: 43, 131). In the case of Uzbekistan, contestations began within the local ulema but spread increasingly to the laity as the Soviet system disintegrated. The established ulema had to create boundaries demarcating their own stance from the diverse alternative readings of Islam in order to maintain hegemony. They did so by falling into line with the government's discourse on "right" and "wrong" interpretations of Islam, and the power of the muftiate was therefore at the disposal of the new secular authorities.

The case of postsocialist Uzbekistan has many distinctive features, but diversification within the religious sphere in the context of changing demographic, economic, and political circumstances has thrown up comparable challenges to established religions the world over. These religions typically attempt to exclude and de-legitimate the newcomers. In Uzbekistan, an intricate dance of cooperation and contest takes place on two levels: that of form, practice, and interpretation, on the one hand, and that of religious dominance, on the other. This contestation takes place within confessional boundaries rather than between them. The new movements deny that locality and tradition can provide the basis for religious hegemony. They argue for doctrinal universalism – that is, for a religious self firmly located in the spiritual community of believers but detached from historically contingent ethno-religious ties and profane local or regional customs and practices.

In their work on secularization, Peter Berger and Thomas Luckmann (1967) predicted a decrease in, or even a breakdown of, the religious hegemony of dominant religions. They understood religious pluralism to be a result of secularization: that is, competition between religions increases, the state withdraws, and the old religious monopoly is abrogated. David Martin (2005: 41) noted that evangelical movements create "an autonomous social space within which people may participate in the creation of a different kind of sub-society". As these enclaves multiply, he argued, religious monopoly breaks down and pluralism replaces it; mediation gives way to direct access; and a competitive religious economy is established. Another sociologist of religion, José Casanova (1994), has drawn attention to the difficulties experienced by traditional churches when confronted by religious congregations with strong salvational doctrines. But how far can these various theories be applied to the religious field in Uzbekistan?

Despite the increasing diversity I have outlined in this chapter, if religious pluralism is understood to mean peaceful, tolerant, egalitarian relations between religions, then Uzbekistan is not evolving towards pluralism. On the contrary, the opposite can be observed: an embryonic diversity did not lead to a breakdown of religious hegemony on the part of the traditional religions but was itself instrumentalized by the existing powerholders.[70] The representatives of state-approved Islam and of Russian Orthodoxy in Uzbekistan forged what they perceived to be a natural alliance to maintain the status quo in both religion and politics (cf. Bourdieu 2000: 97).

The term *tradition* is used in very different ways by the chief rivals in this contest. For some it is a normative category, loaded with political meaning because it implies a *longue durée* congruence of religion and nationality

[70] A similar development can be observed in Russia, where the Russian Orthodox Church advocated the amendment of the law on religions in order to restrict the activities of non-traditional communities alleged to pose a threat to unity and to Russian culture (see Kazmina and Filippova 2005).

in a given territory (Archbishop Vladimir 2000; Peyrouse 2003). In this reading, it is an integral part of the "cultural package" of the respective group, which cannot possibly be matched by any non-traditional community. This is quite different from the use of the term *tradition* with reference to disputes within the religious field concerning questions of doctrine and proper conduct. The new religious movements are to be understood in highly universalistic terms. "Tradition" for them refers to a religious theory and genealogy rather than to a local cultural idiom. It is therefore not surprising that both charismatic Protestants and Muslims promoting a scripturalist interpretation of Islam should deplore the national independence ideology of the postsocialist government.

The conflict can also be illuminated by focusing on the competition between religious specialists, who draw on various sources of knowledge and authority on both the spiritual and political levels to maintain their positions in the religious field. Discussions about the finer points of theology or ideology are integral parts of the competition over sacred authority, for control of symbolic and material resources, and for control of human capital – the believers themselves. In Kokand, the odds have been stacked in favour of those who argue that tradition means the "religious heritage" of the nation, a resource available to be instrumentalized for legitimation purposes in nation-building (Rasanayagam 2006c).

Sergei Abashin (2006) has argued against reducing Muslim diversity to a simple opposition between traditionalism and fundamentalism, because all parties insist that their version of Islam is "correct" and try to present themselves as "real" Muslims (2006: 269). In the following chapter I look more concretely at how tradition and Muslimness are defined in everyday life. In Uzbekistan this simplifying dichotomy has become a central political category: "fundamentalism", and indeed any alternative reading of Islam, is seen as a threat to local customs and traditions.[71] Islam represents only one dimension of this polarity, which has been extended to include the proselytizing new religious movements. The contestation has nothing to do with theology but rather with political control over the religious sphere. The government's categorization has material and juridical consequence for all religious communities, helping some to maintain their hegemony while hindering others.

[71] See Ilkhamov's discussion (2006b) of a Muslim movement in the Ferghana Valley that became known under the name Akromiya.

Chapter 4
Conceptualizing *Musulmonchilik*

> The main difference between us and others is simply that we got detached from our Muslim traditions during Soviet times. We learned how to be good Soviet citizens, but now that we again have the freedom to live our religion openly, we need to learn again what it means to be a Muslim.
>
> – A Sufi *shaykh,* Chor Bakr, July 2004

The new enthusiasm for religion on the part of many citizens of Uzbekistan in the 1990s was expressed in statements such as "Now everything is free [*erk*]", "Our religion was given back to us", and "Thank God we have a law proclaiming freedom of conscience; anyone can choose his or her faith, and no one can reproach me any more for praying". This freedom could be experienced on a day-to-day basis as information about religion became openly accessible through the media, not least over the Internet. Religious organizations opened their doors and offered courses, seminars, and information days for anyone who was interested. The feeling of having the right to practise one's faith led to a sharp increase in mosque and church attendance. The imam of the Jome' mosque in Kokand estimated the number of men attending on Fridays in the early 1980s to be around 200, most of them elderly.[72] A decade later the figure was approximately 3,000 to 4,000.[73]

The public display of Islam was significant at the national level as a clear sign of autonomy from the USSR, as well as at the individual level. Indeed, it was difficult to separate the two. Munir, who worked for a local

[72] Few mosques in Uzbekistan have separate spaces for women. Although not officially prohibited from going to mosque, women generally pray at home (see the discussion of gendered spaces in chapter 6).

[73] Ro'i (2000: 73) cited figures of 2,000–2,500, rising to 5,000 at the major festivals, for Kokand in 1951, figures somewhat lower than those for the other major cities of the Ferghana Valley. He also noted another source for the same period (Ro'i 2000: 220–221), which provides an estimate similar to that which I was given by the imam.

NGO in Kokand, explained to me that to be a "good" Uzbek meant to be a Muslim according to the common-sense understanding of Uzbek society. This included going to mosque, professing the religion of one's ancestors, and reconnecting with what was considered authentic Uzbek culture after more than seventy years of alienation.[74] Munir told me that, like many people he knew, he went to mosque only because "everyone did it". No one wanted to be labelled a misfit or to stand out as a "bad" Muslim and Uzbek. Iroda, who had converted to Christianity in the late nineties, was critical of this attitude: "It was a fashion to go to mosque. It was just a matter of fashion, or people were just going because they were afraid of their reputation in the *mahalla,* so that no one would reproach them for not going to mosque. It was just all about showing off. It was all mendacity".

In this chapter I examine the way people like Munir and Iroda have redefined their notions of being Uzbek and being Muslim in recent years. Factors such as growing national consciousness and neighbourhood social expectations certainly provide a part of the answer. Here, however, I am more interested in the individual; the case of Iroda shows that the sincerely held inner convictions we summarize as "belief" also play a role, as does curiosity about the supernatural.

But before giving voice to four individual Uzbeks – Khushnud, Dilorom, Botir, and Iroda – I want to explain more fully the social context of their actions. In outlining Sevara's story in the previous chapter, I showed how issues of nationality and religious affiliation became contested in the 1990s. To be a good Uzbek, one was supposed go to mosque, or one would be criticized by nationalists and Islamists alike. As the mullah of the small mosque in the *mahalla* where I lived in Kokand explained, many people resented the Islamist critique of local practices and lifestyles that had been transmitted even throughout Soviet times. Uzbek Muslims were being criticized for not performing the ritual prayers correctly, he said. "According to those Wahhabis, it is not right to fold your hands on your stomach. They say, the hands should be laid on the breast. But I think the important thing is that we abide by our *mazhab* [school of law in Islam]. Saudis and Muslims from other nations cannot be telling us how to profess our religion, because they belong to another *mazhab* than the Hanafi, that is ours".

In the early 1990s, militant Islamist organizations assumed not only the functions of law enforcement agencies but also the role of a moral police force. Many people experienced tension as the struggle for doctrinal dominance expanded to affect the lives of ordinary Muslims. The government's

---

[74] In the early 1990s it was common for women in cities of the Ferghana Valley, when walking in public streets, to wear the traditional *paranji,* which covered their bodies from head to toe.

repressive measures affected the Ferghana Valley harder than any other area in Uzbekistan.[75] The valley is geographically separated from the rest of Uzbekistan, and military control posts secure the pass into it. To the south lies Tajikistan, which experienced a protracted civil war in the 1990s, and Afghanistan is just a short distance away. It is well known that many Uzbeks have joined the Taliban and other militant groups, and this is often mentioned when people express their discomfort with all forms of radical religious expression and attitudes.

The aggressive demeanour of many Islamists – for example, when dismissing the Muslims of the former Soviet Union as being only nominal Muslims, who had forgotten the essence of Islam – led to a reaction. Like Sevara, many recoiled from their initial enthusiasm after negative encounters with Muslims and further reflection upon what it actually meant to be a Muslim and a good person in moral and religious terms. Another factor was the "everyday vulnerabilities" (Rasanayagam 2006a) that left most citizens with a feeling of insecurity in relation to state policies and the application of the law. When the government is determined to combat Islamic extremism, ordinary believers can easily become suspect; it is enough to dress according to the Islamic dress code (see Human Rights Watch 2004; Rasanayagam 2006a; McGlinchey 2007).

Although definitions of what it means to be a good Muslim take different shapes for different people, almost everyone I talked to acknowledged a strong sense of obligation to maintain the traditions of the ancestors (Akiner 2003: 101). For a majority, differences and incompatibilities among Muslims were articulated in a comparison between "ours" and "theirs". As Privratsky (2001: 109–110) observed for the Kazakhs, local deviations from sharia are defended by their "Muslimness", meaning their being the "familiar way". A frequent comment in this context was, "Our Muslimness is different [Bizning musulmonchiligimiz boshqacha]".

Musulmonchilik, Muslimness, in the discourses of ordinary Uzbek Muslims, refers to both a local way and the inner essence of being Muslim (see Privratsky 2001; Louw 2006; Rasanayagam 2006b). In common parlance it refers to all the religious heritage and ritual practices transferred by one's forefathers. It is also *din,* meaning religion generally, although in the Uzbek context the term is used mostly with reference to Islam. Muslimness embraces the confession of Islam, the observation of the five pillars, a lifestyle that accords with the norms of Islamic doctrine, the reading of the

[75] The literature on the radical Islamist movements of the Ferghana Valley in the post-independence period is extensive, but most studies confine themselves to security issues. See Human Rights Watch (2004); Lubin (1999); McGlinchey (2006); Rashid (1995, 2003); Sagdeev (2000).

Qur'an, and attendance at mosque. Although contested by Islamists, in the views of many Uzbeks, syncretic practices such as the cult of saints, the lighting of candles at graveyards (derived from Zoroastrianism), and commemoration feasts held twenty and forty days after a person's death (said also to originate in pre-Islamic traditions) are legitimate. The cult of saints and shrine veneration are seen as connecting the present to a cultural genealogy that is not only embodied in the conscience of a people but also inscribed in the landscape itself (cf. Privatsky's discussion [2001: 238] of the shrines of Sufi saints and the cemeteries of ancestors in Kazakhstan).

Local ideas about Islam have been deeply permeated by Sufism, the mystical current of Islam that is tolerant in its interpretations of the faith and focuses attention on the inner self.[76] Indeed, tolerance and the peaceful coexistence of cultures and religions are held to be distinctive features of the whole of Movarounnahr, or Transoxiana.[77] There, Zoroastrianism, Nestorian Christianity, and Manichaeism have all left their traces in local practices such as remnants of the fire cult at weddings and the lighting of candles at graveyards (both deriving from Zoroastrianism) and the commemoration rituals performed on the twentieth and fortieth days after a death (sometimes attributed to Christianity). Even so, the local concept of *musulmonchilik* is grounded primarily in the social and cultural memory of the experience of more than seventy years of Soviet constraints on religious practice.

The movie *To'ylar Muborak* ("May the weddings be blessed") is a comedy about an Uzbek on his way to his wedding ceremony at the ZAGS office, the civil registry.[78] The hero is held up on the way by all kinds of people asking him for help. The film was shot in 1985 and depicts life in modern Tashkent. The characters wear fashionable, European-style clothes, and the wedding reception takes place cocktail-party style in a flat in a modern, multi-storey building. The older part of the city, *eski shahar,* is rarely shown, and then mostly to demonstrate how poor and backward its inhabitants are. I watched the movie with Aziza, a woman in her fifties, who pointed to women wearing tight minidresses and fancy high heels and combing their hair back: "Look, this is how I used to dress up in those days … When I was young, I was *chop-chop*".[79] At this point Farrukh, her husband,

---

[76] Editor's note: At this point in her manuscript Hilgers indicated her intention to elaborate this brief characterization of Sufism with reference to works by Schubel, Louw, and Zarcone.

[77] Movarounnahr (Arab., "on the other side of, or beyond, the river") is the old name for the entire region north of the Amu Darya river, usually known in English as Transoxiana.

[78] The Otdel Zapisi Aktov Grazhdanskogo Sostoyaniya (ZAGS) (Rus.) – literally, the Department for the Recording of Acts of Civilian Status – is the Soviet equivalent of the Registry Office in Britain. In Uzbekistan, it has not changed since Soviet times.

[79] *Chop-chop* means roughly "active, lively, brisk, running around a lot while staying within acceptable moral boundaries".

interrupted to tease her by saying, "And look at her now – she was so beautiful when I met her, and now she looks like a Wahhabi". Aziza at the time knotted a headscarf under her chin and wore a long, loose-fitting dress.

Soviet ideology might not have colonized life-worlds completely, but in Uzbekistan it certainly oriented many people towards a lifestyle they considered to be modern – that is, Western, with mainly Russian role models. The ideology changed what it meant to be a Muslim for all those socialized under the Soviet system. For some of the elderly, Islam was still a "lived religion", and the perpetuation of religious knowledge and practices was central to their Uzbek identity, in opposition to the new, all-encompassing Soviet lifestyle. For the younger generations, however, religion gradually lost its meaning. The great majority of those I talked to told me they had learned about Islam from their grandparents, parents, or both, but a gradual decline in the level of knowledge of Islam was unavoidable, given the pressure from the government, limited access to Muslim literature, and the simple fact that the later generations were unable to read Arabic as a result of the alphabet changes.[80] For many, engagement with religion became unfashionable. To read the Qur'an and observe religious practices was the business of old people and associated with the past. A sixty-three-year-old woman explained:

> My grandmother and my mother read the Qur'an and prayed. They taught us about Islam, but my siblings and I never really cared. It was something for the old people. We learned about Uzbek customs, celebrated Muslim holidays, and identified as Muslims, but without feeling the need or the wish to learn more and get seriously engaged with the belief. One was Uzbek, therefore Muslim, and at the same time a citizen of the Soviet Union.

Islam had become for many a marker of cultural and spiritual identity rather than an active spiritual commitment. Its social significance had been reduced largely to life-cycle rituals (see chapter 6). The religious customs that survived did so under the cover of "national tradition" (Critchlow 1991). Often they were mixed with – or covered by - secular Soviet elements, notably in the way state registration became an integral part of wedding ceremonies (see chapter 5). Stories used to circulate about KGB officers observing Muslim funerals at graveyards; those later identified in the photographs were liable to be dismissed from their jobs.[81] Some people reported

[80] For more information on the political background of the decision to introduce Cyrillic and the wider implications of alphabet changes in Soviet Central Asia, taking Turkmenistan as an example, see Clement (2007).

[81] The KGB was the Komitet Gosudarstvennoy Bezopasnosti (Rus.), the Committee for State Security.

receiving verbal warnings for attending private religious study circles. For the sincerely religious, irrespective of denomination, Soviet controls meant risking exclusion from access to resources, prestigious jobs, and institutions of higher education. As Viktor Mikhailovich, the pastor of the Baptist community in Kokand, explained to me: "Everybody could believe in what they wanted, but if you wanted to become a party member or hold a government job, you officially had to confess that you were an atheist and that God did not exist. Otherwise you had no chance of a career; for that in general you had to be a member of the party. One had to choose between career and belief".

Mikhailovich's formulation describes the official discourse of the Soviet period – an "ideal" case of sorts. The majority of people growing up in the Soviet system aligned their interests and aims to this situation as best they could, striving for a happy life and keeping out of trouble. The account of a *shaykh* of the Naqshbandiya order of his "double life" (his formulation) during the Soviet era illustrates that it was possible to combine being an observant and pious believer with being a state employee, as long as the public and private spheres remained clearly distinct:

> Like all the other religious groups and movements, Sufis were not tolerated under the Soviets and were persecuted. Practising Sufis were dismissed from their jobs or, under Stalin, even deported to labour camps. The Naqshbandiya order survived underground. The possibilities for performing *zikr* [mystical prayer with ritual recitations] of course were limited, but people met in small groups in private houses. We lived a kind of double life. In the morning I left the house in a suit and tie, did my job as a teacher in state employment. In the evening I returned home, exchanged my suit and briefcase for my *chopon* [cloak], *do'ppi* [skullcap], and prayer rug, and read the Qur'an and performed *namoz*. Of course it was difficult to observe all the prayer times, but I tried my best to comply whenever possible.

The best known exemplar of the compatibility of being Soviet and Muslim was Sharof Rashidov, the first secretary of the Uzbek Communist Party from 1959 until his death in 1983 and the most senior Soviet leader to observe the Muslim obligations.[82] Although denunciations took place, there was a kind of tacit agreement in certain circles to keep silent about issues of belief.

---

[82] Sharof Rashidovich Rashidov (1917–1983) died, apparently of a heart attack, after he was accused of being a central player in a large corruption affair later known as the "cotton scandal". Rashidov and the corrupt leadership in Moscow inflated the cotton quota by thousands of tons a year (see Rumer 1989).

Such silencing of belief and domestication of religion (Dragadze 1993) resulted in religiosity's being widely understood as an inner matter of the heart that did not necessarily need to be expressed in rituals as long as it was sincere. Khushnud, whom I introduce at greater length later, explained to me that Islam formed the basis of Uzbek society, and that observing *o'zbekchilik,* Uzbekness, meant automatically observing the social and moral norms of Islam.[83] Sixty-four years old, he argued that if children were taught the morals of Uzbek society from an early age, that would indirectly impart to them knowledge of Islam. His view was strongly challenged by his twenty-one-year-old nephew Botir, who made a clear distinction between *musulmonchilik,* on the one hand, and *o'zbekchilik* and *urf-odat* (local customs), on the other. For Khushnud, who sees Islam as the underlying feature of his being Uzbek and his *urf-odat,* this distinction cannot be drawn. As one woman succinctly summarized: "The occasion and the basis for any celebration is determined by *musulmonchilik,* [and] the way it is done, by *urf-odat*".

Plate 7. Practicing Uzbek hospitality: Female guests pronounce a blessing prayer (*duo*) for the hostess and their relatives prior to the meal.

[83] Editor's note: The manuscript indicated an intention to discuss at this point a definition of Uzbekness put forward by Peter Finke, but I have been unable to trace such a definition in any publication of this author. In his unpublished *Habilitationsschrift* (Finke 2006), he develops a "permeable" concept of Uzbekness, in contrast to an ethnicity given by genealogy.

The Uzbek sociologist Marfua Tokhtakhodjaeva (1995: 65) wrote of a bi-religious society under socialism: the internal religion of Islam became covered over by the "outer communist religion", and in consequence Islam stagnated. This conception of a form of inward, private religiosity that could be reconciled with modernity in the guise of Soviet socialism helped to shape a way of remaining a Muslim, enabling believers to avoid confrontation and to bridge the two ostensibly contradictory worldviews.

Plate 8. Female merchants selling *do'ppi*, the traditional Uzbek headgear and a symbol of *o'zbekchilik*, at a bazaar.

Searching for Spirituality

The surge of interest in religion in the postsocialist countries is frequently explained in terms of a need to fill the ideological vacuum that followed the collapse of Marxism-Leninism (see Polat 2000; Pollack 2001). According to some scholars, the new religious movements have been successful because they have provided people with new meanings and the security they long for (Pollack 2001). Some writers have gone so far as to compare Soviet ideology and scientific atheism to religion (Rzehak 2002). Alternatively, they question the existence of any spirituality at all during Soviet times and suggest the term *spiritual vacuum* to describe an overarching identity crisis (Merdjanova 2002: n. 25). All arguments in this vein imply that the Marxist-Leninist project was successful, and Soviet citizens rejected their former faiths. It is important to probe further into the extent to which Soviet ideology actually penetrated the lives of citizens, and particularly into the meaning of spirituality.

According to the head of the Council for Spirituality and Enlightenment in Tashkent, a spiritual person (*ma'naviyatli inson*) is first and foremost an educated and knowledgeable person. He or she places special emphasis on a kind of secular reading of spirituality, involving knowledge and memory of the past. Spirituality is thereby connected to the ancestors and to what this official called "Uzbek identity", with a focus on intellectual heritage. This emphatically national logic is reminiscent of the Soviet usage of the Russian term *dukhovnost'*, spirituality (Halstead 1994: 428). It refers not only to the relationship between the individual and God but also to a more diffuse moral capacity, courage, wisdom, and social responsibility.

For ordinary Uzbeks of the postsocialist period, the term *spiritual vacuum* indicated feelings of essential insecurity, of being alienated from former social and economic ties, such that they needed to seek alternative normative and ethical frameworks. Scientific atheism proved insufficient. Although it developed its own rituals and symbols, it remained an ideology "without memory", to borrow an expression of Hervieu-Léger's (cited in Giordan 2007: 171). As Wanner remarked (2004: 733), "Religion provides individuals and social groups with a web of ideas, beliefs, and behaviours that can serve as the basis for a social contract and moral code". In this respect, to engage actively with Islam made sense if one wanted to reconnect to one's ancestors and familiar guidelines for living. Others found a new moral compass in alternative ways, including conversion to a faith other than Islam or embracing a radical and politicized interpretation of Islam.

Plate 9. Hare Krishna graffiti on a wall in Kokand.

The underlying motivations of those who actively searched for a new source of spirituality following Uzbek independence are not hard to grasp. A deep wish to connect to the divine was the primary impulse, but in addition they sought to enhance and edify the self by becoming a "good" person in a society they considered superficial and bigoted. This is the sort of spirituality that Kieran Flanagan (2007: 1) described as follows:

> Spirituality signifies an indispensable dimension of what it is to be human. In the spirit, the social actor finds ambition, animation and exultation that all move and mobilise the self to reach beyond itself, to find powers that make humans small divinities pursuing destinies that transcend the mundane necessities of the immediate and the temporal.

Plate 10. Hare Krishna painting in the apartment of a young convert in Kokand.

Scientific atheism could never provide as convincing an explanation of life on earth as could traditional faiths (Halstead 1994: 425). "I always asked myself where the trees came from, and why there is life on earth," said Dilbar when she told me the story of her personal quest for meaning. "The teachers in school always explained it with natural science, but they could never give an answer that was sufficient for me. Science alone was no proof for me." Dilbar, fifty-five years old when I met her, was a teacher and the single parent of a teenage daughter. She had been born into a family of devout Muslim believers and described her parents as typical Soviet Uzbeks. Her mother worked as a chief secretary at the district committee of the Communist Youth League (Raykom Komsomola), where her father was the head of a department. Both held senior positions and performed their public roles as good communists, but, as Dilbar remarked with sarcasm, in their family life they were "not *zamonaviy* [modern, contemporary]". In school

Dilbar learned about the Communist Party, Marxist-Leninist ideology, socialism, and the communist idea that God does not exist and religion is a sign of backwardness. But in her heart of hearts, she explained, she always knew that this could not be the truth: "I always felt that there must be more, and there were so many questions left unanswered, where science had reached its explanatory limits". Socialism to her was a big lie that burst like a bubble.

Disillusioned with the past and searching to fill her spiritual void with content, Dilbar began buying books on astrology and new age movements, in addition to reading books on Islam and the Bible, but nothing seemed really to touch her. She participated in talks and seminars on transcendence, meditation, and Buddhism and visited various religious congregations in Tashkent, among them the Russian Orthodox church, the Hare Krishnas, and some Protestant congregations. "After independence, I was especially interested in Christianity and the teachings of Jesus Christ – first I visited the Russian Orthodox church, the church of the Russians, and then some Protestant communities. But there the people were not really free. There they had their own authorities they followed, and this is what I didn't like because it reminded me too strongly of Islam". In the end she found the answers to most of her questions in the writings of Bahau'lla, the founder of the Baha'i faith.[84] "But if you ask me 'what' I am, I cannot give you an answer. … I can only say that I like the Baha'is the most. I was never interested in Islam. Islam has many bad sides: you should fear God and be anxious. Many who pretend to be Muslims today are involved in the drugs trade and have political interests – but this should not be part of a religion! In Islam there is no love to God".

I heard many stories similar to Dilbar's during my fieldwork. Many people tried out different religious directions in search of something more meaningful in life, either within the frames of their inherited religions (Uzbeks and Russians alike) or outside those frames. Dilbar's critique of the immorality of many self-proclaimed Muslims, including ulema, was by no means unusual. The quest for spirituality could take many forms and lead to very different outcomes, as I illustrate by looking at four persons in detail.

[84] Bahau'lla (1817–1892) was born as Mirza Husayn Ali Nuri. The Baha'is see him as the founder of a new religion, like Jesus and Muhammad, and as the initiator of a new cycle, comparable to the one that began with Adam. The *Kitab-i-Aqdas* and the *Kitab-i-Iqan,* authored by Bahau'lla, are the key scriptures.

Four Ways of Conceptualizing Religiosity

The experiences already sketched provoked many Uzbeks to reflect on what it actually meant to be a Muslim in general and what it meant to be an Uzbek Muslim in particular. There was a consensus that Uzbek Muslimness was bound up with *urf-odat,* customs, but individuals' concepts were neither homogeneous nor static, as the stories of Khushnud, Dilorom, Botir, and Iroda show.[85]

Khushnud: Belonging without Believing

One day during my brief return to Kokand in summer 2005 I found my landlord, Khushnud, age sixty-four, sitting on the couch watching the news program on one of the Russian satellite television channels. Instead of greeting me, he pointed to the TV and told me to sit down next to him: "Irina, you have to see this. They are showing your city, Cologne, on TV". The newscaster was reporting from the Youth Days organized by the Catholic Church in Cologne. The event coincided with the liturgy held by the newly inaugurated Pope Benedict XVI, and viewers could see tens of thousands of young people singing, shouting, crying, and breaking out in hysteria when the new pope appeared. Khushnud shook his head in disbelief: "Look at them. They are crazy! Can you understand this?" Looking at me to see my reaction, he continued: "Do you understand this hysteria? I don't. You know, I don't believe in God, I'm an atheist". He switched off the TV and went on to explain that he was a Muslim by birth and came from a family in which Islam had played a major role. In that sense, he considered himself to be Muslim. Yet he was an atheist by conviction.

After initially studying at the University of Tashkent, Khushnud had continued his studies in Moscow, where he lived for several years. He liked to tell stories about his time in the students' dormitory and his trips to the Black Sea with friends from all over the Soviet Union. Soviet teaching in the natural sciences, scientific atheism, faith in progress and modernity, and the cosmopolitan atmosphere of the university had all left their imprints. Returning to Uzbekistan, Khushnud led several drilling expeditions to identify natural gas and oil supplies. As a respected researcher and leader, he was appointed head of the Geophysics Institute in Kokand, where he still worked during the time of my stay.

---

[85] My conversations with Khushnud and Dilorom were conducted entirely in Uzbek. Botir and Iroda both spoke excellent English, and we talked mainly in that language, sometimes switching to Uzbek.

Khushnud situated himself in the tradition of the Soviet intelligentsia and took a pragmatic view of Islam and religion in general and of Uzbek society in particular. This meant that he participated frequently in events with a religious background. Partly because of his prestigious position, he was often invited as a guest on all kinds of ritual occasions, sometimes to more than one event on the same day.[86] He could not evade these responsibilities. At the circumcision celebration (*o'g'il to'yi*) of his youngest grandson, which took place at his house in the spring, Khushnud was the perfect host as he welcomed the visiting men to the morning *osh* (pilaf, a rice dish with mutton and vegetables).[87] He stood at the entrance to the courtyard, holding a towel for the guests to dry their hands on after their ritual washing. He took care of the seating arrangements at the long tables in the courtyard before himself sitting down next to his friend, the mullah of the neighbourhood mosque, who recited from the Qur'an and led the ritual. During the circumcision itself (which I was asked to record on video), Khushnud continued to fulfil all his obligations as the host of the feast.

Khushnud considered participation in such events a matter of showing respect and following Uzbek *urf-odat.* Not to participate would be to offend the hosts and show disrespect toward Uzbek customs and one's ancestors. What mattered most was to be a humane person (*inson*) and to uphold the norms and morals of his Uzbek culture. For that, he explained, he did not need a religion to tell him what to do and how to behave. But if people wanted to believe, then he would respect their choice. "Look at my wife. She's a real Muslim believer", he explained. "To her, belief in God is important". Apart from his wife, Lola, who prayed five times a day, religion was inconspicuous in the life of his extended family (the house was shared with his thirty-four-year-old son, Sherzod, his wife, and their two young sons). Khushnud saw no contradiction between organizing and participating in events with an undeniably religious dimension and his self-conception as an atheist. Islam was an historical marker of Uzbek identity, the foundation of Uzbek customs and moral standards. Although asserting that *o'zbekchilik* corresponded to Islamic virtues, he detached the religious from the cultural. He conceived of himself as a Muslim, but as a cultural one, socialized in a family and society forged by Islam. To this extent Khushnud followed the

---

[86] In addition, Khushnud was a member of several *gaps*. *Gap* (Uzb., Tajik) means literally "sentence, conversation". In this context it refers to an informal, rotating association of men. See also chapter 6, note 15.

[87] Editor's note: The author indicated at this point that she intended to provide a more detailed description of the morning *osh,* including the patterns of gender segregation, in the final version of this chapter. *Osh* is a synonym for the dish *palov.* The term is also used to refer to celebrations held in the morning, where *osh/palov* is served. The generic term for domestic life-cycle rituals is *to'y.*

Soviet separation of religion and national identity, rather than earlier Uzbek traditions that precluded distinctions such as that between sacred and secular or between the religious and the national (Keller 2001a: 330 ff.). Whereas for other participants in Islamic rituals, the religious meaning was at stake, for Khushnud the meaning was cultural and social rather than religious or spiritual.

Dilorom: Bridging the Old and the New

Dilorom was of the same generation as Khushnud. She lived with her daughter, son-in-law, and teenage granddaughter, Rayhon. They ran a small bed-and-breakfast establishment in Kokand, where I stayed for some time before moving to live with Khushnud. Dilorom and her family and I became close friends. She had a deep knowledge of the religious scene in her *mahalla* and was on good terms with various female and male religious specialists, ranging from a healer and several *otin-oyi*s to unofficial and official mullahs.[88] When I visited Dilorom one day for tea, she told me about her childhood and her relationship to religion during the Soviet era. Her father, an imam at a mosque in Kokand and a pious believer, had suffered under Soviet repression but continued to read the Qur'an and to transmit his knowledge of Islam to his children. Dilorom had been introduced by her mother into numerous female religious practices. She remembered celebrating *mushkul kushod* ("the Solver of Problems") and *mavlud* (the Birth of the Prophet) at home and said she had learned the most when *otin-oyi*s came to explain the *eski-chilik,* the "old ways", by which she meant Islamic practices of pre-Soviet times.

Dilorom was born in the early 1940s in a village near Kokand. She described her early years as a student and young employee as a time full of contradictions. Always conceiving herself to be a Muslim, she felt that she had to "cover her belief up in her heart" and adapt to the system and the circumstances as well as possible. At eighteen she married an Uzbek from Bukhara. The couple moved to Bukhara, where she finished her studies and worked for several years as a geologist for the gas works. "To the outside world", she said, "I adapted to the situation and was a good Soviet citizen, but at home I tried to observe all the rules of *musulmonchilik* I could, performed *namoz,* and read the Qur'an". At that time it was vital to keep this

---

[88] *Otin-oyi* is the standard term in the Ferghana Valley for a female religious specialist with significant knowledge of Islamic texts. In Khorezm the equivalent is *bibi-halpa* or *mullah-oyi;* in Bukhara the term is *bibi-mullah* or *oyi-mullo.* These women seldom have any formal religious education from official Islamic institutions; they are either autodidacts or receive teaching from other religious specialists or from their female relatives. See Fathi (1997, 2004); Kleinmichel (2001); Krämer (2002).

secret, because the whole family would suffer the consequences – for example, in terms of educational opportunities – if it were public knowledge that a state employee was practising her religion. "Therefore it was important to think carefully about how far to profess one's religiosity openly". Her father and an uncle who was a *domla* (Muslim teacher) continued teaching Islam to their close relatives at home, but in Soviet public space they behaved as she did: "They worked in small shops, for the state, and [their religiosity] did not interfere in state affairs, because religion is something private, and it does not pose any opposition to the state. My father continued working for the *kolkhoz* [collective farm], and when I became a member of the Komsomol, he was not against it".

Years later, Dilorom and her family moved back to Kokand, where she worked for the party committee (*partkom*). She was able to separate her work for the party clearly from her belief and was never quizzed about whether or not she believed in God:

> No. I was never asked if I believed in God or not. You would have to know the political structure, the number of members in the party in Uzbekistan, the date the Constitution was issued, and the birthday of Lenin and so on. But no, I was never asked – anyway, most of the people in the party were Muslims themselves, and so nobody asked and there was no malicious gossip-mongering. Belief in God has always been a private matter, inside people's hearts, and it remains there.

When Dilorom's husband died in the 1980s, the family conducted a proper Muslim burial, followed by the customary commemoration feasts, Yigirma ("twenty" – that is, twenty days after the death) and Qirq ("forty"). Dilorom invited a *domla* and relatives and neighbours to attend and, following recitations from the Qur'an, to eat *osh* together. Men were invited in the morning, women separately in the afternoon. "It was no problem to arrange this. Nobody said anything against it".

During the first turbulent years of independence, Dilorom was still working for the party committee and found herself confronted by novel interpretations of Islam:

> We were taught about Islam, even in the office at work, and they told us to learn Arabic, because at the time a switch to the Arabic script was under consideration, so we were summoned and told that all colleagues should know the Arabic alphabet, so as to be prepared. And so after work, at five o'clock, we would sit and take Arabic language lessons from a mullah or an imam. That is how it all started and how I learnt about *namoz* and Islam. The men started attending the mosques. We had thirty-five minutes for our lunch break and

> people used this time to attend the big mosques. Mosques were also opening in *mahalla*s and villages, cities and towns everywhere. So everyone, including children, started going to mosques. .... War started in Tajikistan and Afghanistan, and it came from there mostly. .... Muslims began having conflicts with Muslims, our Friday mosque and that big mosque started disagreeing with each other. And men started to beat the heads of those women who were walking without a headscarf, saying they should cover themselves, and introducing prohibitions, so in the 1990s there were a lot of these Wahhabis [*vahobiylar*]. ... I remember that from time to time when I went out early for sweeping I found leaflets at my door. I read one and it had no meaning in it. It said that when Karimov became president he had taken an oath, and that he had promised this and that at specific parliamentary sessions, but had not delivered – but this was a direct confrontation of the state. These leaflets contained nothing good from the viewpoint of religion and so I burned them. We say, "Do not stamp on the face of those who did good to you", and it was the state which returned our religion to us. Nobody says anything to you when you are performing *namoz,* and you should be grateful for that. The aim of those leaflets was to attract youths. Hezbollah and extremists came from this angle, but I never talked with any of them, and I always avoid them. Thanks to God we were given our religion again. There are things like the *mazhab* where different groups are each trying to recruit more followers. But authentically the Qur'an is one. It is good from the beginning to the end, and we should fulfil its requirements. Those who do so will not lose anything.

By the time Dilorom retired in 1993 she had begun to engage actively with Islam. She attended study circles lead by an *otin-oyi* from the neighbourhood, read all kinds of books, and discussed authors' differing interpretations with her friends. She showed me a small booklet in which prayers and their movements were explained step by step with the aid of illustrations of a properly dressed Muslim woman, and she pointed to the notes she had scrawled in the dog-eared booklet. Although Dilorom had learned how to perform *namoz* and had practised it since childhood, she now considered it important to look up proper practice in a manual and to correct her own practice accordingly.

On one occasion Dilorom invited me, together with some neighbours, around to watch *Klon,* a Brazilian *telenovela.* The love story between the two main characters – Jade, a Moroccan Muslim, and Lucas, a Brazilian businessman – unfolded in Brazil and Morocco. The scenes shot in Morocco showed beautiful women dressed in lavish, Muslim-style robes and jewellery. These scenes captured the attention of the Kokand Muslim women because of the attractive way they depicted everyday life and fashion. To watch *Klon* was more than evening entertainment for them. It seemed to afford them a glimpse into the wider Muslim world and a point of comparison, albeit fictional.[89] Dilorom drew attention to a scene showing the Moroccan family performing *namoz* at home, with men sitting in the front and women at the back, and remarked that for men and women to pray together would be unthinkable in Uzbekistan. This, she concluded, might be a key difference between the Uzbek way and the Moroccan. For Dilorom, it was up to each individual to decide what constituted proper practice, but her own main source of information and guidance was clearly the Hanafi school of Sunni Islam, the Islam she had learned from her father. She regarded a return to a pre-Soviet Islam undesirable but was similarly unsympathetic towards radical scripturalist interpretations that would invalidate certain elements she viewed as integral to the local way and cultural memory, such as saint veneration. Religious practice should be a private matter for each individual. What mattered most, she said to me often, was having the right intention (*niyat*) and believing in one's heart.

Botir: Opting for the Modern

Botir, the twenty-one-year-old nephew of my host family in Kokand, whom I mentioned briefly before, was a student of economics at the polytechnic institute in Tashkent. He spent his semester break with his family in Kokand, and during this stay he often came to visit his uncle's place to play with the children, to give his aunt a hand in preparing food, or simply to chat. One Friday afternoon I met Botir on the street in the city centre, wearing a white skullcap and carrying a prayer rug under his arm. He told me he had just come from the small Friday mosque close to his house, where he had attended the Friday prayers. Curious, I asked him how many people had attended, but instead of giving me a number, he explained that it would be important for me and my work to know that there were basically two kinds of Muslims in Uzbekistan: those who were "real" (*haqiqiy*) believers, who believed in their hearts and prayed out of true faith, and those who called themselves Muslims but did not abide by the rules and who, even if they attended mosque, could not be seen as real Muslims. Botir admitted that for

---

[89] This *telenovela* was aired in Uzbekistan on the Russian channel in summer 2004 and enjoyed great popularity among women of all ages. The Moroccan clothes, jewellery, and way of flinging the headscarf loosely around the head instead of knotting it at the chin became extremely fashionable. *Klon* had a similar effect at the same time in Kyrgyzstan (McBrien 2007).

a long time he had belonged to the second category himself and called himself a Muslim simply because he was born into a Muslim family. In his family, he explained, only his grandmother, who lived in the same house, performed *namoz.* Apart from life-cycle rituals, religion played no important role in the family's life.

Botir's family might be considered upper middle class in terms of income and status. Both parents were academics who attached great importance to education, and all four of their children had gone on to study in Tashkent. Like his elder brother, Botir had attended the Turkish grammar school in Kokand. This school was affiliated with the Nurcu brotherhood; it taught in English and Turkish and had a good reputation. But Botir was unable to graduate from there because the school was closed by the Uzbek government, and he eventually received his high-school certificate from a state-run school.[90] When I raised the issue of the closure of the Nurcu schools, he said that his Turkish teachers had not delved into religious issues. More crucial was his encounter with a visiting Russian Orthodox priest whom Botir helped with some translations. The priest's story about how he had changed from being a nominal believer to a committed one inspired Botir to make a similar move within Islam.

A few years ago, he continued, he had begun to take an interest in his roots, by which he meant not only his family history but also Uzbek culture, history, and ethnicity. He began reading and talking to all kinds of people to gather information about the more recent past. Digging deeper, he came to the conclusion that the essence of being an Uzbek could not be grasped without Islam. In the beginning he had seen Islam as a means to gain a better understanding of culture and history, but the more he read about religion, the more he became interested in what he called his native religion, Islam. He also came to feel that a proper understanding of Islam could not be reached through books alone; only the active practice of Islam would reveal the spiritual side of religion. Botir therefore started to go to mosque for prayers, and from time to time he visited the mullah of his *mahalla* mosque to obtain formal religious instruction by attending the *dar,* the lecture after the Friday prayers. He also started to learn Arabic in order to read the Qur'an in the language of revelation.

---

[90] In the early 1990s, the Nurcular, followers of Bediuzzaman Said Nursi (1876–1960) and his disciple Fetullah Gülen, opened hundreds of schools in the Central Asian states. The schools in Uzbekistan were closed in 1999 following a decree by the president. Although on the surface they appeared to be propagating a moderate, modernized version of Islam, on a more informal level, through extracurricular contacts and the distribution of translations of the texts of Said Nursi, they were suspected of radical proselytizing (Akiner 2003: 109; see also Balcı 2003).

Botir saw the time he began visiting a mullah regularly as the turning point in his life, following which his initial motivation – learning about his roots – became secondary. He emphasized that in advancing in his studies of Islam, his heart was opened by Allah. Praying in the mosque was no longer a mere social obligation but now a personal desire to express his belief in Allah. All the same, he said, he was not yet ready to call himself a 100 per cent Muslim, because he was still in the learning process.

A few days later Botir came to visit our house again and asked me for some information about scholarships in Germany. Earlier, his priority had been to enrol in a master's degree program in the United States, but now, he said, he would consider going anywhere. He just wanted to leave the country as soon as possible, not only to obtain a better education but also because of his deep dissatisfaction with the policies of the Uzbek government towards Muslims, which hindered him in exercising his beliefs. According to the Constitution, he explained, he had the right to profess any religion he wanted, but according to the law on religion, visiting a mullah for tuition in the interpretation of the Qur'an, the most basic knowledge for a Muslim believer, could easily fall into the category of unregistered religious activities and be prosecuted under the criminal code. Even if government officials generally tolerated such sessions, to visit a mullah more than once a week might well attract the attention of the secret police, who would view him as a suspicious Islamist. If that happened, then it would be impossible for him to get the exit visa he needed to leave the country. Botir's complaint was that he could not satisfy the requirements for becoming a "real" believer in his native country, because of its restrictions on access to knowledge and the stigma a practising believer was likely to attract, especially in the Ferghana Valley.

Formal religious training, discussions with specialists, and his study of the scriptures had also changed Botir's attitude towards many everyday religious practices common in Kokand and Uzbekistan in general. Islam was no longer just a component of his cultural package, he asserted; it had become central to his life. He saw it as his personal challenge to draw near to the ideal of a Muslim believer. This ideal could be located only in the canonical interpretation of Islam, which connected Central Asia to the larger Islamic world. He was therefore critical of local practices. When I told him I had joined a group of women to visit a sacred site close to Kokand (see chapter 6), he told me that many people confused traditions with "true" Islamic conduct. To his thinking, the way Uzbek women directly addressed the saint was not in accordance with the teachings of Islam and was simply wrong. Despite this clear opinion, it would be bad manners, in Botir's opinion, to reproach people openly for such practices. He nevertheless maintained a conception of Islam as a pure religious system that must be seen outside of any socio-cultural framework. This opinion led to lively discussions – for instance, with his uncle Khushnud.

Iroda: Choosing Christianity

Iroda came from a family with a long genealogy of religious specialists – her grandfather was a mullah, and her grandmother, an *otin-oyi.* They gave Iroda and her siblings books on Islam and taught them how to read the Qur'an, how to pray, and how to observe Muslim rituals. She remembered that religious studies were conducted at their house, organized by her grandparents, despite the constant threat of their being denounced by neighbours. During school and later in her studies at the city's medical institute, Iroda tried to fulfil her obligations as a Muslim as far as possible, praying regularly and fasting during Ramadan. "I think I was a proper Muslim by that time!" she joked. After graduating from the medical institute, Iroda moved to Tashkent, enrolled in an English language course, and obtained a diploma. Wishing to practise the language, she sought contact with native English speakers and was told about a Christian seminary where an American offered English conversation courses:

> And so I went there only to improve and practice my English, but when I wanted to ask them if I could study there, they asked me, "Do you speak English?" I answered, "Yes". "Can you work as an interpreter for the seminary?" [laughs] So I came there for the first time, got a job, and without knowing Jesus I translated the Bible for the next four months. I didn't want to hear about the Bible. … I, I loved the Bible, but I didn't like what they said that Jesus is God's son, he is God and he is the holy spirit at the same time. So this was my first contact with Jesus.

Iroda began working at the seminary of this charismatic Protestant congregation when she was still in her mid-twenties. She depicted her first four months of work as a period of moral dilemma, uncertainty, and fear:

> When I started to work here, with Christian people, fear came into my heart, because it is written in the Qur'an that if you go and stay with unbelieving people – *kofir* we say in Uzbek – you will lose your future and your spiritual relationship with God. I knew it and I went to my mother and said, "You know, these people asked me to work as a translator, but this is written in the Qur'an – what shall I do?" And so my mother said, "If they need you, you shall help them because they serve to God, too". And so I decided: I'm a Muslim, these

people came to bring unbelieving people – Russian people, Korean people – to God, and I think it will be okay for me to help them. …

But my heart didn't find peace with this decision, and during these four months I had fear in my heart. And it grew, day by day, and it seemed sometimes that I would look behind [me] and I would see someone very dangerous and I [feared I would] lose my life or my mind and that it would be punishment for me because I betrayed my religion and I'm among these unbelieving people. This fear became so big that one day I couldn't take it any more and started praying to God. For this, the pastor about whom I'm talking now – he is a pastor from Samarqand, he gave me a book and I read this book – when he gave it to me, I said, "You know, I don't have time to read and study, but if I find time, maybe after one year, maybe after two years, I will read it", because I was very busy in these times, and [he said], "Okay, so, if you have time, read please!" And I put the book on my shelf.

One night I couldn't sleep and I started to see what could I do [instead]. … I saw this book and I wanted to read it. The author of the book was a Muslim who was from Arabia or Afghanistan … I don't know … and he wrote about his experience, what he felt when he heard about Jesus. And he had this prayer: "God, you have eyes and you see me. You have ears and you hear and you are listening to me. I don't want people to teach me. I want you to teach me – open [enlighten] me right away!" He prayed this way and I read it and I started to pray and I felt myself [to be] very bad and I said to God, "Open me, please – open me." I cried and I went to sleep. And in the morning, God came to me and revealed himself to me, and Jesus talked to my heart. And if people had said [these things] to me, I wouldn't have accepted him, because if Christian people say, "Our book is good, a great book," we would say, "Our Qur'an is better!" [laughs] And if the preacher says, "We have the Holy Spirit," we would say the same thing. But when Jesus came himself … I accepted him. I experienced seeing him and talking to him. And this changed my life. I accepted him in one morning, during three or five minutes. … He had some questions for me, and I answered, and I knew he was the right way.

In the early period after accepting Jesus and becoming a Christian, Iroda found it hard to talk about her new faith because, as she described it, her mind was full of her knowledge of Islam. She decided not to talk about it with her parents and relatives, because she was aware of the problems that would result from her decision. In a dream encounter, Jesus took her by the hand up a staircase to heaven. As she climbed higher and higher, she looked down and saw her relatives going to hell. After this dream, Iroda said, she knew it was not right not to tell them about her acceptance of Jesus. She felt she had a duty to save her relatives from going to hell by telling them about the right way – that is, belief in Jesus.

After this confession, her family refused to speak to her. Four months later, her younger sister also converted and was similarly abandoned by their parents. Some time later their relationship with their mother improved when she became a Christian as well. Iroda herself carried on working with the congregation and became a very involved member of the community. Seven years after joining the seminary she became a pastor herself, holding study circles and delivering sermons in the Uzbek language for the growing community. For many Uzbek converts, she became a counsellor for all questions relating to their "coming out" and the moral dilemmas resulting from their decision to leave Islam.

Iroda's main criticism of Uzbek Muslims was their obstinate adherence to what they conceived of as traditions and culture, without questioning whether or not these practices and norms conformed to their faith: "It is not even interesting for them. For them it is tradition and this is all that matters! Even if they know that God is against it, they will do it, because it is tradition. And people even acknowledge this openly! My mother once told such people that what they do is against the Islamic tradition, and the people answered, 'What shall we do, if it is our tradition?'"

In her new community Iroda did not find a faith that she viewed as intrinsically morally superior to Islam; rather, she found a group of believers whom she viewed as more sincere and devout than the Muslim community – both local Uzbek Muslims and Muslims on the international level. Her criticism of a bigoted society resembles that put forward by certain Muslims, but in Iroda's case it is also marked by the distance she travelled in conversion and by the rhetoric and dogma of the charismatic church.

Narratives of Religiosity

The stories of Khushnud, Dilorom, Botir, and Iroda represent four different ways of conceptualizing what it means, on an individual basis, to be religious or non-religious in Uzbekistan. In each of their biographies we can see processes of decision-making influenced by certain experiences and encounters. I chose these four people because their reasoning and their ways of engaging with questions of religiosity and spirituality exemplify certain patterns that I identified during my fieldwork. Khushnud represents the idea of cultural Muslimness, and Dilorom and Botir illustrate different intensities of the orientation towards a more scriptural interpretation of Islam. Iroda represents the steadily growing minority who decide to leave Islam for another religion. It is important to stress that these are snapshots I took at certain stages in lives that might well move in different directions in the future. And of course all four persons were confronted by me as a researcher and were fully aware of my special interest in the topic.

In his study of Turkish Islamists in Germany, Werner Schiffauer (2000) pointed out that, in the analysis of narratives, one must keep in mind that talk about religion always revolves around decisions between being for and being against something. Intensive religious encounters often result in an awakening of faith or conversion: the whole world appears to be different. People who undergo such experiences tend to structure their lives accordingly, in before and after periods. The period before the experience is commonly presented as an unconscious search for the truth, which finds its fulfilment in the religious encounter. Such people bear witness to their experience when they interpret the past from the position of their new religious orientation. It is important not to view such constructions as distortions, because they are inseparable parts of the experience that give meaning to the event (Schiffauer 2000: 235).

Iroda was a pastor, rhetorically trained by the seminary, and her narrative should be seen in this light. She told me a story that she had probably told many times before, refining it during her seven years of constituting herself as a Christian by reflecting to an audience about her Muslim past.[91] Similar remarks apply in the case of Botir, who did not undergo a religious conversion in the conventional sense of changing his religion but experienced a transformation from expressing a rather indifferent, nominal allegiance to Islam as found in the mainstream to being a highly interested, self-conscious Muslim actively engaging with the principles of his faith.[92]

---

[91] In his analysis of Christian conversion narratives, Peter Stromberg (1993: xi) argued that "it is through the use of language in the conversion narrative that the processes of increased commitment and self-transformation take place. This argument is based upon a view of what language is and how it works that is opposed to certain widespread common-sense understandings of these topics. In fact, … it is precisely these common-sense understandings of language and subjects (the persons who use language) that set up the conversion narrative by placing some members of our society in a contradictory position". See also Wohlrab-Sahr, Krech, and Knoblauch (1998) on approaches to conversion narratives in the sociology of religion.

[92] Editor's note: At this point the author indicated an intention to expand her discussion of "intra-faith conversion or intensification of faith" by examining more cases like that of Botir. For more on conversions to Christianity, see chapter 8.

Rethinking *Musulmonchilik*

Eickelman and Piscatori (1996) coined the concept "objectification of Islam" to characterize what changes when Islam becomes a postulate for conscious believers and is no longer necessarily embedded in a particular culture and social practice. In the process of defining the religion, other essential issues have to be addressed, such as democracy, secularism, and, as in the Uzbek case, the question of Islam as a common good negotiated within the public sphere (see also Roy 2006). In the course of this process, the power to define moves away from a limited number of religious specialists to encompass every believer who wants to become engaged with Islam and what it means to be a Muslim. The formulation, not the content, shapes meaning (Roy 2006: 159). Objectification entails "self-examination, judging others, and judging oneself. The sense of contrast with a past or contrast with the rest of society is at the heart of the self-consciousness that shapes religious style" (Metcalf 1996: 7).

In the cases I have presented in this chapter, the objectification takes place along different lines, but all four narratives present common patterns that are of urgent concern to the society of Uzbekistan, including moral critique, the localization of religion within a given territory, and the juxtaposition of religion and nationality.

Many conscious Muslims in Uzbekistan are concerned about the moral ambiguities present in the behaviour of fellow Muslims and members of the ulema at all levels. Dilorom described a blatant discrepancy between the way people proclaimed their Muslimness and the way they failed to live accordingly – for example, when Muslims killed each other. Dilorom, Botir, and Khushnud all distinguished clearly between Islam as a religious system and Muslims who instrumentalized religion to pursue political aims. Common to all of them was the idea that society should return to a more liberal or ethical Islam (cf. Roy 2006: 155). Iroda, as a Christian convert, took a more radical stance. From her perspective, Islam was an intrinsically negative religion, God in the Islamic conception was an angry one, and Islamic doctrines facilitated evil.

The question of morality also bears directly on religious authority. A believer is expected to show *ishan* (Arab., "perfection, excellence") in the "inner" dimension of Islam, whereas sharia (Arab., "law" or "path") refers to the outer dimension. *Ishan* includes the Muslim responsibility to accomplish excellence in worship and in social action. The individual is expected, on the basis of inner belief and sincere devotion, to strive to become a better person and to seek out the information and knowledge that will enable him to be relatively autonomous in choosing which religious authority to follow. From the statements of Khushnud, Dilorom, Botir, and Iroda, and more generally in the quest for spirituality among Uzbeks at large, it is evident that the established Muslim authorities in Uzbekistan are not considered necessarily authoritative or as providing a role model for ordinary believers. This scepticism is based on perceptions of inconsistency between (outer) deeds and proclaimed morality. Official ulema are suspected of propagating the government's ideological definition of *musulmonchilik,* and unofficial, often self-trained religious figures are thought to have too little knowledge or to be teaching Islam primarily as an economic strategy (cf. Krämer 2002; Fathi 2004). Those promoting "purer" scripturalist models are easily associated with political extremism.

Khushnud tended to block out the religious dimension and locate authority within secular Uzbek norms and customs. Dilorom remained more open and connected to both "traditional" and "modern" ideas and interpretations, while Botir clearly positioned himself towards the latter. He was willing to acknowledge local practices and the worldview and history that lay behind them, but he rejected them for himself. Iroda rejected all Muslim authorities and sought alternatives elsewhere.

If a growing individualization of religious practice is the consequence of a decline in the societal authority of religion, then the very definition of what it means to be a Muslim and the rebuilding of a Muslim community depend on the individual (Roy 1996). The way the believer experiences and formulates her or his relation to religion is crucial. Olivier Roy sees such an individualization as omnipresent in Islam, which follows the same path as Christianity by emphasizing belief and values, the striving for a universal community beyond culture and nations, the local assembly as a basis of socialization, and a critique of alienation in a vain, materialist society. Roy's analysis is based on his studies of changing patterns of religiosity among Muslim migrants in the West, particularly the phenomenon of fundamentalism. But similar developments can be seen in the Uzbek case, as in the moral critique, although the understanding of what it means to be a Muslim seems more diverse in Uzbekistan. While acknowledging that religion is a private matter, a large majority endorses the government's position that it is also closely connected to nationality and local culture.

Uzbek Muslims experience their religion as a set of practices tied closely to society, history, and everyday life. Botir questioned this link and argued for a universalist reading of Islam. Iroda questioned it more drastically by converting to a form of Christianity that places strong emphasis on the trans-local and trans-ethnic character of religion, analogous to the universalist Islamists. Dilorom and Khushnud stand for the larger stratum in Uzbek society that favours a localized reading of Islam. Acknowledging universal aspirations, they nonetheless prioritize the local character of *musulmonchilik* and see it as deeply intertwined with being Uzbek, thereby accepting the postsocialist government's ideology and promoting the nation-building project.[93]

Conclusion

Musulmonchilik and religiosity in general are currently being reappraised in Uzbekistan. The process often summed up in the literature under the umbrella of "re-Islamization" or "resurgence of Islam" is more than a simple revival. People always conceived of themselves as Muslims, although with differing intensities. Rather than a return to an earlier status quo, a more radical re-evaluation of what it means to be a Muslim and an Uzbek has taken place. People have both fallen back on pre-existing, familiar concepts and interpretations and considered new ways of perceiving the world. Khushnud, Dilorom, Botir, and Iroda undertook this re-evaluation in distinctive ways, shaped by their individual biographies and social backgrounds, drawing on various regimes of knowledge as they did so.

The postsocialist Uzbek government has sought to ground national identity by emphasizing, rather narrowly, a distinctive local way of *musulmonchilik* that is largely shared by the majority of Uzbek Muslims. Yet this *musulmonchilik* is not static. It is invested with a certain core meaning, but it remains flexible and open to differing interpretations. For some, local Islamic practice is grounded in the religious genealogy of the region; for others, it is part and parcel of their history and culture but open to a new alignment towards universal, normative Islam.

John Bowen (1998) has written of "Muslim diversities" in his studies of Islam in Java, where Javanese Muslims range from what he calls traditionalists to "modernists". He notes that the "historic shift in highland religious thinking is not a once and for all change, but a process of reflection and rethinking of the old and new" (Bowen 1998: 320). The Uzbek case is difficult to compare, partly because the necessary data from the Soviet era are lacking, but it can be said with certainty that negotiations about what it means to be a Muslim have acquired a new quality and intensity in recent decades. Since the 1980s, diversification has meant that ever larger strata of

---

[93] Editor's note: At this point Hilgers expressed uncertainty about the adequacy of her analysis in this section. She was considering rewriting, paying more attention to the way people obtained and used information concerning religion and preparing a more detailed, "point by point" comparison of where the four individuals stood in relation to a longer list of themes, followed by analysis of their permutations. I imagine she would have added more references back to the themes introduced in earlier chapters. For example, in the light of the earlier historical analysis, the uncle-nephew disagreement would appear as two sides of the same "modernist" coin.

the population are debating matters previously confined to closed elite circles (see chapter 3). But increased access to information also affords access to other belief systems, and new religious movements have become ever more visible, offering alternatives and adding to the pressure for critical re-evaluation – as demonstrated in the complementary cases of Iroda and Botir.

Meanings often emerge in the context of specific large-scale events, but they are also shaped directly by everyday negotiations over orthopraxy and by direct comparison of self with other (Abramson and Karimov 2007: 319). In the following chapters I present three case studies to demonstrate the way "right" religious practice is negotiated in Kokand: first at a life-cycle ritual, then in the reallocation of religious space at a famous shrine, and finally in the confrontation of common standards with alternative religiosities, taking the example of a community of Uzbek Christians.

Chapter 5
How to Conduct a Wedding

In order to explore the way life-cycle rituals become arenas of negotiation for global and local practices of Islam, I draw on data taken from the discourse on the "Islamic wedding" (*islomiy to'y*) in the local Muslim community in Kokand.[94] I show how legitimate religious practice is defined at the local level within a continuum between modernity and tradition and how the alternatives are constrained by internal and external factors.

It has already been demonstrated that in the post-Soviet period, rituals have become a site for the assertion of "authentic" Uzbek identity (Kandiyoti and Azimova 2004). I argue that the same rituals form an arena in which ideas about what constitutes (Uzbek) Muslim selfhood are contested. Life-cycle rituals, in this case weddings, become spaces for the display of religious self-representation and discussion of conflicting ideas about proper or authentic Muslim practice, spaces in which local custom (*urf-odat*) may diverge from normative (orthodox or canonical) Islam. As Johan Rasanayagam (2006b) demonstrated in the case of healers, the frame for negotiating what is perceived as legitimate religious practice is determined by the local community, on the one hand, and state policy, on the other.

I begin with a brief account of a particular wedding party, the unusual features of which sparked intense discussions about the adequate conduct of rituals among Uzbek Muslims in the local community. I then describe the spectrum of opinion about whether this celebration was Islamic or not and about to what degree such new forms of ritual conform to local notions of tradition. The discussions prompted large circles to reflect upon general questions of what constitutes legitimate religious practice. Finally, I locate the local discourse in a larger context, trace its origins, and identify the key factors shaping it today.

---

[94] My analysis is restricted to the urban setting of Kokand. Regional differences are considerable in Uzbekistan, and the wedding practices I describe vary significantly even in other cities of the Ferghana Valley (Ashirov 2000).

The *Islomiy To'y*

In April 2004 I was invited by Dilorom, whom I introduced in the previous chapter, to join her in attending a "real Islamic wedding". I had often heard people talking about the "new" wedding, the *islomiy to'y,* which had first appeared in Kokand in the middle of the 1990s and had become increasingly popular since then. I had a vague idea of what it would be like from the gossip I had picked up. Dilorom, who had been married in the "old way" (*eskicha*) in the 1950s – before the imposition of the secular Soviet wedding at the end of the 1960s – promised to explain the differences between the various types of weddings and help me draw comparisons. When I told the family of Khushnud about this invitation, they laughed and said that such weddings were only for old people or really pious Muslims: "It is boring! Just sitting around, listening to what the mullah is saying, no dancing, no fun, and all those religious people milling around".

The groom's family, who were organizing the wedding party (*bazm*), were distant relatives of Dilorom's who lived in a relatively wealthy area on the outskirts of the city. The bride's family lived in the old part of Kokand, generally thought to be the most conservative neighbourhood in terms of religion. Both families had the reputation of being *dindor kishilar*, pious Muslims who obeyed the laws of Islam.

We were among the first guests to arrive at the groom's house in the afternoon. Preparations for the party were still under way in the house and its courtyard (*hovli*). After being introduced to family members and drinking tea with some of the other early arrivals, I was shown around the house by the teenage daughters of the family. They explained to me that male guests would be seated in the neighbouring *hovli*, which was separated by a brick wall from their house, where the women would be celebrating. The initial idea of dividing the *hovli* by a curtain would have provided too little space to host the 200 or more guests who were expected. This strict gender segregation during an Uzbek wedding party was a new experience for me, although I had heard about it. At other wedding parties I had attended, men and women had shared the same hall or *hovli*, dancing and chatting together although sitting at separate tables. I had also witnessed even this limited separation being repealed in the course of the evening as both men and women switched tables to chat with friends and relatives.

As more guests arrived, the women gathered in a large, lavishly decorated living room where a long table had been laden with sweets, salads, and other side dishes. While nibbling and chatting, some of the older women read a blessing (*duo*) for the new couple. After being served food, we were summoned outside to board two buses, rented for the occasion, and travel to the house of the wife-givers for the symbolic taking of the bride. Men and women were squeezed into the buses together, which surprised me; this was not what I had expected at an Islamic wedding.

Arriving at the house of the bride, the female guests were led into the house by her mother. The men were seated outside in the courtyard, together with male guests from the bride's side. In the hallway, women were personally welcomed by female relatives of the bride, who stood in a line in front of the room that had been prepared for us. As soon as all the guests were seated, food was served by the bride's mother and sisters, all of whom wore headscarves and long, loose-fitting dresses in modest colours. Some elder women in our group performed blessings (*duo*s) and addressed the hosts. An *otin-oyi*, a female religious specialist, recited from the Qur'an. The hosts' attire was noted with surprise and remarked upon as soon they left the room. The guests speculated about whether these women had chosen to wear the headscarf (Uzb., *hijob*) or had perhaps been forced by their husbands to veil themselves. Some women who knew the family commented that the hosts were *islomiy kishilar* (Islamic people) who saw it as their religious obligation to dress in this way.

During this lavish meal, the mullah, sitting with the men in an elevated place in the courtyard, preached a sermon, which could be overheard in the house. We listened silently. After approximately two hours, all the guests were returned by bus to the house of the groom for the wedding party and the official registration, the ZAGS ceremony. Back at the house, guests who had not travelled to the bride's house and some newcomers, men and women together, were standing outside in the street, waiting for the celebration to start.

The bride and her relatives arrived half an hour later by car. She was led into the courtyard by her mother and maid of honour. All the new guests were welcomed by the women of the groom's family, who were lined up at the entrance. Accompanying musicians played the *to'ylar muborak* ("may the weddings be blessed"), the standard wedding tune, with a *qarnay* (a brass instrument), a *surnay* (a woodwind instrument), and a *doira* (drum). While crossing the threshold of the courtyard, the bride and her escort stopped, and the bride performed the *kelin salom* (bridal greeting), bowing three times to show her respect to her future in-laws and the guests. She was led across to the other side of the courtyard, where a special table had been prepared, decorated with flowers and with a rug hanging at the back. Before taking her seat between her sister and her maid of honour, the bride turned around and bowed again three times in the direction of the guests, seated at long tables arranged in rows in front of her.

Plate 11. Older female guests at an (Islamic) wedding pronounce blessings (*baraka*) for the hosts, whilst an *otin oyi*, a female religious specialist, recites *suras* from the Qur'an.

As I took pictures of the bride's arrival, I was surrounded by the teenage girls of the groom's family, who commented excitedly on the "beautiful European style" of the shimmering, light pink wedding dress and the embroidered scarf with glittering pink flowers that covered the young woman's hair. The appearance of the maid of honour also caught the girls' attention. She wore a modern Islamic-style dress with a matching *hijob*, under which she wore a second veil that covered half her forehead with a string of pearls. The host girls, some of whom were wearing the *hijob* themselves, explained to me that this was "Arabian style", and they clearly found this detail beautiful and trendy. I was surprised only that the bride herself was not dressed in a similar way.

Plate 12. Gender segregation at an Uzbek wedding: Whilst male guests sit outdoors in the host's yard, women gather inside the house, protected by a white curtain.

For the civil registration of the marriage, a table with two chairs was prepared in the middle of the dance floor in the women's *hovli*. The groom and his best man entered and sat down next to the bride and her maid of honour. The registrar, wearing a sash in the colours of the Uzbek flag around her chest, made a speech about the importance of marriage and the future of the Uzbek state. After the two signed the documents and exchanged rings, the scarf covering the bride's face was removed, revealing a transparent white veil. The music began, guests went up to congratulate the newlyweds with hugs and kisses, and elderly women uttered *duo*s to wish them a fortunate life. The groom then returned to the men's section to continue the celebrations.

The music in both courtyards consisted initially of popular Uzbek songs played by a disk jockey from minidiscs. Later, a female singer wearing a *hijob* and a loose-fitting overcoat entertained the women, accompanied by music from a stereo. The deejay, a male relative of the groom's family, was positioned near the entrance of the *hovli*, concealed from the women sitting in front of him by a white curtain. From time to time, however, he peered out, chatted to the singer, or accepted a request for a particular song from one of the guests. The white curtain, hung temporarily on a washing line, gradually fell away, and by the end of the party it had been torn down completely.

Food was served to the assembled female guests by girls, while young men hurried back and forth between the courtyards, carrying food across to the men's section. Some women danced during this dinner, and from time to time one would grab the microphone to congratulate the newlyweds, although the groom was no longer present. Following each intervention of this kind, the music started up again and the woman danced in front of the bride, initially alone but then together with other women and girls until the next speaker presented herself. I had seen all this at other weddings, but the usual donation of money to the dancers by other guests or by the newly married couple did not take place on this occasion. This money is usually passed on by the receiver to the wedding band. When I mentioned this to my neighbour, she explained that giving money to the dancers was considered *bid'at* (Arab., unlawful innovation in worship). It might be an Uzbek custom, but it was not good Islamic practice. "You know", the woman explained, "usually at weddings I would give money to acknowledge a good dancer, but this is an *islomiy to'y*, so it is not considered proper".

Compared with what I had seen before, few girls and women danced at this wedding. Usually, women and men crowd onto the dance floor together as soon as the first tunes are played. For many people, having an occasion to dance is among the main motivations for going to a wedding.[95] When I asked some of the girls standing next to me, they admitted that they would like to dance but said it was not considered decent for a Muslim girl to dance in public, and they feared the disapproval of their parents. Later, after most of the guests had left, these girls took to the dance floor.

Towards the end of the feast, I joined Dilorom and three of her cousins, all in their seventies, sitting at a table on the veranda that surrounded the courtyard. Dilorom introduced me, explaining that I was there to learn about wedding celebrations. "So, how do you like our Islamic weddings?" one of the women asked, slightly amused. Without waiting for my response, she continued, "Now look, they announced it as a 'real' Islamic wedding and look what we get – merely separating men and women, having girls walk around *yopilgan* ("closed", i.e. veiled) and a wedding singer who wears a veil does not make for a real [*haqiqiy*] Muslim wedding, or what do you think?"

---

[95] The meanings of the music and dancing at Uzbek wedding parties are vividly described by Sultanova (2005).

Gossip, Rumours, and Opinions

The next day I visited Dilorom to show her the photographs I had taken at the wedding party. As she looked through them, she referred back to her cousin's comment the evening before expressing doubt about the true character of the event. Was it a real *islomiy to'y,* as had been announced, or was it just a normal Uzbek wedding party with a few Islamic trimmings? Dilorom, who identified herself as a practising believer and hosted a religious study circle for women once a week, explained as she sifted through my pictures why many people had criticized this wedding party as non-Islamic. She highlighted the inadequate gender segregation, which I had heard several women criticize during the event. Segregation is a strict rule according to sharia, but at this wedding, men and women had mingled on various occasions, including gathering outside on the street for a chat. In the course of the evening, young men had crossed over to the women's *hovli* to pick up food and cutlery from the kitchen, and girls without headscarves had entered the men's area to serve food.

Some of my pictures showed the deejay entertaining the women by playing popular songs after the civil registration and accompanying the female singer. Dilorom explained that, from an orthodox point of view, it was indecent for a man to watch women dancing. She further remarked that if religious commands were to be taken seriously, then electronic music should be prohibited at Islamic weddings. According to the scriptures, no music should be allowed. In the interpretation of the Hanafi school of law, to which Uzbek Muslims adhere, music is permitted, but only when played on live instruments.

This was by no means the only criticism. On the way to the bride's house, men and women had sat together in the same buses, which again violated Islamic law. In the bus, Dilorom said, it was obvious from the smell and behaviour of some men that they had consumed alcohol, which in Islam is forbidden (*harom*); its consumption is *gunoh,* a sin. At the house of the bride, the female guests had been led into the house while the men were left outside in the courtyard. The mullah's Qur'an recitation and sermon to the men were audible in the room where the women and girls were seated. In strict adherence to Islamic rules, they should have been unable to listen to the mullah's words. Dilorom added that she had seen some boys sitting in the courtyard with the men, although the Prophet Mohammed had advised that only people possessing the necessary knowledge and maturity to correctly understand the message of the sermon should listen to it. The presence of the boys was not, strictly speaking, prohibited, she explained; rather, the Prophet's opinion was extracted from the *tafsir,* the exegesis of the Qur'an. As such, it was not perceived as a command of Allah's, which must be obeyed, but as the advice of the Prophet, which was still imbued with great religious and moral authority.

When she saw a picture of the bride sitting at the table with her sister and maid of honour, Dilorom pointed approvingly at the maid of honour but complained that at a "real" Islamic wedding the bride, too, should have been clad modestly, instead of wearing a European-style wedding dress. Moreover, the bride was not wearing a *paranji* to cover her face, and her white gauze headscarf with glittering embroidery was transparent enough to reveal her face.

Later that day Dilorom took me to the house of a neighbour who had invited us to take part in the first formal reception of the female relatives of the fiancée of their eldest son. The *nikoh,* the marriage ceremony conducted by a mullah, was planned for the beginning of September, almost five months away, but according to Uzbek custom, an elaborate exchange of gifts and invitations between the bride-takers and bride-givers was to be held during this period. Sitting in a large group of married women, all from Kokand and the vicinity, Dilorom told them about the wedding party we had attended the day before and how it differed from older forms of Uzbek weddings. A vivid discussion ensued about what the women called *o'zbekona* (Uzbek style) and the new trend towards conducting "Islamic" (*islomiy*)-style weddings.

The women verified in this discussion what I had heard before – that a definite trend was taking place in the local Muslim community towards conducting religious rituals more rigorously according to scriptural interpretations of Islam, reducing or eradicating elements identified as non-Islamic. But although the number of Islamic weddings had increased, the women said that few such weddings were genuine. "Real" Islamic weddings, they explained, were, in the past, the prerogative of religious specialists such as imams and mullahs. Nowadays many lay people wanting to present themselves as pious Muslims were trying to do the same. One woman interjected: "But only a few are able to conduct a 100 per cent Islamic wedding, because not so many people here know how to do it correctly. And we can't know it, because we have never learned it and still have to learn how to do it. Maybe the next generation will know how to conduct Islamic rituals, but we had no possibility to learn it". Another added, "Nowadays it has become a fashion to celebrate Islamic weddings. People think it is enough to make a few changes to make it look more religious, and they call it Islamic. The majority of Islamic weddings you find here are not real ones. The real ones you find very rarely".

The women agreed that the motives of those who conducted Islamic weddings were dubious and suspected them of hypocrisy. They were Muslims who displayed their religiosity in public only in order to show off, or they were Uzbek nationalists claiming to "go back to the roots". In either case, they had little credibility as true, pious Muslims.

The mother of the groom-to-be told me that the family intended to celebrate a typical Uzbek wedding in the hall of a well-known and rather posh restaurant in the city. They planned to engage a live band and to permit men and women to celebrate together. The bride's mother agreed. She explained that both her family and her future in-laws were *imonli* (believing) people who tried to live according to the teachings of Islam. But at the same time, belief was a personal matter that did not need to be displayed in public: "How to celebrate the *nikoh* was never a question for either of our families, because we felt much more comfortable in conducting the wedding in the traditional Uzbek way, which is also more fun for the guests than these new Islamic ones. At an Uzbek wedding, people can dance, enjoy themselves, drink if they like to, and the whole event is not as stiff as an Islamic wedding".

In these discussions it was obvious that the women did not explicitly confront a universal with a local definition of Islamic practices. Rather, the concomitance of the two was the dominating aspect. The women argued that the Islamic style was the ideal model of religious practice, but they retreated from the realization of this obligation by affirming that they lacked sufficient knowledge of "real" practices, and it was therefore preferable for them to stick to what they knew and what was acknowledged to be mainstream practice. Ramil, a twenty-three-year-old Uzbek student from Kokand who had attended the *islomiy to'y,* gave the following summary of the reasons many Uzbeks refrained from organizing such events and spoke negatively about them:

> An *islomiy to'y* is too decent and, you know, our Uzbeks like it to be chic and to throw a huge celebration with lots of music and dancing. You know, it is a *bayram* [celebration], a festivity. … Besides, it is considered *urf-odat.* There is *urf-odat* and *odat. Odat* is Islamic, and *urf-odat* refers to our current tradition and to traditions from old, pre-Islamic times, for example Turkic or Zoroastrian. And lastly, because people are afraid of the Wahhabi stigma.

Locating the Discourse: Between *Urf-odat* and Wahhabism

Life-cycle rituals are above all communal occasions. They may be an important part of a cultural package and national identity (Kandiyoti and Azimova 2004: 337). Everywhere they tend to activate networks and to be occasions for the display and reproduction of social status within the community.

Talking and gossiping about a wedding are crucial to this mechanism, as Max Gluckman (1963: 313) showed long ago when writing about villagers in colonial Africa:

> They struggle for status and prestige. These struggles have to be kept within bounds, while the general values of the group are asserted, if the group is to survive. The values of the group are clearly asserted in gossip and scandal, since a man or woman is always run down for failing to live up to these values. But the struggles to fulfil those values by individuals and cliques are restrained because the methods of achieving them are defined by gossip and scandal: and these themselves punish any excess.[96]

The Islamic wedding in which I participated triggered lively discussions about legitimate religious practice among the women I met. These discussions were no doubt provoked in part by the presence of a foreign researcher known to be interested in such questions, but they also reflected a general concern within the Muslim Uzbek community since independence over reassessing Uzbek customs and Islamic practice.

In the 1990s, weddings became occasions on which the return to "authentic" Uzbek forms was clearly in evidence (Kandiyoti and Azimova 2004: 337). Yet the definition of what made for authenticity remained unclear and became highly politicized on both the national and local levels. Some traditionalists claimed that a return to the religious practices of pre-Soviet times would constitute authentic Uzbek Muslim practice. They were opposed by sharia-oriented Muslims who asserted that those rituals were intertwined with non-Islamic practices and therefore unacceptable, or *bid'at.*[97] Rather than merely going back in time for a yardstick, they demanded an orientation towards universal Islamic norms as prescribed in the sunna, the body of Islamic customs and practices that became codified as the Hadith, and in the sharia.

In the understanding of the majority of Uzbeks whom I met in Kokand, "Uzbek" rituals were predominantly Muslim in character while containing a range of pre-Islamic elements from religions such as Zoroastrianism, as well as later secular and European features adopted under Soviet rule. The aggregate was perceived as *urf-odat*. Kandiyoti and Azimova

---

[96] Editor's note: At this point in her draft the author inserted two further quotations from the same Gluckman article, without elaborating clearly how his functionalist arguments concerning gossip as an instrument of social control were to be applied in her analysis in this chapter.

[97] Bringa (1995: 224) defined sharia-oriented Muslims in the Bosnian case by saying that "they approve of practices which are codified and disapprove of those which are not, and they make a clear distinction between Muslim customs which are 'according' to Islam and [those] which are not".

(2004: 329) have described Soviet inventions in the domain of rituals in Central Asia as having a dual nature: Soviet officials aimed to eliminate rituals grounded in religion and to replace them with a Bolshevik ceremonial system and a Europeanization of local customs (cf. Levin 1993).[98] In practice, this Europeanization and secularization of rituals from above remained superficial. It modified certain public aspects of weddings without substantially dislodging the Muslim frame. In April 2004, Dilorom described this phenomenon to me in local terms:

> *Yangicha* [Uzb., new, modern-style] weddings started here in Kokand and the region only in the 1970s.[99] Especially in the villages, weddings were conducted in the old way until 1970, which differed from the cities, where the new way of conducting weddings had begun earlier. In 1970 we were the first in the village to organize a red wedding [*qizil to'y*], for my brother. It was a new style of wedding where people sat at tables, but even then the bride was arguing and refused to come out. … A lot of intelligent and educated people came then, and we were the first to do this type of wedding. … There was an artist at the Hamza theatre who acted as master of ceremonies throughout the evening, and he made a round of the tables where people were sitting – men and women mixed – to make the wedding more enjoyable. But even then, none of the girls came forward to dance. The ZAGS ceremony was held during the wedding party in the evening. But before that, my brother and his wife had been married by a mullah.

During the Soviet period, Dilorom and her family ranked among the intellectual elites and were active party members. She and her husband both had university degrees and worked for the state oil company. Nevertheless, their Muslim background remained an important element in their everyday lives. Dilorom, who had married a few years before her younger brother, remembered her own wedding as *eskicha* – that is, retaining the old customs of the pre-Soviet era, which were dominated by Muslim rituals and strict gender segregation.

Other people recalled how the new Soviet elements were juxtaposed with traditional Muslim ones: the civil marriage ceremony at the ZAGS

---

[98] On the former aspect, see also the study of changing life-cycle rituals under Soviet rule among Durmen-Uzbeks in Tajikistan by Borozna (1984) and Annaklychev's study (1984) of Turkmen workers in Turkmenistan. The Europeanization of local customs is often referred to as Russification or simply modernization. I prefer to follow Levin (1993: 52) in using the term *Europeanization*, because "it was specifically European models that Soviet ideologists had in mind as they planned the cultural future of Central Asia".

[99] The weddings introduced under the Socialist regime were also known as *qizil to'y* (red weddings) and *komsomol*, or simply communist, weddings.

office became an integral element of the public wedding party, but the *nikoh* was performed beforehand by a mullah.[100] Before the wedding party, the parents and elderly relatives and neighbours would recite *duo*s to bless the couple, who then left, accompanied by a few close friends, to pay a visit to the central war memorial or a statue of Lenin. The white "European" wedding dress and white gauze veil came into fashion at this time, generally replacing the colourful long dress of atlas silk and the *paranji* worn by brides at old-style (*eskicha*) weddings. The consumption of alcohol, musical accompaniment in the form of a singer who performed popular songs accompanied by a heavily amplified band combining traditional Uzbek instruments with a synthesizer, and men and women dancing together were the features that people tended to highlight when looking back on the wedding parties of Soviet times (Levin 1993; Kandiyoti and Azimova 2004; Sultanova 2005). Videotaping weddings became popular in the 1980s. During my fieldwork I found that these features were still seen as integral elements of a typical Uzbek wedding, except that Soviet symbols had been replaced by Uzbek national symbols such as statues of Amir Timur, poets, and Muslim philosophers. These monuments are the places now visited by the new couple and their friends before the commencement of the party.

Kandiyoti and Azimova (2004: 323) wrote of a process of long-term "nativization" of pre-Islamic, Islamic, and Soviet elements through their incorporation and assimilation into indigenous modes of thought and action. In the light of the discourses that emerged in the 1990s, as reported to me by local people, it might be argued that nativization has entered a new phase in which secular and Soviet elements are being abandoned in favour of Islamic ones. As Shikhberdy Annaklychev (1984) showed in the case of Turkmen workers during the Soviet period, wedding rituals among them, too, were subject to moral critiques by the older generation, who condemned the young for violating the customs of their ancestors. In this way the elderly became the custodians of the old way. "Keeping the traditions for the future" and "doing it as our forefathers did" are arguments frequently heard from Uzbek Muslims calling for a return to pre-Soviet Muslim practices. But the generations that organize life-cycle rituals nowadays were brought up under Soviet rule, and their only information about the old ways comes from the narratives of their parents and grandparents. It is much easier for the great majority to reproduce religious rituals and celebrations the way they them-

---

[100] Babadjanov (1999) noted that according to the statistics of the Uzbekistan Communist Party Central Committee for 1982, 65 to 66 per cent of newly married couples in the Ferghana Valley went through both the civil marriage ceremony and the *nikoh*, the religious consecration.

selves learned and practised them, a way that had become, in their understanding, collective cultural property by the end of the Soviet era.[101]

Another reason why many people prefer to hold onto what they know and consider to be their tradition pertains to current socio-economic and political realities. Life-cycle rituals reproduce social status within the community through the medium of consumption. They require generous outlays of food and gifts. The quantity and quality of the food provided, the number of guests (often ranging in the hundreds), and the popularity of the singer and the wedding band are decisive in the social evaluation of a wedding.[102] Fifty-eight-year-old Aziza, who had organized the weddings of her daughter and son in recent years, explained why people invested in elaborate wedding celebrations: "It is important how people talk about your wedding party. If they liked it, if there was enough good food, if everything looked nice and they could enjoy themselves – that's what people expect and pay attention to at weddings, and they will talk about later".

Families display their wealth and generosity through the elaborate exchange of invitations and material gifts.[103] Wedding feasts are the major expenditure in the household's budget (Kandiyoti and Azimova 2004: 336), but they are also occasions when alliances are perpetuated and new ones created. In short, they generate social capital (Bourdieu and Wacquant 1994). Meeting their costs has, however, become increasingly difficult in Uzbekistan in a time of economic decline and uncertainty. Many people cannot afford an elaborate wedding feast without going into debt. For poorer people, an Islamic wedding is an effective way to reduce the expenditure. Not only is the scale of an Islamic wedding generally much smaller than that of an Uzbek wedding, where the number of guests can rise beyond 500, but also at an Islamic wedding no alcohol is provided, and in extreme cases no musicians are engaged, thereby greatly reducing costs. Young people may

---

101 Editor's note: At this point Hilgers added a quotation, apparently from Babadjanov, which we have been unable to trace. She evidently intended to work the point into the final version of the foregoing section. The point was that not everyone accepted the secularization and Europeanization of rituals in the Soviet period; religious specialists ("theologians") remained hostile.

102 It is common to have an Uzbek pop star perform at a wedding; this indicates the status and wealth of a family. Other significant factors are the attendance of members of the elite, with their speech-making, and the presence of foreigners. I was sometimes invited to wedding celebrations by people I did not know, because the presence of a German who could extend her congratulations to the couple in Uzbek was evidently valued. The social hierarchy is usually reflected in the order of the speakers.

103 For further details on the social meaning of weddings and the general significance of exchange, see Werner (1997) on household economies in Kazakhstan, Kuehnast (1997) for Kyrgyzstan, and Yalçın-Heckman (2001) for a wedding in Azerbaijan.

stay away from the *islomiy to'y* because it is considered "no fun", as was implied by Ramil's statement, quoted earlier.

Islamic weddings often become associated with the wealth of the respective families. Bobur, age twenty-four, a member of a professional wedding band, summed it up this way: "The reasons for organizing Islamic weddings [are] that they don't have a lot of money. Sometimes I used to hear people saying, 'We decided to organize an Islamic wedding due to financial problems on both sides' [i.e. in both families]. … I would say that for me the people who celebrate *islomiy to'ylar* are either devout Muslims or poor Uzbeks". If this is the case, then the fact that Islamic weddings are associated with poverty, combined with their disutility in generating social capital, surely constitutes a good reason why even people who define themselves as pious Muslims might refrain from celebrating weddings in this way. On the other hand, such people's social status among like-minded Muslims and perhaps more generally in a Muslim community presumably rises if religious obligations are visibly respected.

In the case of the Islamic wedding described earlier, the groom's family was known as relatively successful in economic terms and as pious and sharia oriented. Because of this reputation and the way the event was announced beforehand, people had expected the reception to be conducted in the Islamic style, emphasizing the religious aspects rather than the secular. Hence the criticism in the aftermath that this expectation had not been met. At the same time, precisely the Islamic elements of the wedding were perceived and gossiped about as not being in line with Uzbek traditions. The definition of acceptable religious practice and its reconciliation with Uzbek customs are blurred and continually renegotiated in discourses on the local and national levels. In practice, much depends on the context and the personal religious orientations of the actors in each case. In general, the directive to be "pious but not too pious" applies to the Muslim community in Kokand in the same way that Maria Louw diagnosed for Bukhara (Louw 2004: 216). The danger of showing excessive zeal is that one might be labelled a Wahhabi who rejects all elements of Uzbek cultural heritage, including ancient Zoroastrian and recent Soviet accretions.

Evaluations of socially acceptable forms of religious expression and practice in the local community are also influenced by state policy, specifically by the measures taken in recent years to counter the "Islamic threat", which have induced fear and insecurity in the lifeworlds of ordinary Muslims (Louw 2004: 217). Citizens are constantly exposed to news of arrests and trials of Muslim extremists, closures of mosques, and so forth, both in the official media and through gossip or personal experience. Government employees are charged with monitoring suspect behaviour such as wearing the *hijob,* for women, growing a beard, in the case of men who are not mullahs or imams, and taking private religious instruction (Human Rights Watch 2003). *Mahalla* committees are required by law to carry out surveillance of this kind and to pass on information to law enforcement agencies. Politically reliable local residents, called *posbon*s, are recruited to support the police in these matters, and the *posbon* law passed in 1999 enhanced the role of the *mahalla* in controlling religious activities. This surveillance of everyday religious practice creates a "witch-hunt paranoia" (Louw 2004: 217) and makes people extremely cautious in practising their faith.

I later learned from an *otin-oyi* who had also attended the wedding feast I observed that the eldest son of the groom's family had been convicted and jailed for his membership in a radical Islamic organization. According to the *otin-oyi,* people close to the family were convinced that the Wahhabi accusation was some kind of set-up by a personal enemy, while others believed it to be true. In her opinion, the family would have been unable to organize a real Islamic wedding even if they had wanted to, because of the imprisonment of their son for religious reasons. Such a wedding would have raised even greater suspicion. This was why the family had decided to organize the wedding more in line with the common Uzbek style, although with a certain Islamic colouring.

Conclusion

The encounter with new notions of Islam, in Uzbekistan as elsewhere, prompts not only a redefinition of Muslim selfhood, as was shown in the previous chapter, but also a renegotiation of religious practice and rituals. Ruth Klein-Hessling (1999: 230) showed in her study of mourning rituals in northern Sudan how competing definitions of "true" Islam generate a climate of insecurity, and how common local practices become defined as un-Islamic. A climate of insecurity also becomes visible in discourse on the conduct of rituals in Uzbekistan. Local concepts of Uzbek Muslim selfhood and religious practice are questioned by those oriented towards a universal, scriptural interpretation of Islam. Many people are now aware that their local religious practice is not in accordance with sharia and contains non-Islamic elements, which at the same time are perceived and positively valued as cultural heritage and tradition. Depending on their individual interpretation of Muslim selfhood, some people orient themselves towards a more scriptural interpretation of Islam, and others pay more attention to the proper practice of religious rituals. In their effort to "Islamize", in the sense of bringing local religious practices into line with Islamic law, these actors are constrained by internal and external factors including social relations in the local community and the political ideology that defines acceptable Muslim practice in terms of Uzbek traditions.

Uzbeks' interpretative frameworks are products of their individual experiences, and in constructing themselves as Muslims, they routinely combine multiple ideas of Muslim selfhood and practice (Rasanayagam 2006b). Rasanayagam's observation concerning healers – that frames for negotiating legitimate practices are determined by both the local community and state policy – applies also to life-cycle rituals, where multiple ideas, experiences, and role models are brought into play. The precise details of the alignment of religious practice to one's understanding of what constitutes "right" Muslim practice is framed in large part by government policies, the ideas it promotes concerning tradition and cultural heritage, and the insecurity it creates through manipulation of the "Islamic threat". This alteration of religious practice is not to be seen as an invention of tradition in the sense of Hobsbawm and Ranger (1983). Rather, Uzbeks "actualize" (Saktanber 2002: 237) religious rituals according to their understanding of Muslim selfhood. Many amend ritual practice to highlight certain Islamic elements, but they do so in the sense in which Michel de Certeau (1984) adapted the concept of *bricolage* and make no clear-cut distinction between scripturalist interpretations and local customs. In the case of wedding rituals, Islamic, secular-Soviet, and non-Islamic elements are rearranged, eliminated, or emphasized according to individual understandings, but within frameworks of local social evaluation and national political propaganda.[104]

---

[104] Editor's note: In a long list of self-admonitions ("To do"), the author indicated that she intended to work further on this chapter. Among other improvements, she intended to provide more ethnographic detail on the case study and the discourse it generated. She also saw a need to probe further into general patterns, to examine the concept of authenticity more carefully, to go deeper into the distinction between pre-Soviet and contemporary Islam, to elaborate on the context of the new nation-state project, contemporary "global practices of Islam", and weddings as a focus of attention in the public sphere, and a great deal more. Materials in her file for the concluding chapter of the book suggest that she would also have drawn on additional source materials such as works by Yaacov Ro'i.

Chapter 6
The Gendered Dimension of Religious Space: Pilgrimage at the Shrine of Bibi Ubayda

Muslim practice in Uzbekistan seems at first sight to be clearly and rigidly differentiated along gender lines. As in other parts of the Muslim world, the mosque and institutions of official Islamic learning are strongly associated with male religiosity, whereas rituals related to the domestic space, including many situated on the margins of canonical interpretations of Islam, are assigned to the female domain (Tapper and Tapper 1987; Abu-Lughod 1993; Tett 1995; Doumato 2000). Shrine veneration is frequently cited in this context: it belongs to the female domain and often forms the core ritual of local Islamic practices, in contrast to the universal, scriptural Islam of the mosque, which is allegedly the domain of men (Tapper 1990; van Bruinessen 2004). In Central Asia, shrine practices often fall outside the parameters of scriptural interpretations (Bennigsen and Wimbush 1985b; Poliakov 1992; Privratsky 2001). Boundaries, however, can be transgressed – for example, when men engage in religious practices associated primarily with the female sphere, such as the rites of *bibi seshanba* and mushkul kushod,[105] when they consult healers, and when they visit sacred sites (cf. Kehl-Bodrogi 2006a; Louw 2006). It is true that women in Uzbekistan are largely excluded from the public sphere of Islam, and the space where women receive religious education is the domestic one. As in the larger Muslim world, decision-making in the official institutions of Islam is dominated by men. The main change in recent years has been that, although still few in number, female students can now graduate from official institutions of higher Islamic learning such as madrasas and the Al-Bukhari Islamic Institute.[106]

---

[105] The rites of *bibi seshanba* (Lady Tuesday) and *mushkul kushod* (Solver of Problems) are categorized as female rituals. See Krämer (2002) and Kandiyoti and Azimova (2004) for accounts of the *mushkul kushod* ritual.

[106] At the time of my research, the Al-Bukhari Islamic Institute in Tashkent had about 20 female students out of a total of 140 students. In addition to the Islamic Institute, there were three official madrasas for girls in Tashkent and Bukhara.

Most studies of Muslim women in Central Asia, both Western and Soviet, present female religious practices as less prestigious than those of men, as representing vestiges of pre-Islamic beliefs, or both (Bennigsen and Lemercier-Quelquejay 1968; Snezarev 1969, 1974, 2003). Underlying this categorization is an assumption that female religious practices are resistant to change and more conservative than the Islam of the mosques, which is necessarily connected to the outside Muslim world (see, e.g. Khalid 1998 on the Jadid movement). Ingrid Pfluger-Schindlbeck (2005) has dismissed this approach towards female religiosity, which relies on the paradigm of "male is to female as public is to private". In her work on religion and gender in Azerbaijan, she criticized the analytical frame that privileges male-defined discourses and leaves ethnic and religious identities "frozen" in the domestic, female sphere (2005: 6). To understand strategies of adaptation and the appropriation of local traditions in debates over new ideas in religious thought and practice, she called for going beyond simple dichotomies based on gender differences. Pfluger-Schindlbeck made a powerful case for looking again at narratives of gendered spaces. But was she able to offer plausible alternatives for understanding a society as outwardly dominated by gender discourses as that of Uzbekistan?

My aim in this chapter is to illuminate the underlying emic conceptions of male and female, public and private, in Uzbekistan rather than elaborate on actual male and female religious practices there. A well-known pilgrimage site serves as a lens to show how the spaces assigned to the male and female domains of religious activity function in the conceptualization of Muslim practice and ritual. Bu Mozor is a sacred site near Kokand dedicated to a female saint (*avliyo*),[107] and it is precisely the absence of men there that provides insights into the use of gendered religious spaces.[108] The physical and sacred landscape of the site provides a microcosm of what are considered to be essential aspects of religiosity. Although meaning is inscribed in the place through narratives and practices (Low and Lawrence-Zúñiga 2003: 129), the example of a pilgrimage group shows how women actively move within the realms of a more complex "sacred geography" (Tapper, cited in Eickelman and Piscatori 1990: xiv) in order creatively to define religious activities and spaces.

---

[107] *Avliyo* (Uzb.) originates in the Arabic word *awliya,* meaning "friend of God" in Sufism (Schimmel 1994: 253). It applies to any saint or holy person, male or female.

[108] *Mozor* is the generic term for a holy tomb or shrine. I give the name "Bu Mozor" as I heard it spoken locally. When written it changes to Buvi Mozor, "the tomb of the grandmother".

Bu Mozor: Topography of the Sacred and Profane[109]

Bu Mozor is the name of the shrine of the female saint Bibi Ubayda and its adjacent graveyard.[110] It lies forty kilometres north-east of Kokand. Regional buses and *marshrutki* (Rus., collective minibuses) depart several times a day from the central bus station in Kokand for the village of Buvayda. At the bus stop in the village, local taxis await visitors who do not want to walk the relatively long distance to the *mozor*. The cars stop in front of the entrance to the complex, and pilgrims then make their way along a small path lined on both sides by stalls selling all kinds of souvenirs, sweets, and beverages as well as religious items. At the end of the path, pilgrims enter the complex through a huge stone gate and arrive in a large park with shady trees, benches, and wooden cabins that visitors can rent for the day. Sufi masters (*shaykh*) and female healers and diviners (*folbin*) sit on wooden platforms or in shady corners, waiting for pilgrims to approach them for blessings or healing. In front of the white *maqbara* (domed mausoleum) of the saint, a dead mulberry tree and a large brown stone, both directly related to the saint, Bibi Ubayda, who is buried there, are the most prominent markers in an otherwise rather empty landscape. In the middle of the park, between the *maqbara,* the graveyard, and the picnic area, a large statue of a kneeling soldier commemorates the victims of World War II. Close by this monument, two photographers offer to take visitors' pictures in front of a big red papier-mâché heart bearing the inscription "Bibi Ubayda 2004".

A leaflet written by local historian, Muzaffar Mirzo (2004), obtainable at the shrine, informs visitors about its historical background and the biography of Bibi Ubayda. She was the wife of a local ruler (*podshoh*). In 665, she and her husband had to flee to Medina, where he died some years later. Bibi Ubayda and her children returned to their homeland in 735 and settled in the village of Buvayda, where she died in 742 at the age of ninety-five. According to Mirzo, Bibi Ubayda was not credited with any curative powers during her lifetime. Like many other saints, her high status was grounded in her piety and knowledge of Islam (see Tyson 1997: 16ff.).

---

[109] I travelled to Bu Mozor twice. The material that forms the basis of this chapter was gathered during a visit in May 2004 that I made with my colleague Paweł Jessa from the Institute of Ethnography of the Adam Mickiewicz University in Poznan, Poland, who was conducting doctoral research on Sufism and shrine veneration in Uzbekistan and Kazakhstan.

[110] The term *bibi* (Uzb., from the Turkic: literally, "old lady") was used as an honorific title, "lady", for high-ranking or educated women, especially those at court, in pre-Soviet Central Asia. The term *bibi-eshon* (lady-master) was applied in pre-Soviet times to denote women who were active in Sufi orders (Fathi 2006: 308). Today the term is applied to female saints within Sufism.

Odina, an *otin-oyi* working at Bu Mozor, presented a somewhat different account of Bibi Ubayda's life, telling the saint's story in a way that underscored her extraordinary qualities and her miracles: "My *buvi* [Uzb., grandmother; here an honorific title] escaped from Medina, where she was persecuted.[111] She brought back a stone and was supporting herself with a walking stick. Then she put her stick and the stone on the ground so that people could be healed by them in the future. After doing that, the earth opened up and she disappeared into the ground. Fifteen centuries have passed since that time".[112]

By the twelfth century Bibi Ubayda had achieved saintly status, and she was reburied in a mausoleum built by an Arab master from Kokand in 1113. The building was destroyed during the Mongol invasion and then rebuilt by local masters from Buvayda around 1413. In 1890, the mother of the khan of Kokand, Khudoyar Khan, initiated the shrine's reconstruction.[113] The *maqbara* was then left to decay until 2000–2001, when, on the initiative of the female mayor of Buvayda, a major renovation of the main building and its forecourt was initiated.

The structure of the complex and the clear division within it of the sacred from the profane date from Soviet times, when shrine veneration became the target of numerous anti-religion campaigns. Perceived as the "seat of every kind of superstition" (CARC report 1951, cited in Ro'i 2000: 369), religious property was confiscated by the regime, shrine keepers were persecuted, and often the shrine itself was destroyed or de-sacralized through conversion to "profane" uses. Those classified as significant architectural monuments, such as the necropolis of Shohi Zinda in Samarqand and the shrine of the Sufi saint Bahauddin Naqshband in Bukhara, were turned into museums and given the status of "national architectural heritage", a reminder of an earlier stage in the development of the culture (Louw 2006: 325; cf. Bennigsen and Wimbush 1985b). Monuments not included in this category, including smaller village shrines, were either turned over to secular use such as storage or the stabling of animals or simply ignored by local officials.[114]

The changes experienced by Bu Mozor were fairly typical. It gradually lost its meaning as a sacred, spiritual site and was transformed into a

---

[111] Pilgrims coming to the shrine of Bibi Ubayda use the term *buvi* (grandmother) as a respectful form of address to the saint.

[112] Trees emerging from the stick of a saint are a common legend motif throughout the Muslim world, wherever saint veneration is practiced (Kriss and Kriss-Heinrich 1960: 20ff.).

[113] For more information on the history and myths surrounding this sacred site, see Abdulakhatov et al. (2003).

[114] Similar policies towards holy places were applied by the communist regime of China in Xinjiang; see Zarcone (2002) and also the contributions of Minoru and Pantusov in the same volume.

park for weekend tourists from Buvayda and adjacent areas. Wooden huts, sanitary facilities, benches, and buildings for the administration were added to the existing infrastructure, which included cooking facilities for the preparation of the *khudoyi,* the sacrifice. The World War II memorial was erected in the middle of the complex, close to the graveyard, juxtaposing a secular shrine with the sacred one of Bibi Ubayda.[115] As noted in the previous chapter, visits to such memorials became an integral part of wedding rituals for Russians and Uzbeks alike. In this case the monument functioned as a cover for pilgrims coming to Buvayda to pay respect to the saint.

Although the secular, touristic aspects of Bu Mozor became more visible over the years, measures to reduce religious activities were not entirely successful. Women looking back on their visits during the Soviet era emphasized their religious motivation. Their pilgrimage (Uzb., *ziyorat;* Arab., *ziyārat;* literally, "visit") had to be disguised as tourism or a "day out" (*dam olish*), but some took the opportunity to see a mullah or *otin-oyi* or to consult a healer for treatment. The site retained its significance as the most important holy place for women in the region and as one of the many sacred spaces that were never completely sanitized and controlled by the state (Tyson 1997; Ro'i 2000; Louw 2006).[116]

After independence, Bu Mozor was officially reopened within the frame of the new government's policy of rehabilitating Sufi saints and holy places. The new significance of Sufism and shrine veneration was presented as part of traditional Islamic practice in the nation-building project. Unlike many other holy places, Bu Mozor today is not administered by the muftiate of Tashkent. It receives no funding from the Muslim Board of Uzbekistan, and no imam is officially employed as guardian. Instead, it has the status of a national historical monument and is protected by the Oltin Meros (Golden Heritage) Fund. Oltin Meros maintains the *maqbara* – the mausoleum – and its forecourt but does not interfere in religious or administrative issues pertaining to the shrine. Administration is the responsibility of the village

---

[115] Kleinmichel (2001, vol. 1: 64) described the transformation of a sacred place into a political one at another Ferghana Valley site, Shoh-i Mardan. Connected originally to the Sufi saint Safed Bulan, this site was renamed Hamza-abad by the Soviets in honour of the poet Hamza Hakimzoda Niyaziy, whom they elevated to the rank of revolutionary martyr. Kleinmichel described how the site was thereby invested with a double spirituality: visitors paid their respects both to the shrine of the saint and to the local hero (see also Ro'i 2000: 372).

[116] Muminov (1996: 366ff.) observed similar developments for shrines in Turkestan oblast in Kazakhstan, where sacred places lost their official standing during tsarist and Soviet times but continued to exist outside the framework of official, institutionalized Islam. The dogged persistence of shrine veneration is also documented by Louw (2006, 2007) for the Bahauddin Naqshband complex in Bukhara, by Kehl-Bodrogi (2005) for Urgench and its surrounds (Khorezm), and by Tyson (1997) for Turkmenistan; see also Ro'i (2000).

administration of Buvayda. Obidjon, the guardian of the complex, took up this position after retirement in order to secure an extra income for his family. He oversees the maintenance of the shrine and administers donations, but he is not a religious specialist. (At the majority of shrines throughout Central Asia, the guardian is a specialist, usually known in Uzbek as *shaykh*). I was told that the fees collected from the vendors and religious specialists who work at the place and the rent paid by pilgrims for using the facilities largely suffice to finance the complex.

According to Mirzo (2004), the shrine of Bibi Ubayda is the only shrine in the Ferghana Valley dedicated to a female saint. Although men are allowed to visit Bu Mozor, the *maqbara* itself is open only to women, a gendered discrimination that reflects Sufi shrine veneration practices common in other parts of the Muslim world (Schimmel 1975: 253). In the course of my two visits to Bu Mozor, I rarely observed men on the premises, apart from the male staff who worked there – religious specialists, the two photographers, some vendors, and Obidjon, the caretaker. Female pilgrims explained that men would drop them off but did not stay at the site. Men conducted *ziyorat* at one of the many other sacred sites that are open to men and women alike, or they went to the *mozor* of Yigit Pirim, near Buvayda in the area of Namangan, which is dedicated to a male saint. Like Bu Mozor, Yigit Pirim is visited mostly by groups of friends spending the day out together. The religious dimension is important, but so, too, is the social aspect of recreation.[117]

Ziyorat at Bu Mozor

With my Polish colleague Paweł Jessa, who was carrying out ethnographic research on Sufism at the time, I met a group of female pilgrims as they sat on a small stone wall in front of the entrance to the mausoleum of Bibi Ubayda. There, a *shaykh* recited the *fotiha,* the first sura, or chapter, of the Qur'an, asking for the acceptance of the women's visit by Allah and the saint, before they moved on to the inner part of the shrine. The women, curious about us and our interest in the shrine, invited us to join them to learn about the conduct of *ziyorat* and to get a "view from within". Later we learned that the twelve women belonged to the "Pilgrimage Club of Massiv Navoiy". They lived in Massiv Navoij, the largest contiguous, Soviet-style *mikrorayon* (micro-district) in Kokand, consisting mainly of multi-storey buildings erected in the 1970s in the north-eastern part of Kokand, in the

[117] I owe this information on Yigit Pirim, as well some details on the Massiv Navoiy (see below), to Olaf Günther. For more on the history of Yigit Pirim, also known as Posho Pirim, see Abdulakhatov et al. (2003).

vicinity of the Yangi Bazar (new bazaar), the city's largest market. At the time, these standardized flats, all with running water and central heating, were a symbol of the Soviet modern way of life, but their prestigious image had gradually declined as a result of the general economic crisis since independence.

Most members of the pilgrimage club spent most of their time at home. Some had lost their jobs in the sewing factory or in the bazaar and had failed to find alternatives because of the high rate of unemployment in the city and because the economy was increasingly male dominated (Kamp 2005; Sancak and Finke 2007).[118] Others, such as Yulduz, who was married to an imam, were housewives because this was the wish of their husbands. Sayyora, in her mid-seventies and the oldest member of the group, was long retired. Some, such as Gulzoda, who brought her two pre-teenage daughters along for the day, engaged in piecework production from their homes for craft factories or private customers. They sewed, baked cookies to sell to bazaar vendors, or prepared the catering for celebrations such as birthdays, weddings, and anniversary parties for friends and neighbours. The only women working outside the home were Umida, a divorcée who lived with her teenage son and was employed as a shop assistant, and Nargiza, an administrator.

The women were neighbours and indeed relatives (mostly distant), but they preferred to emphasize friendship as their reason for getting together every month for a *gap*.[119] Excursions to holy sites in the region provided an additional opportunity to escape from their homes and engage in activities that would be countenanced by their husbands. They had visited the shrine of Bibi Ubayda several times already. On this occasion in May, they had gathered early in the morning on the main street in their neighbourhood to await their vehicle, a minibus owned by the husband of one of the women, who would collect them again in the evening. They had brought along all the kitchen utensils and food they would need for the day, including tea, soft

---

118 According to a report on gender equality from the United Nations Development Programme (UNDP), registered unemployment among women in Uzbekistan in 2004 was 45.5 per cent, and that of men, 54.5 per cent (UNDP 2005: 68ff.). Constantine (2007: 123) estimated that actual (registered and unregistered) female unemployment was about 50 per cent higher than male unemployment.

119 The term *gap,* literally meaning "conversation", usually refers to rotating credit associations, made up of any group of friends, neighbours, classmates, age mates, colleagues, and so forth, predominantly of the same sex. Many Uzbeks belong to more than one. Usually they meet at regular intervals in a rotating system, each member paying a fixed amount of money to the host of the meeting. Some *gap* groups undertake excursions or spend summer weekends together. For more details, see Kandiyoti (1998) and Koroteyeva and Makarova (1998). See also Snezarev (1963) for a Soviet ethnographic account of *gap*s in Khorezm.

drinks, salad, fruit, vegetables, meat, and cream cakes. After arriving at Bu Mozor, they rented a room in the house next to the park entrance. Some of the women started to unpack their bags and prepare the room, while the others set off at once to visit the shrine of Bibi Ubayda, which was where Paweł and I first met them.

In the following sections I outline chronologically the day spent by the Pilgrimage Club of Massiv Navoiy at Bu Mozor. Although certain performances and sequences at the sacred site are inscribed in the practice of *ziyorat,* pilgrims' movement from one station to the next is not rigorously prescribed. They are encouraged to wander around freely and to make use of specific religious symbols and services as they personally see fit.

Station I: Visiting the Saint

After the *shaykh* had blessed their visit, the group went inside the *maqbara* to visit the saint, inviting me to join so that I could see what happened inside. Denied access, Paweł waited outside, chatting to the *shaykh.* Upon entering the shrine, three of the women stayed in the entrance hall and rolled out their prayer rugs at the wall facing south-west to conduct the ritual prayer. The others headed straight for the tomb of the saint. In a narrow room containing two sarcophagi, the women circled the tomb of Bibi Ubayda three times, touching it with their hands while murmuring their requests. They placed headscarves and notes of 100 so'm on top of the sarcophagus and at its base, where plentiful offerings from earlier pilgrims were visible.[120] The women then paid their respects to the smaller tomb, that of Badi'ga-bonu, the saint's daughter-in-law. Unlike Bibi Ubayda's tomb, which was covered with a purple, velvet-like material and white linen decorated with braid, that of her daughter-in-law was draped with a simple white sheet and had no visible donations. In the corner at the head of Bibi Ubayda's tomb, the *otin-oyi* called Odina, a woman in her sixties, was sitting on a quilt (*ko'rpacha*), and the group sat down in a row along the wall next to her. They held their hands open to pray, and Odina recited from the Qur'an and followed up with a *duo* to invoke a successful outcome to the pilgrimage:

> The Qur'an we recited, and Allah's name we remembered; we dedicated it to the soul of Buvijon and Shahzoda her daughter-in-law. Oh, dear Buvijon, we address you to ask Allah to ease and help in whatever demand and request these ladies have. Let them be with their spouses when old, let them spend what they find for good, and hold festivities, be in health and wisdom. Let their visit be accepted,

[120] In 2004, 1,000 so'm equalled US$1.

> let their children be happy, and let them see the happiness of their children. Let their future be wonderful. Let their belief be stronger. Let Buvijon support them to achieve higher levels. Allohu Akbar.

The women then ended the prayer with an *omin,* a gesture in which they brushed their faces with the palms of their hands, and each gave a donation to the *otin-oyi* by shoving so'm notes under her quilt. The group rushed out of the main room and paid a short visit to the second room, which held the tomb of Bibi Ubayda's grandson, Shahzod Shokhruhbiy. At the base of this small tomb was a pink plastic bucket, into which the pilgrims put their donations. Obidjon later told me that he collected the money from this bucket twice daily.

Station II: "Portable Spirituality"

Back in the entrance hall of the *maqbara,* Umida and Latofat invited me to join them as they approached another *otin-oyi,* who was sitting next to the entrance of the tomb, to obtain small packets of blessed tea and salt to take home. We sat down on *ko'rpacha*s placed around a white cloth on which rested the small packages of tea and salt, which are thought to be saturated with *baraka,* divine blessing power. Taking them home enables one's house to "take part" in the *ziyorat,* protects it against evil spirits, and perhaps frees it from *issiq-sovuq,* or black magic (literally "hot-cold"), in a practice called *qaytariq.*[121] The sacred spirit is held to exercise benign influence over everyone who consumes the blessed tea and salt.[122] The *otin-oyi* recited a *duo* in which she asked Allah and the saint to allow the women to be blessed and healthy, and their requests to the saint to be heard. She then handed a package of salt and tea to each of the women, who in return passed a 100-so'm note under the *otin-oyi*'s quilt. Latofat explained that she had brought some of her children's toys for the same purpose, and on behalf of her household she symbolically placed a soft drink bottle at the base of Bibi Ubayda's tomb, where it could absorb the blessing (*baraka*) of the saint.

---

[121] Derived from the verb *qaytarmoq,* meaning to give or take something back.

[122] The idea of the "transportability" of the spirit of a holy place is also to be found at Christian holy places. As Jill Dubisch (1995: 35) noted in her study of a Greek island shrine, "this power can not only be experienced by the pilgrim who visits such places; it can also be taken home in one form or another – whether as a feeling of spiritual renewal, as a healed illness, as a physical object imbued with the sacred power of the pilgrimage site, or as a transformation in one's social status".

Station III: The Stone from Medina

As we left the *maqbara*, some members of the group were still waiting for us; others had gone back to the house to prepare lunch or had set out for a walk. I joined Gulzoda and her daughters. Gulzoda, who was in her late twenties, was suffering from migraine and wanted to touch the brown stone opposite the entrance of the *maqbara* – purportedly brought back from Medina by Bibi Ubayda – hoping to be cured. As in the wider Muslim world, it is believed by Uzbek Muslims that *baraka* is manifested in objects directly related to a saint. Moreover, objects and places close to a shrine are exposed to the *ruh* (spirit, soul) of the saint and therefore are saturated with spiritual power (Kriss and Kriss-Heinrich 1960; Bhardwaj and Rinschede 1988). *Baraka* can be obtained by staying at a holy place and by practising rituals such as circumambulating, touching, and kissing the grave. Such *baraka* can ward off evil spirits, improve fertility, and cure persons from sicknesses (Kriss and Kriss-Heinrich 1960; Fartacek 2003: 169).

Plate 13. Doing *ziyorat* at Bu Mozor: Kissing and touching the 'healing stone of Medina' promises alleviation from illness and suffering.

At the shrine of Bibi Ubayda, the stone and the adjacent leafless mulberry tree are believed to possess healing power because of their association with the saint. Gulzoda and I had to queue up in a row of women. While waiting, we observed how women touched the big brown stone with their foreheads. Gulzoda explained that the curative power of the stone was especially effective for the treatment of headaches. When it was her turn, Gulzoda, too, bent down and touched the stone with her forehead, while the *otin-oyi* sitting next to the stone mumbled blessings and recited from the Qur'an. Gulzoda had consulted numerous doctors and tried various medications and traditional healers to cure her migraine. She was optimistic that touching the stone would have a positive effect on her ailment, at least easing the symptoms.

Station IV: The Party

After Gulzoda's treatment, we went back to the house, where the others were already sitting around a table covered with sweets, soft drinks, salads, fruits, bread, and tea. After lunch the women switched on a tape recorder, and after a discussion about what sort of music to play, they agreed on a tape of Uzbek pop music. Some immediately got up to dance. Others sang, clapped their hands, or, if they remained seated, at least moved to the rhythm of the music. Everyone was in a joyful mood, making jokes about the presence of Paweł as the only man in the group and asking him to promise not to tell their husbands that they were having a party instead of engaging in serious religious issues. When they decided to take a break from dancing and singing, they went for a stroll. Some wanted to visit other pilgrimage groups where they had spotted acquaintances, and others wanted to buy souvenirs for their families.

Leaving the house, we discovered a group of elderly women celebrating a *mavlud*, a ritual commemorating the Prophet's birthday, as part of their *ziyorat*. Sitting around a long table, these women invited me to stay and listen to the recital of the *otin-oyi*. One of them told me, "Our *buvi* is buried here, and we come every year. We come here to conduct *ziyorat* and to pay our respect to her. She gives everything you ask, whether it is a child, or a *davlat* [Pers., money and estate] or a long life. She gives it all. That's why we make a *ziyorat*, my daughter".

At the end of the recitation, Umida, who had stayed behind with me, and I followed the rest of our group into the neighbouring courtyard. There, a different world opened up: young people from the village of Buvayda and vicinity were celebrating a birthday party. A deejay was playing the latest hits and interjecting comments and jokes while young men and women danced together or sat around chatting and flirting. Some of the women of our group joined in the dancing, and others stood aside to watch.

After leaving the party, the women wanted to have a group picture taken in the park next to the war memorial. For the background, the photographer invited us to choose between a huge red heart in papier-mâché and some large stuffed animals or plastic flowers. The development of the picture took an hour, so we went back to join the others in the meantime for more tea, candy, and dancing.

Plate 14. After *ziyorat*: Female pilgrims amuse themselves at a birthday party in a yard near the Bu Mozor pilgrimage site.

Station V: Reciting Namoz

While the others began to prepare the evening meal in the house, four of the women invited me to join them for *peshin*, the afternoon prayer. The five of us went to the sanitary facilities for the ritual washing and then continued to the *maqbara* in search of a suitable place to pray. On the way we passed other women rolling out their prayer rugs along the walls of the mausoleum. Asked to decide the appropriate spot, Yulduz, the imam's wife, spoke critically about her friends who, earlier in the day, had placed commodities next to the sarcophagus of Bibi Ubayda or had obtained blessed objects:

> We, the women who perform *namoz,* do not believe in healing power or in *folbin.* Whoever wants to believe in such healing power is free to do so, but we believe only in what is said in the Qur'an. I for instance have come to this place because praying close to a saint enables you to feel closer to God. Here at Bu Mozor we can perform the *namoz* in public, and besides it is a spiritual place where a saint is buried. This is why we have chosen to come to Bu Mozor and why we pray inside and outside the tomb of the saint.

After finishing the *namoz*, we walked around the *maqbara*. The women touched the wall with their hands, reciting prayers and requests in low voices. On our way back, one of them ventured the thought that, after *namoz*, she always felt "light" (*yengil*). "Here", Yulduz explained, "we can pray outside. At home we can pray only within the house". Another woman added that she was the only one in her family who prayed regularly: "My husband claims to be an atheist. This has to do with his job – he used to work for the Soviet army. My sons are teenagers and not really interested in religion anyway. So I mostly have to pray alone. Here I can pray in the company of my friends and other women. This is a new experience for me". Later I learned that the daily ritual prayer was not considered part of a *ziyorat*. I was unable to find any information concerning women's performance of *namoz* outside the mosque or at their homes.[123]

Station VI: Returning Home

Back at the rented room, the others had prepared dinner to honour the saint and mark the end of the *ziyorat*.[124] Pilaf was served with side dishes of salads, fruits, sweets, and cake. An *otin-oyi* who had been invited beforehand joined us later for tea. She was asked to recite from the Qur'an and to bless the group to ensure a successful journey and the fulfilment of everyone's wishes. At the end of a short sermon, she handed out packages of tea and

---

[123] At the Bahauddin Naqshband complex in Bukhara there is a separate mosque for women, but only four women were praying there at the time of my visit, whereas the two mosques for men were bursting at the seams at prayer times. I never observed women praying in the open at other holy places in the Ferghana Valley or other regions of Uzbekistan. This observation was confirmed by my colleague Krisztina Kehl-Bodrogi, who conducted research on shrine veneration in Khorezm between 2003 and 2005 [editor's note: see Kehl-Bodrogi 2008].

[124] Preparing a meal at the pilgrimage site is common in Muslim *ziyorat* and indeed in the Christian tradition of pilgrimage. No specific reason need be given: the meal is to honour the saint and further cement the bonds between the community of pilgrims and the saint (see Tyson 1997).

salt, for which the women gave her a 100-so'm note, just as I had observed earlier.

After she left, the women prepared everything for their departure. The driver was waiting outside at the small bazaar at the agreed time of seven o'clock. During the journey the women talked about everything they had experienced during the day, including details of the party and how they had danced and sung. They were all highly excited, and the wife of the driver asked him to turn up the volume of the radio so that they could sing along, gesticulate, and even get up from their seats to show how they had danced at the party. Arriving at Massiv Navoiy, the women were greeted in the street by neighbours and relatives passing by and questioned about the day. Some of the husbands helped to unload the car. Before dispersing, the pilgrimage club members discussed their next excursion, scheduled for June, but postponed the final decision until the following Saturday, when they would gather again to celebrate Nargiza's birthday.

Using Spaces: Interpretations and Analysis

Having outlined the main stations of the day as they unfolded, I want now to look more carefully at the emic conceptions of the members of this pilgrimage group. During a conversation that took place during lunch at Bu Mozor, the women tried to explain why they had come and what they expected. Yulduz, the imam's wife, explained that for her the most important aspects were to relax and to have a day out with her friends: "I do not believe in such things as healing and so on. I believe only in Allah. I only came to see". Sayyora, the oldest member of the group, commented, "Some of us come here because they believe in the power of the saint, some believe in Allah only. Each of us has her own idea about piety, but only those who have faith in their hearts come here". Umida agreed with Sayyora but stressed the social aspect, which was her main motivation for coming to Bu Mozor: "We come here just to have a rest, to sit at a table as a group of friends and have a good time. Someone reads from the Qur'an for the soul of those buried here, but I do not know very much about the history of this place. When I was a kid, our mothers and grandmothers took us here and I watched what they did. I come here every year just to relax".

Despite having different opinions and diverging expectations, the women of the pilgrimage club agreed that three elements were important for a successful *ziyorat*: the experience of a day out with friends, the spiritual aspect of proximity to God and to the saint, and the obtaining of a blessing (*baraka*). Individually, they emphasized the elements differently, some highlighting the religious and spiritual aspects, and others, the social and recreational. For some, such as Gulzoda, healing was the main motivation for the trip. Here as elsewhere in the world, participation in a pilgrimage can embrace a triple dimension: the spiritual, the social-recreational, and the supplicatory (Umbelino 1999). The women experienced Bu Mozor as a place where the sacred and the profane came together in a flexible and mutually reinforcing reality. Fulfilling an obligatory Islamic ritual such as *namoz* in no way contradicted the pleasure obtained through dancing and singing. Both the sacred and the profane were perceived as inherent in the "package" of the *ziyorat*.

The first dimension, the spiritual one, is that of belief. Although motivations for conducting *ziyorat* vary, it is the physical and visual contact with the saint that provides common ground. Touching and kissing the walls, the tomb, and the objects related to the saint, a spiritual successor to the Prophet, circling her or his tomb, and taking home consecrated objects allow people to experience the divine and establish a reciprocal relationship with the saint (Trimmingham 1971). Their localized activities create significant sites for meaning and reflection (Louw 2006: 50). A visit to Bu Mozor presupposes knowledge of the basic rites and belief in the myths and the spirituality ascribed to the place. In this setting, the saint and God himself can be not merely imagined but actually experienced more closely by the believer than in the more abstract setting of a mosque (McChesney 1996; Privratsky 2001: 243).[125]

Although practices such as touching the walls and stones of the *maqbara*, donating money, and consulting a healer, let alone participating in a party, can hardly be reconciled with canonical Islam, the sacrality of the site and its spiritual power are unquestioned by the women who come to Bu Mozor. This is not to deny a certain ambivalence in their relationship with shrines (cf. Louw 2006 on shrines in Bukhara). But even those who acknowledge that *ziyorat* practices are out of line with the sunna (perhaps qualifying as *bid'at*, a heretical innovation, or *shirk*, idolatry) consider shrines to exude spirituality and to be the embodiment of the region's Muslim past and customs (Fathi 2004; Louw 2006; Kehl-Bodrogi 2006b). As Christopher Taylor (1990: 80) showed in his study of Muslim saints in medieval Egypt, such local practices establish direct access to the sacred past in order to engage the holy in immediate time and space. Yulduz and the other women who performed *namoz* might have been sceptical towards many of the devotional practices surrounding the shrine and said that they believed only in Allah, and not in the miraculous powers ascribed to stones,

[125] Editor's note: At this point Hilgers signalled her intention to insert a quotation from one of the pilgrims in which she explained why women who adhered more strictly to "scriptural Islam" would never take part in such a pilgrimage.

trees, and the healers practising around the shrine, but they nevertheless acknowledged the spiritual power of the place itself. In their understanding, their visit conformed to their conception of *musulmonchilik*, which is orientated towards canonical practices including the pre-eminence of the Qur'an and the pilgrimage to Mecca.

The second dimension, the social and recreational, can be summed up as "having fun". Nancy Tapper (1990: 247) touched upon this in her work in Turkey, noting that "when women speak of *ziyorat* visits, they usually refer to the relaxed occasions when they visit a shrine with a group of kinswomen, friends and neighbours". Much the same can be said about the Pilgrimage Group of Massiv Navoiy. Getting away from their families and domestic duties and being together with friends, meeting other people, shopping for souvenirs, and exchanging news, advice, and ideas about religion were among the motivations the women gave for their visit to Bu Mozor. People do not conduct *ziyorat* only when their individual situation is characterized by transition and uncertainty (Louw 2006: 93). They also do so to enjoy themselves, fusing profane motivations with religious ones.[126] The monthly excursions of this pilgrimage club are supported and encouraged by the women's husbands, as became clear after our ride home, when the men welcomed their wives, and in the jokes and comments of the men who attended Nargiza's birthday celebration the following Saturday (see also Wilcke 2001).

The third dimension is that of blessing and healing. Pilgrimage is based on the belief that certain places have special power, which can be experienced in situ and then taken home in the form of blessed objects. This power can generate a transformation of the individual's social status as well as feelings of spiritual renewal and the healing or alleviating of an illness (Dubisch 1995; Kehl-Bodrogi 2006b). Doing *ziyorat* is believed to help one to ward off evil spirits through the intercession of the saint with God, the blessing of goods with *baraka*, or the help of healers who capitalize on the spiritual powers of the sacred site to cure both physical and mental illnesses.[127] Gulzoda was not content with touching the sacred stone; she also asked an *otin-oyi* to read an appropriate sura to cure her of her migraine. Other women consulted a *kinnachi*. These healers, concentrated at the saint's

[126] Again, this observation has much wider validity. See Doumato (2000) on the Gulf States, Dubisch and Michalowski (2001) and Turner and Turner (1978) on Christianity, and Taylor (2004) on Buddhism in Vietnam.

[127] In the doctrines of official Islam, saints are mediators who can intercede with Allah to obtain grace for the supplicant. Uzbek women, however, imagine the role of saints and their curative and blessing powers differently. Some believe the saint herself performs miracles and address her directly; others take more care to respect canonical practice.

mausoleum, used a range of techniques. One treated women with back problems by giving them a massage, and another symbolically cut the body of the sick person with a knife, murmuring prayers to exorcise evil spirits. These healing practices are legitimated by the practitioners as being in the service of God (see Rasanayagam 2006b).

Many women come to Bu Mozor for help in resolving fertility problems. Young women are under pressure to get pregnant in their first year of marriage, and there is a strong preference for sons. Infertility or a lack of male offspring can constitute grounds for man to divorce or to take a second wife. Women deposit their written petitions with the *shaykh*, and if they are successful, they return to the *mozor* and leave a curl of the baby's hair wrapped in a white cloth, representing the child's bond with the saint. This will be passed on by the *shaykh* to the next woman coming to ask for his assistance with fertility (see Kriss and Kriss-Heinrich 1960).

Women's motives for visiting sacred sites are not limited to their individual well-being but reflect their domestic and social environments. One example is the bringing of objects related to familial space to have them blessed by the saint. Women often advance requests on behalf of a husband or a son – for a cure, perhaps, or help in improving his material situation.

Plate 15. A female healer, or *kinnachi*, performs curative services for women with back problems and other physical ailments in front of the mausoleum of Bibi Ubayda.

New Meanings in Defined Spaces: Performing *Namoz*

Women in Uzbekistan are largely excluded from mosques and institutions of higher Islamic education. The spaces regarded as legitimate for women to conduct rituals in are to be found, according to local cultural conceptions, at cemeteries and shrines and inside the household, where women may also organize private lessons. As Sayyora explained to me: "It was always like that. Although we know that it is different in other Muslim countries, women in Uzbekistan never went to the mosque. Uzbeks think that women should stay at home, and learn and pray there – this is how we learned it and this is why women do not want to go to mosque. And even if we would like to go to mosque, it never would be approved by men".

When I asked whether they would like to go to mosque, the women I talked to said they would not, and they referred to the general lack of space there. Moreover, few mosques in Kokand have separate spaces for women.[128] To circumvent this problem, women sometimes gather in nearby houses where they can listen through an open window to what is being said inside.[129] In Tashkent, my host Aziza belonged to a study circle that met regularly at the home of an *otin-oyi*. The women went regularly as a group during Ramadan to hear the sermons in the newly built Friday mosque close to their *mahalla*. Although there was a section for women, Aziza said that they never went there on Fridays, giving as a reason the strong presence of men, coupled with the fact that men would be bound to disapprove. Her husband added that the mere knowledge that women were present in the mosque, even if they were not visible, would distract Uzbek men from concentrating on their prayers. Although he said this jokingly, to provoke his wife, his words actually represent a prevalent social norm. A mullah in Kokand quoted a statement from the Hadith saying that it is three times more rewarding for a woman to stay at home than to pray in a mosque, and I later heard this often from women themselves.

One may conclude that it is cultural disapproval rather than any objective lack of space that inhibits women from attending mosque. Both men and women in the Ferghana Valley have deeply internalized the norm that performing *namoz* in the mosque falls in the male domain. Only rarely do women express the wish to go to mosque. It is a male-dominated space

---

[128] The exclusion of women from mosques because of the lack of separate space is by no means limited to the Uzbek case; it can be observed also in Xinjiang, China (Ildikó Bellér-Hann, personal communication; see also Doumato 2000).

[129] Harrison (1924) reported similar strategies by women in Wahhabi Islam in the Persian Gulf at the beginning of the twentieth century.

analogous to the tea house (*choykhona*) or the football stadium.[130] The same applies to religious education. The madrasa has (at any rate until very recently) been regarded as an exclusively male establishment. The majority of girls are taught at home by their parents, an *otin-oyi*, or some other religiously educated person.

It was not always like this. In the early thirteenth century, women attended Friday prayers in the mosques in Samarqand (Tokhtakhodjaeva 1995). At the turn of the twentieth century, women gathered on religious holidays in some mosques in Bukhara, although segregated from men. Special mosques for women operated in Tashkent until the Bolshevik revolution. Marfua Tokhtakhodjaeva (1995: 23–24) interpreted women's later absence from the mosque as "the logical conclusion of women's general inequality within the family and in society". Similarly, Habiba Fathi (2006) has pointed out that nowadays the religious status of Muslim women is often confused with or derived from their social status, although the Qur'an specifies that women should fulfil the same basic religious duties as men. Prayer performed exclusively at home does not fulfil the highest standard of orthodox worship, "which requires regularity, a knowledge of correct prayers, and, at least on Fridays, praying with a group in the mosque. These are standards that can be wholly fulfilled only by men" (Doumato 2000: 94).

Except during *qurbon hayiti*, the Sacrifice Festival, and *ramazon*, or *ro'za*, *hayiti*, the festival marking the end of Ramadan, women's presence in the mosques is accepted. They can attend prayers sitting in the rows behind the men or in separate rooms outside the main mosque enclosure. In practice they seldom bother, and their accounts make it clear that the reasons lie in cultural ideas about shame and morality rather than in the simple concern over deprecation by men or an alleged lack of space. Women told me repeatedly that they did not feel comfortable praying in public, by which they meant spaces associated with official Islam and the male sphere. One reason for the feeling of shame was women's uncertainty about how to perform *namoz* correctly: many could only mimic the prostrations silently because they did not know or could not pronounce the Arabic words.[131]

In rural Tajikistan, a similarly strong emic distinction is drawn between the public and the private spheres, between space where one can be seen by anyone and the space that is bounded by the household (Tett 1995:

---

[130] When I expressed interest in going to watch international football games during my stay in Tashkent, I was told that women did not go to the stadium because it was considered too dangerous. Apparently, in the 1970s a Russian woman had her dress torn when the local team won a big game.

[131] Editor's note: At this point the author intended to insert a quotation from a woman explaining that to her it would "feel strange" to be observed by men when performing *namoz*.

139). The relative absence of men at the Bu Mozor complex creates an environment that women experience as semi-public. There they feel free to profess their religiosity in ways that, in other settings, would cause them to feel ashamed. For the four women of the Pilgrimage Club of Massiv Navoiy who, unusually, performed *namoz* during their *ziyorat*, the absence of men at the site enabled them to conduct a ritual normally confined to the domestic sphere. It clearly helped that they were participating in a female community, able to support and learn from each other. Bu Mozor became a kind of protected area where women could appropriate existing spaces to fulfil their ritual obligations, without having to worry about “getting it right”.

Conclusion

The use of space at Bu Mozor, with its spiritual and profane topography and multi-layered meanings, depends to a great extent on the individual’s conception of *musulmonchilik* and personal relations with the divine. The pilgrimage group members presented in this chapter held certain assumptions in common, but their practices and interpretations were diverse. The *mozor* had something to offer for everyone. The women used the shrine in different ways according to their individual understandings of what it meant to be a religious person.

The conduct of *ziyorat* is more than just a pleasant day off. It gives insight not only into the gendered use of space but more generally into the dynamism of religious practices in “flexible Islam” (Eickelman and Piscatori 1996). Although many details of the practices of saint veneration have been more or less standardized and remained relatively stable throughout Uzbek history, this does not imply that their meanings have remained fixed or frozen (Pfluger-Schindlbeck 2005; see also Louw 2006). This is consistent with Mark Saroyan’s observation (1997c: 106) that religious practices have regularly violated the categorical boundaries of Islam.

In Uzbekistan, women do not merely maintain but actively shape religious spaces on the basis of their conceptualizations of religious practices. The evidence from Bu Mozor shows that religious practice in Uzbekistan cannot be neatly divided into female religiosity, demarcating the sphere of heterodoxy and superstition, and male religiosity, associated with scriptural interpretations and the mosque. The spheres have long intersected. Yet for women to perform *namoz* outside the domestic space, as I observed at Bu Mozor, is a novelty of recent decades and a new element in the conduct of *ziyorat*. This practice in the open air is an approximation of male religious practice, but it does not transgress or challenge culturally determined gendered spaces. It shows women’s growing interest in canonical Islam and reflects their growing self-awareness as religious persons. They do not lay claim to male spaces per se, but they creatively appropriate the space available to them within moral norms. By adapting spaces historically associated with female religiosity, the women carve out a more public niche for themselves according to their changing conceptions of *musulmonchilik*.

This does not mean that concepts of gendered religious spheres have become obsolete. For one thing, the semi-public performance of *namoz* that I observed remains exceptional – perhaps a pioneering trend, but not yet the mainstream. Indeed, only a minority of the pilgrimage group performed *namoz* at the *maqbara* of Bibi Ubayda. For another, Bu Mozor is primarily female space, and the women who visit it do not trespass the culturally and religiously defined boundaries of male and female realms. The continued exclusion of women from male religious spheres reflects cultural conceptions of female morality, tradition, and social norms; it shows the enduring importance of gendered religious spaces in Uzbek society.

It is important to note, however, that the women I met in the course of my fieldwork did not perceive gendered religious spaces as discriminatory. Indeed, the opposite was the case: women attached importance to rituals associated with the female sphere of religiosity and did not necessarily devalue them as inferior to male practices at the mosque. Men seemed to share this view, and sometimes they even tried to appropriate female rituals.[132]

---

[132] For example, in the early 1990s the men of the Ferghana Valley began to conduct the *mavlud,* a ritual associated primarily with women and domestic space, in the mosque (Kandiyoti and Azimova 2004).

Chapter 7 Uzbek Christians: A Question of Tolerance?[133]

I showed in earlier chapters how Islam has been packaged as the national religion of Uzbeks in the postsocialist national ideology. President Islam Karimov sees Islam as the spiritual-religious foundation of the nation and as the basis for moral consolidation and self-identification during nation-building (Karimov 1997: 89). I also argued that it would be incorrect to see this ideology as orchestrated entirely by the government, because the basic idea that religion should be nationally (ethnically) determined is still dominant in Uzbek society: Uzbeks are Muslims, and Russians are Christians. Religions are seen as substantial parts of respective ethnic cultures. During Soviet times, religious customs survived under the cover of "national tradition" (Critchlow 1991), and religion served as an important vehicle for the

---

[133] Editor's note: This chapter is based on a published article (Hilgers 2007). The author had intended to write an entirely new paper on this subject for her dissertation, but this was not accomplished. The file for this chapter opens with eight pages of notes and extracts from her fieldwork diaries, which she had evidently planned to incorporate. I have done my best to implement her intentions by incorporating a section on "Tolerance", as highlighted in her formulation of the title of the chapter; but it was unclear how she intended to proceed with regard to a further planned subsection, "Moralities". She summarized the key tasks in revising the chapter as follows:

- *show that Muslim criticism of the establishment ("anti-clericalism?") is actually the same as the Christian critique;*
- *show that people insist that there is only one God, and that the main thing is to be a "good person";*
- *show in more detail what Muslims say about Christians, e.g. point out that most are not even aware that there are new, non-traditional Christian communities in their city, and find it absurd that Uzbeks are converting.*

In her entire manuscript, Hilgers used the formal name "Church of Uzbek Christians" for the people she discusses here only once, in chapter 3. I have nonetheless retained this name in this chapter as a convenient way to refer to the community she describes, which was unregistered with the state and therefore had no official name. It is likely that the group referred to itself by this name.

preservation and transmission of ethnic identities, in opposition to the national policies of the Soviets (Bruce 2002: 96; Lankauskas 2002: 321).

Yet at the same time, with the 1992 Uzbekistan Constitution, the new government created the legal basis for a new religious pluralism based on freedom of conscience. In addition to a revival of the old, established religions, many new religious currents entered the country. In the Uzbekistan example of global processes of religious mixing (Chambers 2004: 71), the main "traditional" religions, tied to ethno-national identities, have been particularly hostile to newcomers (Peyrouse 2004a). The expanding religious marketplace offers people a wide range of products, from orthodox to charismatic and transcendental. These may be attractive to Uzbeks who perceive themselves as cultural Muslims, who do not necessarily have a strong emotional identification with their inherited religious affiliation, and who have unfulfilled spiritual needs. As they make use of the newly gained right to choose their religion, they necessarily renegotiate their personal selves and the concept of being Uzbek (Snow and Machalek 1983; Krech and Schlegel 1998). The government, however, remains wedded to the concept of a national religion and fears that tension and instability are bound to ensue if national identity and traditions are threatened.

In this chapter I explore these tangled issues with reference to a case study, that of a young Christian community in Kokand, the Church of Uzbek Christians. I show how "Uzbekness" and "Muslimness" as sine qua nons of Uzbek identity are being negotiated by individual converts and how the discourse of a national Uzbek identity is integrated into the doctrine of this community. I also demonstrate the significance of the new local religious organizations, which are highly dependent on the personal relationships and social, cultural, and economic networks maintained by their members outside of their religious community (Davie 1994: 18; Chambers 2004: 71). At the same time, these religious communities are subject to trans-local constraints, which prescribe doctrines and organizational structures to which the local congregations must adhere. Those predominantly foreign religious denominations are "deterritorialized" (Appadurai 1998: 37). With postsocialist liberalization of the religious sphere, individual religious affiliation was de facto privatized and de jure protected. But in practice the Uzbek who turns away from Islam and converts to a non-Islamic religion faces a dilemma in reconciling his new faith, which public opinion regards as not "ours" (i.e. Uzbek), with tradition and national identity. First-generation Uzbek Christians perform a precarious balancing act between their local identities and integration into a universal Christianity.[134]

[134] Editor's note: At this point in her draft, Hilgers inserted the phrase "trauma and conversion", followed by this quotation: "The emotional trauma of breaking with one's neighbours

Uzbek *Musulmonchilik* and the Christian Encounter

In the first years after Uzbek independence, the strength of radical Islamic movements in the Ferghana Valley confirmed the region's long-standing reputation for religious conservatism (Babadjanov and Kamilov 2001). Apart from small Russian Orthodox congregations and a few Baptists and Armenian Orthodox Christians, Islam was absolutely dominant, and this was reflected in the large number of mosques and madrasas. The first charismatic Christian communities were established in the Ferghana Valley by missionaries from South Korea and the United States only in the 1990s, whereas in Samarqand, Bukhara, and Tashkent the first such groups dated from the early years of perestroika. The missionaries at first confined their activities to the Russian-speaking population, but later they attracted increasing numbers of ethnic Uzbeks.

Alisher, age forty-two when I got to know him, was the founder and pastor of a congregation of Uzbek Christians in Kokand. His first contact with Christianity had come in 1997, during his military service in Russia.[135] A year later he and his wife, Mohira (thirty-six), were baptized. Alisher had hitherto considered himself a Muslim, performed *namoz,* and attended Friday prayers at the mosque. Like so many other Uzbeks, he perceived himself to be a Muslim for cultural reasons, rather than a devout Muslim whose belief stemmed from conviction, or "from the heart":

> By that time I did not know what it meant to be a Muslim. We were born in a Muslim country and family; our ancestors were Muslims; we did not possess the knowledge and understanding and thought that everyone else apart from Uzbeks and Arabs were *kofir* [Arab., "unbeliever"] – for example, Russians or Koreans or Americans. The word *kofir* was used often then, and we thought our nation superior to others. ... They [the Uzbeks] don't understand the meaning of the word Muslim. It means one who believes in and submits to God, a person who fulfils his orders. Islam also means to obey what God has prescribed. But those who consider themselves Muslims are drinking alcohol, smoking, offending people, divorcing whenever

---

and publicly professing a new faith, moreover, forced the youths to take their own actions seriously. Before going public with the news of their conversion, most reflected long and hard on the purpose and likely consequences of their commitment" (Hefner 1993: 117).

135 Alisher had met a Russian soldier who openly confessed his Christian belief. Alisher was impressed by the soldier's strict compliance with Christian doctrine in everyday life. He remembered the soldier and his belief when Christian missionaries came to his village in 1997, spreading the gospel and distributing religious literature. Following these encounters with Christians, Alisher bought a Bible, though he started to read it only a year later.

> they want to; they also do not look after their children, leaving them on their own, yet they always affirm that they are Muslims.

Mohira added, "They say this because our ancestors were Muslims. … For the majority of Uzbeks, Islam is primarily a signifier of ethnic or national commitment and inseparable from Uzbek ethnic identity. Therefore those who turn away from Islam face many obstacles and risk social exclusion". Alisher amplified her point by explaining: "People in the village as well as our own families perceived our acceptance of Jesus as a sin and betrayal of our culture. Because of our decision to leave Islam, we faced a lot of difficulties. The connection between being Uzbek and Islam is very strong, and for Uzbeks it is unimaginable that someone can leave Islam and turn to another faith".

After accepting Jesus and openly confessing their new faith, the family had to move several times to other villages. As soon as people got to know about their Christianity, they were met with hostility and were accused of betraying their culture and ancestors: Uzbeks had to be Muslims; they could not adhere to a religion often referred to as "the religion of the Russians".[136]

Christianity: The Religion of the Russians?

In 1999 Alisher and Mohira, harassed in the countryside, moved into the relatively anonymous nearby city of Kokand, where some new Protestant churches had already been established. They joined the Evangelical church but soon began organizing Uzbek-only gatherings in private houses. Eventually they split from the Evangelical church to found their own Christian community, the Church of Uzbek Christians. Alisher was chosen to be the *cho'pon* (Uzb., "shepherd") of the congregation, because of his good reputation and engagement on behalf the community. He had no formal theological education. Membership was open only to ethnic Uzbeks, and Uzbek was the community's lingua franca, mainly because many converts to Christianity, in the city as well as the villages, were not fluent in Russian. Alisher said that the widely accepted idea that Christianity was the national religion of the Russians, the equivalent of Islam for the Uzbeks, was the main reason for excluding other ethnicities:

---

[136] Editor's note: At this point the author inserted a note concerning a similar situation among the Baha'is with whom she spent some time in Tashkent. The parents of a convert had gone with him to the Baha'i Centre to discuss the problem with "those responsible". The Baha'is tried to mediate between the convert and his parents, but they were unsuccessful, and he was obliged to move out of his family home and *mahalla*. See the discussion in the later section "Tolerance".

> Some were saying that they did not hear about Jesus; they say that they knew that Jesus was a prophet, that he came to Russians. There is such a dominant idea among Uzbeks that every nation has its own prophet. David for the Jews, Jesus for Russians, and Mohammed for Uzbeks. … We wanted to show that Jesus came not only to Americans or Russians, but that he came for all, for Russians, but also for Uzbeks. We wanted to prove it, so we started gathering separately with our relatives and neighbours, and we wanted to show that we are not just converting to some religion, because Jesus did not come to establish a religion, he came for all. It is written in the revelation that many nations, in many languages, will be reciting his name, and so we also wanted to recite his name in Uzbek and praise his name. For this reason we gathered an Uzbek national community to profess in Uzbek.

The community was also exclusionary in the way it conducted its meetings and services, in *o'zbekona* – Uzbek style. When they met as small groups of believers in private houses, they wore "national" Uzbek clothes and played "national" Uzbek instruments. At the time of my fieldwork, the movement had about 100 members, subdivided into several house groups in the city itself and in four villages. To participate in their meetings it was necessary to receive an invitation from one of the members, and this could be issued only if everyone in the group agreed. Members were obliged to recruit in this way because they were unregistered with the Ministry of Justice (see chapter 2). They were not allowed to conduct religious teaching or celebrate divine services, but thanks to their good relations with the local authorities, their prayer meetings were tolerated. The personalized recruitment procedure also helped to secure the anonymity of members, an important consideration for those who feared repression from Uzbek Muslims or simply ostracism by their relatives if their conversion to Christianity become public knowledge.

I asked Alisher how his family and friends in Tashkent had reacted when they learned of his conversion.

> *Alisher*: They did not respect me any more. They had a bad opinion of me, saying that I had become Russian and so on. And once I was reading a part of the Bible where it is said that we should be very patient. I was insulted. People laughed at me, and I even left my house, because I was kicked out from home, but I did not pay much attention to that and was strong in my belief. The time came and now everyone in my family respects me. …
>
> *Hilgers*: Why did your father say that it was wrong?
>
> *Alisher*: He would say that it is the God of the Russians. …

> *Hilgers*: What is your opinion of the idea that Uzbeks should belong to Islam?
>
> *Alisher*: This is a false concept. God is one for everyone. Saying Uzbeks are Muslims and Christianity is for Russians is not true and it is incorrect. God has given everyone the right of choice, and to choose is in everyone's hands. Russians can be Muslims, and Uzbeks can be Christians.

Alisher's mother and sister followed him in converting to Christianity. His father remained a devout Muslim who attended mosque regularly and performed *namoz,* but he, too, began reading the Bible. Although rejecting Christian belief for himself, he acknowledged that Jesus was a "perfect person" and accepted his son's new belief. Alisher described himself as a believing Muslim before his conversion. He performed *namoz* only once a day (for his sins to be forgiven, as he put it), but he went to mosque every Friday and observed all the Islamic holidays. He had learned about Islam from his parents since early childhood. A private teacher he visited later had to flee the country because of accusations of being an Islamist.

It is important to see the limitations of the "choosing" to which Alisher refers in the preceding transcript. Talal Asad (2006: 239–240) has recently argued:

> Thus it is that the human in modern secular society comes to be endowed with particular capacities for self-awareness, autonomy, and responsibility that make her capable of acting (an agent). These capacities do not necessarily depend on one another – they are contingent – but the human individual defined by them lies ideologically at the center of capitalist political economy – as worker, consumer, and citizen. And as the follower of various modern liberal religions. Because religion's ultimate justification is now widely believed to reside in the individual's experience of "the sacred" and his/her desire to connect with "transcendence", he/she now assumes an absolute right to choose in such matters. The agent is ultimately responsible for himself or herself because he or she is now presumed to have a self that can be inspected, evaluated, and guided autonomously. In previous epochs, the individual was often an integral part of family and institutions and his substance derived from particular places and kin.

My fieldwork data provide no support for this position. That the individual can make choices does not render him or her autonomous. On the contrary, the Uzbek individual remains "an integral part of family and institutions", which is why the sanctions applied to converts are often extended to their families. This in turn helps us to understand why many families, unlike Alisher's, show little tolerance of the individual member's "absolute right to choose".

Tolerance

If Uzbek converts to charismatic Christianity tend to be objects of intolerance from the Muslim majority, they themselves vacillate between inclusionary and exclusionary orientations. I discussed this with Iroda, the Christian convert whom I introduced in chapter 4. She emphasized that people of many nationalities attended her prayer house and that Jesus did not discriminate. Jesus "accepts everyone, whether he is Russian, Uzbek, Kazakh, German, Japanese, or Korean. There are many Koreans, by the way. Everyone will be my children. But if a Russian goes to a mosque, he will not be accepted there; they think that Islam is only for Uzbeks. It is people's illiteracy. The level of their minds is low".

Iroda's contention is valid in the sense that new currents asserting a universal Islam, freed from all local, ethnic bonds and privileging the choices made by individuals, are not yet accepted by most Uzbeks. In the same conversation she told me that there were basically two kinds of Muslims: those who persecuted converts and those who paid no attention to them. She evidently felt that the former were still a substantial majority. Perhaps for this reason, she was adamant that born-again Christians should marry within their community. It was relatively easy for her to live as a Christian in Tashkent, said Iroda, but at home in the Ferghana Valley, in an almost completely Muslim environment, it was difficult to deal with the pressures from one's family.

Iroda illustrated these pressures by telling me the story of her brother Rustam's failed marriage plans. He had fallen in love in Tashkent with a fellow student from Kokand, who had no problem with his Christianity. It seems that the girl's mother, too, was prepared to agree to their marriage, but her father was resolutely opposed. Rustam's mother intervened to point out that her son had become a "better person" since his conversion, having given up smoking and drinking alcohol. Was it really better, she asked, to give one's daughter to a man who performed *namoz* but who might not be such a good person?

Her arguments were to no avail. The father insisted that he had nothing against Rustam personally, or against Christians; but a Christian son-in-law was unacceptable in his family – and then there was the question of what the neighbours would say. Iroda had the impression that the latter consideration was uppermost in the father's mind. He was afraid that allowing his daughter to marry a Christian would reflect badly on him as a Muslim, for others would comment that he obviously had not raised her properly.[137] A nominal tolerance towards Christians ceased at once when one's own family and status were at stake.

I found similar attitudes towards Uzbeks who had converted to religions other than Christianity. Bobur told me the story of his elder brother, Sardor, who had converted to the Hare Krishna movement after a trip to India. Since then he had lost interest in a career (for which he had good educational qualifications) and in material goods, given away much of his property, and maintained that only spiritual values mattered to him. Bobur said that his brother was "living for the moment". Sardor's wife, too, had converted, and the couple were raising their young daughter in accordance with the ideals of the Hare Krishna community.

The family had worried about their son, especially when he began to dispose of his property. They saw themselves as to blame for his abandoning Islam. According to Bobur, their parents had never spoken much about religion or insisted on regular performance of *namoz* or reading the Qur'an, and now they reproached themselves for this neglect. They also experienced the reproaches of others in the family and the *mahalla* that they were no longer "decent" and had failed as parents. The conversion clearly affected the entire family. Bobur himself remained a devout Muslim and prayed daily that his brother would return to the "right path". When I asked if I might contact his brother, Bobur hesitated and said he was afraid that explaining himself to me might only work to strengthen his brother's self-justification. Bobur had not given up hope that his brother would see the error of his ways and accept the truth of the Prophet. (It was his duty, he told me, to draw my attention to the ultimate truth of the Qur'an – but only once, for Islam was not an aggressive, missionizing religion.) As for the rest of the family, they tended to view the elder son's conversion as a form of mental aberration and hoped he would sooner or later recover.

Some time after this I got to know Sardor himself at the Krishna community centre. The problems in the *mahalla* had intensified, and he had moved outside the city and no longer had much contact with his parents. Bobur told me that his brother would be able to live much more comfortably if he would only accept the opportunities offered to him by their parents, but Sardor was uncompromising. Almost a year later I met both brothers at a family celebration. Sardor and his wife and daughter performed the prayer gestures along with everyone else. As vegetarians, they were not offered the

---

[137] A Muslim religious teacher (*domla*) whom I interviewed in Kokand laid much stress on this parental responsibility.

specially prepared food that included meat.[138] There was no discussion of the couple's commitment to the Krishnas, but they were treated cordially, and there was a great deal of interest in what he had to say about India. He explained that, although an engineer by training, he preferred to make his living by making sweets (I had tasted some of his products at the Krishna meetings, and they were delicious). He said he didn't mind baking and could cook for up to 200 people. His young daughter was included in a group photograph along with her many Muslim cousins, a sign that the parents had just about come to terms with their son's apostasy.

I also spent some time with members of the Baha'i community. There, too, some members reported problems of acceptance in their families. These problems were attributed to a lack of information and a herd-like mentality formed in the Soviet era, when faith was limited largely to the established religions and tied to ethnicity. The Baha'is were still thought of by some as a radical Islamic sect and were confused with Wahhabis. Conversion was stigmatized as a betrayal of one's family and traditions. For Muslim families, beyond the theological implications, it brought a loss of social prestige and the risk of exclusion from important social and economic networks. This led people to keep their conversions secret.[139]

We Are Christians, Not a Religion!

When I asked Alisher which direction of Christianity he and his community were following, he answered, "We don't pay much attention to that, we only follow what is written in the Bible. … People think that Christianity is a religion, but it is not a mere religion. Christianity is the divine way, Jesus was sent by God the saviour".

In its definition of religion, this community resembled other charismatic Protestant congregations in its emphatic anti-ritualism. The Russian Orthodox Church and the Roman Catholic Church were designated as religions because they were highly ritualized, stressed their traditions, venerated icons, and displayed a strongly hierarchical order in their clergy. Islam, too, was a religion, which for them was too dogmatic, lacking soul and spirit. Alisher once told the priest of Kokand's Russian Orthodox church that he should pay less attention to vestments, icons, and rituals and more to the words of the Bible. Those affiliated with religions were perceived to conduct

---

[138] The mother of two female converts to the Hare Krishnas commented that one purely practical complication arising from their new faith was the difficulty she now experienced in cooking for them.

[139] Students had a further reason for maintaining secrecy. It was reported during my fieldwork that several Hare Krishnas had been expelled from their courses for no reason other than their new faith.

prescribed rituals at fixed times, but without any strong emotional commitment.

This critique was usually put forward by Uzbek Christians as one reason for leaving Islam. Whereas in a traditional religion, one entered the community by being born into it, membership in a new religious community had to be achieved by the individual by displaying the proper beliefs, sentiments, and actions (Bruce 2002: 107). Uzbek Christians responded to what they perceived to be contradictions between religious moral standards and everyday life. Too many people called themselves pious Muslims but did not live by their doctrines. Uzbek Christians saw the proof of their superiority in the commitment a person had to show in everyday life, both to improving the spiritual self and in relation to others. They followed the general evangelical understanding of Christianity as "religion of the heart", a state in which the believer has a continuous sense of the saving presence of Jesus Christ and of the enthusing power of the Holy Spirit. Converts might be intellectually convinced of the scheme of salvation, but the real touchstone of its worth was the "warm" or "lively" inward emotional state, which came from having accepted Christ as one's saviour (Peel 2000: 250). This, they claimed, was what mere "religions" were lacking.[140]

At the time of my fieldwork in Kokand, the Evangelical church, the Neo-Baptists,[141] and the Pentecostals were attracted to the idea of uniting the new Christian congregations of the city. Christianity was, after all, they argued, a universal religion whose believers were unified by a sacred fictive kinship (Toulis 1997: 123). The topic was frequently discussed at their meetings and addressed by pastors in their sermons. Alisher's Uzbek Christians, however, preferred to remain separate and did not participate in the discussions about uniting. They rarely took part in joint activities with other churches; for example, they did not attend the screening of the movie *The Passion of Christ* that I mentioned in chapter 3, although some Russian Orthodox Christians and even Muslims did so. Alisher justified this anti-ecumenical stance on the grounds that Christianity was originally supposed

[140] Editor's note: At this point Hilgers inserted a note pointing out that there were "committed" and "conscious" Muslims who deployed the same critique of the contradictions and compromises made by the majority. This is an appropriate place to mention another caveat of the author's, in the raw notes she left in the file for this chapter. She wrote that it would be "too easy" to classify converts as "social misfits" merely because some of them had experienced a personal or financial crisis; unfortunately, this was the way they tended to be perceived by members of the established religions and by certain scholars (e.g. Hefner 1993).

[141] The Neo-Baptists were a small group of young believers who split off from the Baptist church in the city following a disagreement over the conduct of the service (see chapter 3). They were closer to the Pentecostals in the way they expressed themselves during the divine service.

to be a religion reserved for "others", notably Russians and Koreans, and not for "us", Uzbeks. "For example", he said, "if we go to the prayer house, where it is mostly Koreans and Russians who gather, the majority [Uzbek Muslims, but Christians as well] might think that we [the Uzbek Christians] had converted to another religion, which is not true. And because of this, we prefer to gather ourselves in [our members'] homes".

Alisher did not mean to reject the other congregations, with whom in fact he was on friendly terms, but he wanted to avoid giving the impression to the Muslim majority that the Uzbek Christians had become members of a "Russian" church. This would imply a loss of authenticity. Alisher valued the status of being shepherd to an independent Christian community with predominantly Uzbek traits. A fusion and confusion between "Russian Christians" and "Uzbek Christians" had to be avoided.

Alternative Identities

The Uzbek Christians of Alisher's congregation generally attached importance to maintaining their social networks and to remaining in close contact with their kin. Their social obligations and moral code left little space for individuality. People were dependent on their kin, and social control by the extended family and neighbourhood affected everything they did. Inappropriate behaviour was sanctioned by gossip.

These Uzbek Christians always stressed in interviews that they wished to respect the norms and values of Uzbek society. Their decision to leave Islam was not meant as an expression of protest against Uzbek society and tradition itself, but rather was the result of a search for spirituality and the enhancement of the self. Members of the Church of Uzbek Christians were careful to appear modest in public, not to provoke conflicts with Muslims, and not to stand out through dress or behaviour. Dressing in the "Uzbek style" was not compulsory, but it was a way of showing their commitment to their culture. Women tended to wear long dresses and the headscarf called *ro'mol,* which was usually hung loosely over the head. Men wore the black and white Uzbek skullcap (*do'ppi*) and on special occasions the *chopon,* a long quilted coat. At their meetings and divine services, the Uzbek Christians integrated Uzbek symbols, as in the way they held their hands and made *omin* at the end of a prayer or intercession. This was the same gesture that Muslims made, but, like women's wearing of the headscarf, it was perceived not as being Islamic but as being part of Uzbek tradition and culture. Muslims would not have disagreed.

The Christians of Alisher's congregation did not perceive their belief as being contrary to Uzbek traditions. They acknowledged that Uzbek identity was closely connected to Muslimness, but they saw no contradiction between their Christian belief and their fulfilling of social obligations. For them, too, *o'zbekchilik* incorporated a set of customs and rules that had been historically constituted and transferred over the generations. The teachings of Islam had been integrated. Alisher explained that he and his family were still invited to Uzbek celebrations, and they participated in them even if they were Islamic. It was their social and Christian obligation to attend such gatherings. As Mohira explained: "If we know the people, or if we are invited, we will go there. Otherwise, people could feel insulted by our behaviour, and we don't want that".

Nasiba, twenty-six, who had become a born-again Christian ten years earlier, told me that some members of the Church of Uzbek Christians observed the Ramadan fast:

> Of course I also love doing *ro'za*. Because if I am praying and they are doing *ro'za* it is even better … it is good! Yes, of course I also will be doing this. All of us believers are doing this, because we all love our Muslims very much. We love our Uzbek people and we never will be fighting with them just because we are Christians. No, because it is our duty to show them our love, our respect, because Jesus loves them too … It will not be good if I live with my family and say, "I'm sorry – I'm a Christian, you are Muslims". That's not good – no, that's not possible!

According to these converts' understanding of Christianity, fasting at Ramadan does not contradict their belief, because it is written in the Bible that Jesus himself fasted. Even among the Muslims of the Ferghana Valley, fasting tends to be viewed not as a religious obligation but as a decision for the individual. I observed in many Muslim families that some kept the fast while others did not. It is much the same among the Uzbek Christians, and by aligning their fasting period to that of the Muslims, they symbolize their unity with Muslim Uzbek society.

Members of the Church of Uzbek Christians engaged actively in social and public life. If a mullah or *otin-oyi* recited from the Qur'an at a celebration, these Christians did not withdraw but sat and prayed silently, addressing their intercession to Jesus instead of Allah. But although they participated in most rituals and customs, they drew the line if they themselves were made the subject of an Islamic ritual by their Muslim kin. Alisher explained:

> For example, there is a custom that when a woman is in the seventh month of her pregnancy a *kalla* [Uzb., head of a sheep] should be cooked, and one has to give headscarves and the like as presents. But we, for example when we had our second child, did not do any of

> those customs; we did not call a mullah, nor did we whisper the *azon* [the call for prayer] into the ear of the baby.[142] People say if this is not done he will not be a Muslim, but he is quite healthy and all right, has not been in hospital so far. Now our child is five years old and we don't need such traditions. These traditions and customs are mostly unnecessary.

Some of these rituals, unnecessary to Alisher, are perceived as important religious life-cycle rituals by Christians' Muslim kin. Alisher reported cases in his community in which not only the convert but also his or her Muslim relatives suffered from gossip in the *mahalla.* Mixed confessional families could reckon with a decline in social prestige, just as the parents of converts could count on accusations of not having fulfilled their religious and moral educational duties.

Beyond gossip, more fundamental problems emerge for these families. An Uzbek Christian, for example, cannot be buried in a Muslim graveyard, together with his or her ancestors. Marriage poses further challenges. In Uzbekistan, most marriages are arranged by the parents, female elders, or both, and people older than twenty-six are usually said to be too old to get married (Tabyshalieva 1997: 52; Werner 1997: 606). The reputation of the family is an important factor in the acceptability of a potential spouse, alongside education and employment, and few Muslim families are willing to give their child to a non-believer. Christians ideally marry other Uzbek Christians or Muslims whose families accept their faith. Mohira described the situation this way:

> We had a girl in our community who waited and worshipped a long time, and finally a believing [i.e. Christian] man from Samarqand married her. In that case, the sisters and neighbours, together with the parents of the girl, were all insisting that she should get married, and after a long time even her mother, who was a believer, started to worry for her, as time was passing and she was getting older, and insisted that she should get married, even if [the husband] was a non-believer [i.e. Muslim]. The girl had younger sisters and they also wanted to get married, but according to Uzbek tradition, they couldn't get married until their elder sister was married. But we talked with the family and insisted that the girl should marry only a believer. She married a believer from Samarqand. This boy came here for an internship. They found each other, prayed together, and now they are getting married.

---

[142] This is a widespread Muslim custom.

Alisher added, "Now we are trying to organize and gather money for a festival in the valley, in order to gather the youth, to give speeches to the families, and also to give young people the possibility to meet each other. All the Uzbek communities will be invited".

Alisher's congregation regularly organized meetings at which members shared experiences and discussed questions of the right behaviour for Christians in everyday life situations in a society shaped by Islam. Often, as in the case of matchmaking, but also in questions of the moral education of children, Uzbek Christians have no clear reference points in situations where cultural ideas collide with Christian ethics. Expert assistance was sometimes brought in from the capital. Alisher said, "We have teachers in Tashkent who can lecture or teach on the true believing family, show how a believing husband and wife should behave, basing their attitude towards each other on the Bible".

According to Nicole Toulis (1997: 127), the person is a culturally constructed, moral entity, and there always exists "a cultural idea of morality or ethics, which decrees what are the correct interests, motivations, choices and actions that the person must posses". Uzbek Christians want and need to comply with the moral responsibilities prescribed by their Uzbek culture, for two reasons. First, they wish to avoid the social stigma of being perceived as "bad" people, which has negative effects not only for the individual but for the family as a whole, Muslim members included. For example, the family may be regarded as unsuitable for marriage alliances, which affects all the unmarried siblings of the convert. Second, it is in the interest of Uzbek Christians to convince non-believers of the rightness of their Christian belief, to legitimate their choice, and to set an example of good behaviour, in order to convince other people to accept Jesus. Because there is widespread antagonism towards "two-faced" Muslims, and because many people, both Muslims and Christians, harbour doubts about the credibility of Muslim authorities, the strategy has brought results. Alisher told me:

> Many of our relatives who heard about Jesus and saw that our lives changed for the better after accepting him got convinced and followed our example. My father was one of them. Before, he was a devout Muslim who prayed *namoz*, read the Qur'an, and went to mosque. At first when he heard about my decision, he shouted and insulted me. But when he saw that Jesus had helped me to live a better life and to become a better person, he started reading the Bible too.

This response is typical. Many of my Christian informants in the Ferghana Valley told me that they had decided to accept Jesus after seeing that the life of a Christian relative or friend had changed for the better.

Uzbek Christians stand precariously between rejection and acceptance in Uzbek society. Rejection is an ever-present threat, given the government's manipulative equation of national unity and social stability through playing on tradition and the congruence of ethnicity and religion. Yet Christians such as Alisher also experience acceptance and admiration from some Uzbek Muslims for the authenticity of their faith, which they demonstrate in their daily lives and behaviour.

Conclusion

Conversion from Islam to other religions is still a marginal phenomenon among Uzbeks, and ethnic churches like the one described in this chapter are exceptional among converts. Nonetheless, the Church of Uzbek Christians gives valuable insights into more general negotiations of national and self-identity, of tradition and modernity, in this postsocialist society in transition.

Conversion involves a radical questioning of subjects previously taken for granted. After the suppression of religiosity during the Soviet period, the new possibility of religious pluralism offered people an alternative basis for constructing identities and for distancing themselves from their traditional settings. A new religious affiliation, however, does not necessarily involve a radical change of the social and cultural matrix, including symbols, customs, worldviews, and institutions. The contents of customs and rituals perceived as Islamic can be rejected or simply exchanged for Christian contents while the forms of traditional Uzbek rituals are preserved.

But despite the Uzbek Christians' attempts to remain integrated in society, perceptions of tradition are inevitably challenged by the new religious pluralism. These challenges for society are expressed not only in the change of faith but also in the questioning of established social forms and the communality of Uzbek society. The first reaction of the society is to reject alternative identities such as "Christian Uzbek" as subversively modern and a threat to stability. Yet for the congregation of Uzbek Christians, their religion guarantees their ethnic identity, even if it is a modified form of *o'zbekchilik* that places them at the margins of Uzbek society. With their exclusionary stance towards other ethnicities, they seek to legitimate their ethnic interests (Bruce 2002: 107) and demonstrate that Christianity can reach across national borders. Perhaps it is not too far-fetched to describe this phenomenon as a new form of myth-making. The "myth of the chosen people" has often been crucial in ensuring long-term ethnic survival in the course of nation-building (Smith 1996: 189). The same idea can be applied to smaller social entities, such as the Uzbek Christian community I have focused on here. Their belief that Jesus came to all people, including Uzbeks, enables them to create their niche in the religious landscape of Uzbekistan and to earn public recognition as Uzbek Christians.

The very notion of an exclusively Uzbek Christian identity appears to contradict the common unifying experience of shared Christian beliefs, where religious symbolism is supposed to transcend ethnic, racial, and cultural differences. The Uzbek Christians of Alisher's congregation acknowledge this inclusive dimension, but they cannot afford to assimilate to a universal Christian identity and lose their selfhood. They see themselves as living in a transitional period, in which their first task is to overcome, by the example of their lived faith, the prejudice of nationally determined religions and to prove to society that Christianity is not a Russian religion. In affirming their marginal position as Uzbek Christians in Uzbek society, they have raised their collective consciousness and welded members together to form a new moral community. A new, "modern" self-definition and identification have been constructed, without the church members' becoming detached from national and traditional forms.[143]

[143] Editor's note: In her preliminary notes for revising this chapter, Hilgers included the following quotation from John Bowen's analysis of Muslims in Indonesia. She did not indicate exactly where she wished to introduce the comparison, but it seems directly relevant to her concluding observations: "And yet, the detachment of Gayo modernists from village life, though broad, has always been partial. Modernists have not conjured images of a new mode of life, free of village constraints, as James Siegel (1969) describes for Aceh reformists. Instead, they have carved out a distinct religious sphere of activity which would also allow for the continuation of nonreligious activities and ties (largely in the villages)" (Bowen 1998: 37).

Chapter 8
Conclusion

Editor's note: This chapter was planned to be a relatively short conclusion in which the author would summarize the main arguments of her book and perhaps point the way forward to new research questions. Unlike the introduction, the drafting of which was assuming its definitive shape, the conclusion had barely been begun. The chapter file opened with the following outline:

1. On history, ideology, and religion
2. The making of the religious self
3. Negotiating religiosities

None of these sections was written, even in part. There followed seven pages of notes on various authors, most of whom had already been incorporated into the discussions of preceding chapters (Hilgers had to endure her supervisor's pedantic insistence that she should not introduce new materials in the conclusion). Some of these authors are Central Asia specialists. It is clear that Hilgers intended to focus one last time on the close relationship in this region between religious and secular identities, as encapsulated in her dissertation title, and on the Soviet legacy. She also meant to suggest that the initial postsocialist efflorescence of religion was over, and religion was now retreating from the public sphere. In other words, it was again becoming "domesticated" or "privatized". There could be no question of a "tabula rasa" after the demise of the Soviet Union, or of a simple return to pre-Soviet "roots". Rather, she urged recognition of complex layers of historical determination, including the impact of Soviet modernization. On this point she quoted her colleague Mathijs Pelkmans (2006) and also from Paul Werth's study of the Kräshens (2000), although she was not quite sure she wanted to endorse the implications of the latter's proposition that "religion, especially in the colonial context, can serve as a vehicle for inducting sub-

jects into modernity" (Werth 2000: 514). General theories of colonialism might also have some limited comparative usefulness in this context.

The most substantial passages in Hilgers's notes again take off from Bruce Privratsky's study (2001) of Islam as it is actually lived in Kazakhstan, from which she quoted extensively in her introduction to the book. This time she is slightly critical, or rather, she suggests that the Uzbek case might be different in the sense that orthodox Islam is there more thoroughly integrated into the mainstream "lived religion" than Privratsky found among the Kazakhs, who historically have been more oriented towards pastoralism:

> I argue that exactly what Privratsky calls the familiar way of "Muslimness" is called into question by one part of the population in the course of the objectification of belief and the re-thinking and defining of the concept of Muslimness in contemporary Uzbekistan. Others, however, reassert this concept and try to hold onto it and defend it against attempts to amend it – for instance, by purifying it or by breaking the imagined synthesis of ethno-religious affiliations, as happens through religious conversion or through the adoption of a universalist interpretation of belief according to which the *umma* [Arab., universal community of Islam] is not defined nationally.
>
> I do not agree [with Privratsky] that orthodox Islam is confined to the mosques and so on. As the examples given in this dissertation show, these ideals find their way into believers' minds and their everyday conceptions. People become more conscious about the orthodox form of Islam by learning more about it in study groups, from missionaries, and from booklets. … While some people do not consider it to be the predominant expression of their belief, others orientate themselves towards it and give it a more dominant position in their religious life. Maybe it is accurate for Kazakhstan to say that it is not the predominant expression of religious life, but one has to differentiate and look deeper: although for many Uzbeks, local Islamic practices that are seen as connected to the cultural and the ethnic are considered the spiritual homeland, that does not mean that these Uzbeks completely deny the orthodox side of faith.

In addition to this engagement with literature pertaining to the region, it is equally evident that Hilgers intended in her closing pages to open up a wide-ranging comparative discussion, with reference to recent work on identification (she preferred this term to identity) among Muslim migrants in the West (Barbara Metcalf, Sophie Gilliat-Ray) and the Muslim world in general. She quoted approvingly the argument of Dale Eickelman and Armando Salvatori (2006: 104):

> In short, there is no singular public Islam, but rather a multiplicity of overlapping forms of practice and discourse that represent the varied historical and political trajectories of Muslim communities and their links and influences with society elsewhere. The debates in the public sphere about the common good encompass both words and actions. They are also profoundly shaped by new practices, new forms of publication and communication, and new ways of thinking about religious and political authority.

Hilgers proceeds in these final notes to highlight the sociological value of the concept of spirituality in an increasingly "individualist" and democratic world. Here she follows an argument put forward recently by Giuseppe Giordan (2007). She expands the discussion to include classical studies in the sociology of religion, past and contemporary, among them those of Max Weber, José Casanova, and Danièle Hervieu-Léger. At one stage of her planning, Casanova's concept of the "de-privatization" of religion stood in the title of this conclusion. Whereas he had focused primarily on the return of religion to the public sphere, she was more interested in explaining why, in the case of Uzbekistan, individual religious choices were not purely private but matters of burning concern for people's families and for society. She indicated support for John Bowen's application of Weber's ideas of "rationalization" in his analysis of a new Islamic public sphere in highland Indonesia (Bowen 1998).

In the middle of this bricolage of notes, Hilgers gives the following lapidary summary of her position:

> Religion in Uzbekistan is not reducible to ideas and practices that are either modern or traditional. There is a complex and even contradictory consciousness involved.

Bibliography

Abashin, S. 2006. The Logic of Islamic Practice: A Religious Conflict in Central Asia. *Central Asian Survey* 25 (3): 267–286.

Abdulakhatov, H., et al. 2003. *Bibi Ubaida Tarixi.* Ferghana: Farg'ona Nashriyoti.

Abduqodirov, P. 2004. Qo'qon Latif Madrasalari. *Qo'qon Aslar Silsilacida. Respublika ilmyi nazaryi konferenzyiasi* 14 May 2004: 255–261.

Abduvakhitov, A. 1993. Islamic Revivalism in Uzbekistan. In D. F. Eickelman (ed.), *Russia's Muslim Frontiers: New Directions in Cross-Cultural Analysis,* pp. 79–97. Bloomington: Indiana University Press.

——. 1996. The Jadid Movement and Its Impact on Contemporary Central Asia. In H. Malik (ed.), *Central Asia,* pp. 65–76. London: Macmillan.

Abramson, D. M. 1998. *From Soviet to Mahalla: Community and Transition in Post-Soviet Uzbekistan.* PhD dissertation, University of Michigan. Ann Arbor, Michigan: UMI Dissertation Service.

——. 2001. Socialism's Bastard Children. *PoLAR* 23 (1): 49–64.

Abramson, D. M., and E. E. Karimov. 2007. Sacred Sites, Profane Ideologies: Religious Pilgrimage and the Uzbek State. In J. Sahadeo, and R. Zanca (eds.), *Everyday Life in Central Asia, Past and Present,* pp. 319–338. Bloomington: Indiana University Press.

Abu-Lughod, L. 1993. Islam and the Gendered Discourses of Death. *International Journal of Middle East Studies* 25: 187–205.

Adams, L. 1998. What Is Culture? Schemas and Spectacles in Uzbekistan. *Anthropology of East Europe Review* 16 (2): 65–71.

Akiner, S. 1996. Islam, the State and Ethnicity in Central Asia in Historical Perspective. *Religion, State and Society* 24 (2–3): 91–132.

——. 2003. The Politicisation of Islam in Postsoviet Central Asia. *Religion, State and Society* 31 (2): 97–122.

Albrow, M. 1997. The Impact of Globalization on Sociological Concepts: Community, Culture and Milieu. In J. Eade (ed.), *Living the Global City: Globalization as a Local Process,* pp. 20–36. London: Routledge.

Alimova, D. 2004. The Turkestan Jadids' Conception of Muslim Culture. In G. Rasuly-Paleczek, and J. Katschnig (eds.), *Central Asia on Display: Proceedings of the VII Conference of the European Society for Central Asian Studies,* pp. 143–147. Vienna: LIT Verlag.

Allworth, E. (ed.). 1999. *Central Asia: One Hundred Thirty Years of Russian Dominance. A Historical Overview.* Durham, North Carolina: Duke University Press.

Anderson, J. 2002. *Religion, State and Politics in the Soviet Union and Successor States.* Cambridge: Cambridge University Press.

Annaklychev, S. 1984. The Wedding Ceremonies of the Turkmen Workers. In T. Dragadze (ed.), *Kinship and Marriage in the Soviet Union: Field Studies,* pp. 15–40. London: Routledge and Kegan Paul.

Appadurai, A. 1998. *Modernity at Large: Cultural Dimensions of Globalization.* Minneapolis: University of Minnesota Press.

Archbishop V. 2000. Christianity and Islam in Central Asia. In R. Sagdeev, and S. Eisenhower (eds.), *Islam and Central Asia: An Enduring Legacy or an Evolving Threat?*, pp. 95–115. Washington, DC: Center for Political and Strategic Studies.

Arslanzoda, P. 2004. Qu'qonda Ilk Madrasalarining Barpo Etilish Sanasi Hususida. *Qo'qon Aslar Silsilacida. Respublika ilmiy nazaryi konferenzyiasi* 14 May 2004: 54–58.

Asad, T. 1996a. The Idea of an Anthropology of Islam. In J. A. Hall, and I. C. Jarvie (eds.), *The Social Philosophy of Ernest Gellner,* pp. 381–403. Amsterdam: Rodopi.

——. 1996b. Modern Power and the Reconfiguration of Religious Traditions. Interview by Saba Mahmood. *Stanford Humanities Review* 5 (1), www.stanford.edu/group/SHR/5–1/text/asad.html.

——. 2006. Responses. In D. Scott, and C. Hirschkind (eds.), *Powers of the Secular Modern: Talal Asad and His Interlocutors*, pp. 206–241. Stanford, California: Stanford University Press.

Ashirov, A. A. 2000. *Farg'ona Vodiysi Aholisi Turmush Tarzida Qadimyi Diniy E'tiqodlar Izi: Tarix Fanlari Nomzodi Ilmiy Darajasini* [Relics of Ancient Religious Beliefs among Residents of the Ferghana Valley]. PhD dissertation. Tashkent.

Babadjanov, B., and M. Kamilov. 2001. Muhammadjan Hindustani and the Beginning of the "Great Schism" among Muslims of Uzbekistan. In S. A. Dudoignon, and H. Komatsu (eds.), *Islam in Politics in Russia and Central Asia: Early Eighteenth to Late Twentieth Centuries,* pp. 195–219. New York: Kegan Paul.

Babadjanov, B. 1999. The Fergana Valley: Source or Victim of Islamic Fundamentalism? *Central Asia and the Caucausus: Journal of Social and Political Studies* 5 (4), www.ca-c.org/dataeng/10.babadzh.shtml.

——. 2002. Religious Opposition Groups in Uzbekistan: Religious Extremism in Central Asia, Problems and Perspectives. In *Materials of the Conference of Dushanbe,* pp. 43–63. [Publisher unknown.]

Bacon, E. E. 1966. *Central Asians under Russian Rule: A Study in Cultural Change.* Ithaca, New York: Cornell University Press.

Balcı, B. 2003. Fethullah Gülen's Missionary Schools in Central Asia and Their Role in the Spreading of Turkism and Islam. *Religion, State and Society* 31 (2): 151–177.

Barker, E. 1997. But Who's Going to Win? National and Minority Religions in Post-Communist Societies. In I. Borowik, and G. Babiński (eds.), *New Religious Phenomena in Central and Eastern Europe*, pp. 25–62. Kraków: NOMOS.

Becker, F. 2001. *Ankommen in Deutschland: Einwanderungspolitik als biographische Erfahrung im Migrationsprozeß russischer Juden.* Berlin: Reimer.

Bennigsen, A., and M. Broxup. 1982. *The Islamic Threat to the Soviet State.* London: Croom Helm.

Bennigsen, A., and C. Lemercier-Quelquejay. 1967. *Islam in the Soviet Union.* London: Pall Mall Press.

Benningsen, A., and S. E. Wimbush. 1985a. *Muslims of the Soviet Empire: A Guide.* London: C. Hurst.

——. 1985b. *Mystics and Commissars: Sufism in the Soviet Union.* London: C. Hurst.

Berger, P. L., and T. Luckman. 1967. Aspects sociologiques du pluralisme. *Archives de Sociologie des Religions* 23: 117–127.

Bergne, P. 2003. The Kokand Autonomy, 1917–18: Political Background, Aims and Reasons for Failure. In T. Everett-Heath (ed.), *Central Asia: Aspects of Transition,* pp. 30–44. New York: Routledge.

Bhardwaj, S. M., and G. Rinschede (eds.). 1988. *Pilgrimage in World Religions.* Berlin: Dietrich Reimer Verlag.

Bobrovnikov, V. 2006. "Traditionalist" versus "Islamist" Identities in a Dagstani Collective Farm. *Central Asian Survey* 25 (3): 287–302.

Borozna, N. G. 1984. Some Features of the Traditional Wedding Ceremony of the Uzbek-Durmen of the Southern Raions of Tadzhikistan and Uzbekistan. In T. Dragadze (ed.), *Kinship and Marriage in the Soviet Union: Field Studies,* pp. 60–73. London: Routledge and Kegan Paul.

Bourdeaux, M., and A. Popescu. 2006. The Orthodox Church and Communism. In M. Angold (ed.), *The Cambridge History of Christianity,* vol. 5, pp. 558–579. Cambridge: Cambridge University Press.

Bourdieu, P. 2000. *Das religiöse Feld: Texte zur Ökonomie des Heilsgeschehens.* Konstanz: UVK Universitäts Verlag Koblenz.

Bourdieu, P., and L. J. D. Wacquant. 1994. *An Invitation to Reflexive Sociology.* Chicago: University of Chicago Press.

Bowen, J. R. 1998. *Religions in Practice: An Approach to the Anthropology of Religion.* Boston: Allyn and Bacon.

Bringa, T. 1995. *Being Muslim the Bosnian Way: Identity and Community in a Central Bosnian Village.* Princeton, New Jersey: Princeton University Press.

Bruce, S. 2002. *Religion in the Modern World: From Cathedrals to Cults.* Oxford: Oxford University Press.

Carrère d'Encausse, H. 1981. *Réforme et révolution chez les Musulmans de l'Empire Russe.* Paris: Presse de la Fondation des Sciences Politiques.

Casanova, J. 1994. *Public Religion in the Modern World.* Chicago: University of Chicago Press.

Castells, M. 1996. *The Information Age: Economy, Society and Culture.* Cambridge: Blackwell.

Chambers, P. 2004. Religion, Identity and Change in Contemporary Wales. In S. Coleman, and P. Collins (eds.), *Religion, Identity and Change,* pp. 69–83. Aldershot, UK: Ashgate.

Clement, V. 2007. Alphabet Changes in Turkmenistan: State, Society, and the Everyday. In J. Sahadeo, and R. Zanca (eds.), *Everyday Life in Central Asia: Past and Present.* Bloomington: Indiana University Press.

Constantine, E. A. 2007. Practical Consequences of Soviet Policy and Ideology for Gender in Central Asia and Contemporary Reversal. In J. Sahadeo, and R. Zanca (eds.), *Everyday Life in Central Asia: Past and Present,* pp. 115–126. Bloomington: Indiana University Press.

Corcoran-Nantes, Y. 2005. *Lost Voices: Central Asian Women Confronting Transition.* London: Zed Books.

Corley, F., and I. Rotar. 2006. Uzbekistan: Quantity of Mercy Constrained. Forum 18 News, 10 October, www.forum18.org/Archive.php?article_id=852.

Critchlow, J. 1991. *Nationalism in Uzbekistan: A Soviet Republic's Road to Sovereignty.* Boulder, Colorado: Westview Press.

Davie, G. 1994. *Religion in Britain since 1945: Believing without Belonging.* Malden, UK: Blackwell.

——. 1999. Europe: The Exception that Proves the Rule. In P. Berger (ed.), *The Desecularization of the World: Resurgent Religion and World Politics*, pp. 65–84. Grand Rapids, Michigan: Eerdmans.

de Certeau, M. 1984. *The Practice of Everyday Life*. Berkeley: University of California Press.

DeWeese, D. 2002. Islam and the Legacy of Sovietology: A Review Essay on Yaacov Ro'i's *Islam in the Soviet Union*. *Journal of Islamic Studies* 13 (3): 298–330.

Djumaev, A. 2002. Nation-Building, Culture, and Problems of Ethnocultural Identity in Central Asia: The Case of Uzbekistan. In W. Kymlicka, and M. Opalski (eds.), *Can Liberal Pluralism Be Exported? Western Political Theory and Ethnic Relations in Eastern Europe*, pp. 320–343. Oxford: Oxford University Press.

Doumato, E. A. 2000. *Getting God's Ear: Women, Islam, and Healing in Saudi Arabia and the Gulf.* New York: Columbia University Press.

Dubisch, J. 1995. *In a Different Place: Pilgrimage, Gender, and Politics at a Greek Island Shrine.* Princeton, New Jersey: Princeton University Press.

Dubisch, J., and R. Michalowski. 2001. *Run for the Wall: Remembering Vietnam on a Motorcycle Pilgrimage.* New Brunswick, New Jersey: Rutgers University Press.

Eade, J., and M. J. Sallnow. 2000. *Contesting the Sacred: The Anthropology of Pilgrimage.* Urbana: University of Illinois Press.

Eickelman, D. F. 1992. *Knowledge and Power in Morocco: The Education of a Twentieth-Century Notable.* Princeton, New Jersey: Princeton University Press.

Eickelman, D. F., and J. Piscatori. 1996. *Muslim Politics.* Princeton, New Jersey: Princeton University Press.

Eickelman, D. F., and A. Salvatore. 2006. Public Islam and the Common Good. *Etnográfica* 10 (1): 97–105.

El-Zein, A.-H. 1977. Beyond Ideology and Theology: The Search for the Anthropology of Islam. *Annual Review of Anthropology* 6: 227–254.

Erşahin, S. 2005. The Official Interpretation of Islam under the Soviet Regime. *Journal of Religious Culture* 77: 1–19.

Fartacek, G. 2003. *Pilgerstätten in der syrischen Peripherie: Eine ethnologische Studie zur kognitiven Konstruktion sakraler Plätze und deren Praxisrelevanz.* Vienna: Verlag der Österreichischen Akademie der Wissenschaften.

Fathi, H. 1997. The *Otin*, the Unknown Women Muslim Clerics of Central Asian Islam. *Central Asian Survey* 16 (1): 27–43.

------. 2004. *Femmes d'autorité dans l'Asie centrale contemporaine: Quête des ancêtres et recompositions identitaires dans l'Islam postsoviétique.* Paris: Maisonneuve and Larose/IFEAC.

——. 2006. Gender, Islam, and Social Change in Uzbekistan. *Central Asian Survey* 25 (3): 303–317.

——. 2007. *Femmes d'Asie centrale: Genre et mutations dans les sociétés musulmanes soviétisées*. Montreuil: Éd. Aux Lieux d'Être.

Featherstone, M., S. Lash, and R. Robertson (eds.). 1995. *Global Modernities*. Thousand Oaks, California: Sage.

Finke, P. 2006. *Variations on Uzbek Identity: Concepts, Constraints and Local Configurations*. PhD dissertation, University of Leipzig.

Flanagan, K. 2007. Introduction. In K. Flanagan, and P. C. Jupp (eds.), *A Sociology of Spirituality*, pp. 1–21. Aldershot, UK: Ashgate.

Frank, A. J. 2001. *Muslim Religious Institutions in Imperial Russia: The Islamic World of Novouzensk District and the Kazakh Inner Horde, 1780–1910*. Leiden: E. J. Brill.

Fumagalli, M. 2003. Elite Perspectives on Identity Formation in Uzbekistan: Exploring the Dimensions of O'zbekchilik. A Work in Progress. *International Journal of Central Asian Studies* 8 (1): 154–164.

Gellner, E. 1981. *Muslim Society*. Cambridge: Cambridge University Press.

——. 1992. *Postmodernism, Reason and Religion*. London: Routledge.

Giordan, G. 2007. Spirituality: From a Religious Concept to a Sociological Theory. In K. Flanagan, and P. C. Jupp (eds.), *A Sociology of Spirituality*, pp. 161–180. Aldershot, UK: Ashgate.

Gluckman, M. 1963. *Order and Rebellion in Tribal Africa: Collected Essays with an Autobiographical Introduction*. London: Cohen and West.

Hann, C. 1997. The Nation-State, Religion and Uncivil Society: Two Perspectives from the Periphery. *Daedalus* 126 (2): 27–45.

Harrison, P. 1924. *The Arab at Home*. New York: Crowell.

Hedin, S. A. 1898. *Through Asia,* vol. 1. London.

Heelas, P., S. Lash, and P. Morris (eds.). 1996. *Detraditionalization: Critical Reflections on Authority and Identity*. Cambridge: Cambridge University Press.

Hefner, R. W. 1993. Of Faith and Commitment: Christian Conversion in Muslim Java. In R. W. Hefner (ed.), *Conversion to Christianity: Historical and Anthropological Perspectives on a Great Transformation,* pp. 99–125. Berkeley: University of California Press.

Hilgers, I. 2006. The Regulation and Control of Religious Pluralism in Uzbekistan. In C. Hann and the Civil Religion Group, *The Postsocialist Religious Question: Faith and Power in Central Asia and East-Central Europe,* pp. 75–98. Berlin: LIT Verlag.

——. 2007. Defining the "Uzbek Christian": Conversion to Christianity in the Ferghana Valley. In P. Sartori, and T. Trevisani (eds.), *Patterns of Transformation in and around Uzbekistan,* pp. 121–138. Reggio Emilia: Ed. Diabasis.

Hobsbawm, E., and T. Ranger (eds.). 1983. *The Invention of Tradition.* Cambridge: Cambridge University Press.

Horvatich, P. 1994. Ways of Knowing Islam. *American Ethnologist* 21: 811–826.

Human Rights Watch. 2003. *From House to House: Abuses of Mahalla Committees.* New York: Human Rights Watch.

——. 2004. *Creating Enemies of the State: Religious Persecution in Uzbekistan.* New York: Human Rights Watch.

Husniddinov, Z. 2002. Religion and Religious Extremism: Combat of Ideas and Interests. *Seventafziz "Democratization and Human Rights"* 15–16 (3–4): 96–99.

Ilkhamov, A. 2001. Uzbek Islamism: Imported Ideology or Grassroots Movement? *Middle East Report* 221: 40–46.

——. 2002. *Ethnic Atlas of Uzbekistan.* Tashkent: Open Society Institute.

——. 2006a. Archeology of Uzbek Identity. *Anthropology and Archeology of Eurasia* 44 (4): 75–79.

——. 2006b. The Phenomenology of "Akromiya": Separating Facts from Fiction. *China and Eurasia Forum Quarterly* (Central Asia–Caucasus Institute and Silk Road Studies Program, Johns Hopkins University, Washington, DC) 4 (2): 39–48.

Kamp, M. R. 1998. *Unveiling Uzbek Women: Liberation, Representation, and Discourse, 1906–1929.* PhD dissertation, University of Chicago.

——. 2005. Gender Ideals and Income Realities: Discourses about Labor and Gender in Uzbekistan. *Nationalities Papers* 33: 403–422.

Kandiyoti, D. 1998. Rural Livelihoods and Social Networks in Uzbekistan: Perspectives from Andijan. *Central Asian Survey* 17 (4): 561–578.

Kandiyoti, D., and N. Azimova 2004. The Communal and the Sacred: Women's Worlds of Ritual in Uzbekistan. *Journal of the Royal Anthropological Institute* 10: 327–349.

Karimov, I. 1997. *Uzbekistan on the Threshold of the 21st Century.* Richmond, UK: Curzon Press.

——. 1999. *Alloh qalbimizda, yuragimizda.* Tashkent: Uzbekiston.

Kaschuba, W. 2001. Geschichtspolitik und Identitätspolitik. In B. Binder, W. Kaschuba, and P. Niedermüller (eds.), *Inszenierung des Nationalen: Geschichte, Kultur und die Politik der Identitäten am Ende des 20. Jahrhunderts,* pp. 19-42. Cologne: Böhlau.

Kazmina, O., and O. Filippova. 2005. Re-Imagination of Religion in Post-Soviet Society: Challenges and Responses (Russian and Ukrainian

Case Studies). *Journal of the American Academy of Religion* 73 (4): 1049–1076.

Kehl-Bodrogi, K. 2005. Shrines in Khorezm: Coincidence of "Global" and "Local" Islam. Presentation made at the Max Planck Institute for Social Anthropology, Halle/Saale, February.

——. 2006a. The Reassertion of Religious Healing in Post-Soviet Uzbekistan. *Asian Anthropology* 5: 111–129.

——. 2006b. Who Owns the Shrine? Competing Meanings and Authorities at a Pilgrimage Site in Khorezm. *Central Asian Survey* 25 (3): 235–250.

——. 2008: *"Religion Is Not So Strong Here": Muslim Religious Life in Khorezm after Socialism.* Münster: LIT Verlag.

Keller, S. 2001a. Conversion to the New Faith: Marxism-Leninism and the Muslims in the Soviet Empire. In R. P. Geraci, and M. Khodarkovsky (eds.), *Of Religion and Empire: Missions, Conversions, and Tolerance in Tsarist Russia,* pp. 311–334. Ithaca, New York: Cornell University Press.

——. 2001b. *To Moscow, Not Mecca: The Soviet Campaign against Islam in Central Asia, 1917–1941.* Westport, Connecticut: Praeger.

——. 2007. Going to School in Uzbekistan. In J. Sahadeo, and R. Zanca (eds.), *Everyday Life in Central Asia, Past and Present,* pp. 248–265. Bloomington: Indiana University Press.

Khalid, A. 1998. *The Politics of Muslim Cultural Reform: Jadidism in Central Asia.* Berkeley: University of California Press.

——. 2003. A Secular Islam: Nation, State and Religion in Uzbekistan. *International Journal for Eastern Studies* 35 (4): 573–598.

Kim, G. N. 2005. Koreans in Kazakhstan, Uzbekistan, and Russia. In M. Ember, C. R. Ember, and I. Skogga (eds.), *Encyclopedia of Diasporas: Immigrant and Refugee Cultures around the World,* vol. 2, pp. 983–992. New York: Springer.

Klein-Hessling, R. 1999. Wo endet die Trauer? Soziale Praktiken im Diskurs über islamische Identität im Nordsudan. In S. Nökel und K. Werner (eds.), *Der neue Islam der Frauen: Weibliche Lebenspraktiken in der globalisierten Moderne,* pp. 229–248. Bielefeld: Transcript-Verlag.

Kleinmichel, S. 2001. *Halpa in Chorezm (Hwarezm) und Atin Ayi in Ferghana: Zur Geschichte des Lesens in Uzbekistan im 20. Jahrhundert.* 2 vols. Berlin: Das Arabische Buch.

Koroteyeva, V., and E. Makarova. 1998. Money and Social Connections in the Soviet and Post-Soviet Uzbek City. *Central Asian Survey* 17 (4): 579–596.

Krämer, A. 2002. *Geistliche Autorität und islamische Gesellschaft im Wandel: Studien über Frauenälteste (otin und xalfa) im unabhängigen Usbekistan.* Berlin: Klaus Schwarz Verlag.

Krech, V., and M. Schlegel. 1998. Auf der Suche nach dem "wahren Selbst": Über den Zusammenhang von Konversion und der Konstitution religiöser Identität. In H. Knoblauch et al. (eds.), *Religiöse Konversion: Systematische und fallorientierte Studien in soziologischer Perspektive,* pp. 169–191. Konstanz: Universitätsverlag.

Kriss, R., and H. Kriss-Heinrich. 1960. *Volksglaube im Bereich des Islam,* vol. 1. Wiesbaden: Otto Harrassowitz.

Kuehnast, K. 1997. *Let the Stone Lie Where It Has Fallen: Dilemmas of Gender and Generation in Post-Soviet Kyrgyzstan.* PhD dissertation, University of Minnesota.

Lankauskas, G. 2002. On "Modern" Christians, Consumption, and the Value of National Identity in Post-Soviet Lithuania. *Ethnos* 67 (3): 320–344.

Lash, S., and J. Urry. 1994. *Economies of Sign and Space.* London: Sage.

Levin, T. 1993. The Reterritorialization of Culture in the New Central Asian States: A Report from Uzbekistan. *Yearbook of Traditional Music* 25: 51–59.

Louw, M. E. 2004. *"The Heart with God, the Hand at Work": Being Muslim in Post-Soviet Bukhara.* PhD dissertation, University of Aarhus.

——. 2006. Pursuing "Muslimness": Shrines as Sites for Moralities in the Making in Post-Soviet Bukhara. *Central Asian Survey* 25 (3): 319–339.

——. 2007. *Everyday Islam in Post-Soviet Central Asia.* London: Routledge.

Low, S. M., and D. Lawrence-Zúñiga. 2003. *The Anthropology of Space and Place: Locating Culture.* Malden, Massachusetts: Blackwell.

Lubin, N. 1999. *Calming the Ferghana Valley: Development and Dialogue in the Heart of Central Asia. Report of the Ferghana Valley Working Group of the Centre for Preventive Action.* New York: Century Foundation Press.

March, A. F. 2002. The Use and Abuse of History: "National Ideology" as Transcendental Object in Islam Karimov's "Ideology of National Independence". *Central Asian Survey* 21 (4): 371–384.

Martin, D. 2005. *On Secularization: Towards a Revised General Theory.* New York: Ashgate.

Massell, G. J. 1974. *The Surrogate Proletariat: Moslem Women and Revolutionary Strategies in Soviet Central Asia, 1919–1929.* Princeton, New Jersey: Princeton University Press.

McBrien, J. 2007. Brazilian TV and Muslimness in Kyrgyzstan. *ISIM Newsletter* (International Institute for the Study of Islam in the Modern World) 19: 16–17.

McChesney, R. D. 1996. *Central Asia: Foundations of Change.* Princeton, New Jersey: Darwin Press.

McDonnell, M. B. 1990. Patterns of Muslim Pilgrimage from Malaysia, 1885–1985. In D. Eickelman, and J. Piscatori (eds.), *Muslim Travelers: Pilgrimages, Migration, and the Religious Imagination,* pp. 111–130. Berkeley: University of California Press.

McGlinchey, E. M. 2006. Islamic Leaders in Uzbekistan. *Asia Policy* 1: 123–144.

——. 2007. Divided Faith: Trapped between State and Islam in Uzbekistan. In J. Sabadeo, and R. Zanca (eds.), *Everyday Life in Central Asia, Past and Present,* pp. 305–318. Bloomington: Indiana University Press.

Melvin, N. J. 2000. *Uzbekistan: Transition to Authoritarianism on the Silk Road.* Amsterdam: Harwood Academic.

Meixler, L. 2000. Uzbeks Encouraging Mystics in Fight against Fundamentalism. Associated Press, 28 August 2000, http://lists.topica.com/lists/eurasia/read/message.html?sort=a&mid=1302874526.

Meneley, A. 1996. *Tournaments of Value: Sociability and Hierarchy in a Yemeni Town.* Toronto: University of Toronto Press.

——. 2007. Fashions and Fundamentalism in Fin-de-Siècle Yemen: Chador Barbie and Islamic Socks. *Cultural Anthropology* 22 (2): 214–243.

Merdjanova, I. 2002. *Religion, Nationalism, and Civil Society in Eastern Europe: The Postcommunist Palimpsest.* New York: Edwin Mellen.

Metcalf, B. D. 1996. Introduction: Sacred Words, Sanctioned Practice, New Communities. In B. D. Metcalf (ed.), *Making Muslim Space in North America and Europe,* pp. 1–27. Berkeley: University of California Press.

Mirzo, M. 2004. Bibi Ubaido (Buvimozor). Tarix Haqida qichasa ziyoratchilarga malumot. Buvaida.

Muminov, A. 1996. Veneration of Holy Sites of the Mid-Sirdar'ya Valley: Continuity and Transformation. In M. Kemper, and A. von Kügelgen (eds.), *Muslim Culture in Russia and Central Asia from the 18th to the Early 20th Centuries,* pp. 355–367. Berlin: Klaus Schwarz Verlag.

——. 2005. Traditional and Modern Religious Theological Schools in Central Asia. *Central Asia and the Caucausus: Journal of Social and Political Studies,* www.ca-c.org/dataeng/09.muminov.shtml.

——. 2007. Fundamentalist Challenges to Local Islamic Traditions in Soviet and Post-Soviet Central Asia. In T. Uyama (ed.), *Empire, Islam, and Politics in Central Eurasia,* pp. 249–262. Sapporo, Japan: Slavic Research Center, Hokkaido University.

Munawwarow, S. 1999. Der Islam in Usbekistan: Vergangenheit, Gegenwart, Zukunft. In *Wostok Spezial: Usbekistan, Land zwischen Orient und Okzident,* pp. 68–72. Wostok-Verlag.

Nahaylo, B., and V. Swoboda. 1990. *Soviet Disunion: A History of the Nationalities Problem in the USSR.* London: Hamilton.

Naumkin, V. V. 2005. *Radical Islam in Central Asia: Between Pen and Rifle.* Lanham, Maryland: Rowman and Littlefield.

Northrop, D. T. 2004. *Veiled Empire: Gender and Power in Stalinist Central Asia.* Ithaca, New York: Cornell University Press.

Oh, Chong Jin. 2006. Diaspora Nationalism: The Case of the Ethnic Korean Minority in Kazakhstan and Its Lessons from the Crimean Tatars in Turkey. *Nationalities Papers* 34 (2): 111–129.

Olcott, M. B. 1995. Islam and Fundamentalism in Central Asia. In Y. Ro'i (ed.), *Muslim Eurasia: Conflicting Legacies*, pp. 21–40. London: Cass.

——. 2007. *Roots of Radical Islam in Central Asia.* Carnegie Papers 77. Washington, DC: Carnegie Endowment for International Peace.

Pantusov, N. 2002. Le mausolée de Mawlânâ Yûsuf Sakakî (ou Shakakî). In T. Zarcone, and E. Isin (eds.), *Saints and Heroes on the Silk Road,* pp. 183–198. Paris: Jean Maisonneuve Successeur.

Papas, A. 2005. *Soufisme et politique entre Chine, Tibet et Turkestan: Études sur les Khwaja Naqshbandis du Turkestan oriental.* Paris: Librairie d'Amérique et d'Orient Jean Maisonneuve.

PAPU (Press Agency of the President of Uzbekistan) 2004. http://2004.press-service.uz.

Peel, J. D. Y. 2000. *Religious Encounter and the Making of the Yoruba.* Bloomington: Indiana University Press.

Pelkmans, M. 2006. Asymmetries on the "Religious Market" in Kyrgyzstan. In C. Hann and the Civil Religion Group, *The Postsocialist Religious Question: Faith and Power in Central Asia and East-Central Europe,* pp. 29–46. Berlin: LIT Verlag.

Perrin-Wagner, H. 1999. Cultural, Social, and Political Identities in Central Asia. *Harvard Asia Quarterly* 3 (4), http://www.asiaquarterly.com/content/view/50/40/.

Peyrouse, S. 2003. *Des chrétiens entre atheism et islam: Regards sur la question religieuse en Asie centrale soviétique et post-soviétique.* Paris: Maissoneuve et Larose.

——. 2004a. Religious Diversity in Post-Soviet Central Asia. *ISIM Newsletter* (International Institute for the Study of Islam in the Modern World) 14: 48–49.

——. 2004b. Christianity and Nationality in Soviet and Post-Soviet Central Asia: Mutual Intrusions and Instrumentalizations. *Nationalities Papers* 32 (3): 651–673.

Pfluger-Schindlbeck, I. 2005. *Verwandtschaft, Religion und Geschlecht in Aserbaidschan.* Wiesbaden: Reichert.

Polat, A. 2000. The Islamic Revival in Uzbekistan: A Threat to Stability? In R. Sagdeev, and S. Eisenhower (eds.), *Islam and Central Asia: An Enduring Legacy or an Evolving Threat?*, pp. 39–57. Washington, DC: Center for Political and Strategic Studies.

Poliakov, S. P. 1992. *Everyday Islam: Religion and Tradition in Rural Central Asia.* Armonk, New York: M. E. Sharpe.

Pollack, D. 2001. Modifications in the Religious Field of Central and Eastern Europe. *European Societies* 3: 135–165.

Polonskaya, L., and A. Malashenko. 1994. *Islam in Central Asia.* Reading, UK: Ithaca Press.

Poujol, C. 1993. Approaches to the History of Bukharan Jews' Settlement in the Ferghana Valley, 1867–1917. *Central Asian Survey* 12 (4): 549–556.

Powell, D. E. 1977. Religion and Secularization in the Soviet Union: The Role of Antireligious Cartoons. In D. J. Dunn (ed.), *Religion and Modernization in the Soviet Union*, pp. 136–201. Boulder, Colorado: Westview Press.

Privratsky, B. 2001. *Muslim Turkistan: Kazak Religion and Collective Memory.* Richmond, UK: Curzon Press.

Randeria, S. 2004. Verwobene Moderne: Zivilgesellschaft, Kastenbindung und nicht-staatliches Familienrecht im (post) kolonialen Indien. In S. Randeria, M. Fuchs, and A. Linkenbach (eds.), *Konfigurationen der Moderne: Diskurse zu Indien,* pp. 155–178. Baden Baden: NOMOS.

Rasanayagam, J. 2006a. "I am Not a Wahhabi": State Power and Muslim Orthodoxy in Uzbekistan. In C. Hann and the Civil Religion Group, *The Postsocialist Religious Question: Faith and Power in Central Asia and East-Central Europe,* pp. 98–124. Berlin: LIT Verlag.

——. 2006b. Healing with Spirits and the Formation of Muslim Selfhood in Post-Soviet Uzbekistan. *Journal of the Royal Anthropological Institute* 12 (2): 377–393.

——. 2006c. Introduction. *Central Asian Survey* (special issue) 25 (3): 219–233.

Rashid, A. 1995. *The Resurgence of Central Asia: Islam or Nationalism?* Karachi: Oxford University Press.

——. 2002. *Heiliger Krieg am Hindukusch: Der Kampf um Macht und Glauben in Zentralasien.* Munich: Droemer-Knauer.

——. 2003. *Jihad: The Rise of Militant Islam in Central Asia.* New Haven, Connecticut: Yale University Press.

Robertson, R. 1992. After Nostalgia? Wilful Nostalgia and the Phases of Globalization. In B. S. Turner (ed.), *Theories of Modernity and Postmodernity,* pp. 45–61. London: Sage.

Ro'i, Y. 2000. *Islam in the Soviet Union: From the Second World War to Gorbachev.* New York: Columbia University Press.

Rorlich, A.-A. 1991. Islam and Atheism: Dynamic Tension in Soviet Central Asia. In W. Fierman (ed.), *Soviet Central Asia: The Failed Transformation,* pp. 186–218. Boulder, Colorado: Westview Press.

Rotar, I. 2006. Uzbekistan: Religious Freedom Survey, May 2006. Forum 18 News Service, www.forum18.org/Archive.php?article_id=777.

Roy, O. 1996. *The Failure of Political Islam.* Cambridge, Massachusetts: Harvard University Press.

——. 2000. *The New Central Asia: The Creation of Nations.* London: I. B. Tauris.

——. 2006. *Der islamische Weg nach Westen: Globalisierung, Entwurzelung und Radikalisierung.* München: Pantheon Verlag.

Rumer, B. 1989. *Soviet Central Asia: A Tragic Experiment.* Boston: Unwin Hyman.

Rzehak, L. 2002. Bolschewismus als Glaubensform: Über Absichten und Wirkungen des sowjetischen Atheismus in Mittelasien. In A. Strasser, S. Haas, G. Mangott, and V. Heuberger (eds.), *Zentralasien und Islam/Central Asia and Islam,* pp. 30–58. Hamburg: Deutsches Orient-Institut.

Sagdeev, R., and S. Eisenhower (eds.). 2000. *Islam and Central Asia: An Enduring Legacy or an Evolving Threat?* Washington, DC: Center for Political and Strategic Studies.

Saktanber, A. 2002. *Living Islam: Women, Religion and the Politicization of Culture in Turkey.* London: I. B. Tauris.

Sancak, M., and P. Finke. 2007. Konstitutsiya buzildi! Gender Relations in Kazakhstan and Uzbekistan. In J. Sahadeo, and R. Zanca (eds.), *Everyday Life in Central Asia, Past and Present,* pp. 160–177. Bloomington: Indiana University Press.

Sanikidze, G. 2007. Islamic Resurgence in the Modern Caucasian Region: "Global" and "Local" Islam in the Pankisi Gorge. In T. Uyama (ed.),

Empire, Islam and Politics in Central Eurasia, pp. 263–280. Sapporo, Japan: Slavic Research Center, Hokkaido University.

Saroyan, M. 1997a. The Islamic Clergy and Community in the Soviet Union. In M. Saroyan, *Minorities, Mullahs, and Modernity: Reshaping Community in the Former Soviet Union,* E. W. Walker (ed.), pp. 43–57. Research Series no. 95. Berkeley: University of California, International and Area Studies.

——. 1997b. The Reinterpretation and Adaptation of Soviet Islam. In M. Saroyan, *Minorities, Mullahs, and Modernity: Reshaping Community in the Former Soviet Union,* E. W. Walker (ed.), pp. 58–82. Research Series no. 95. Berkeley: University of California, International and Area Studies.

——. 1997c. Ambivalence, Authority, and the Problem of Popular Islam. In M. Saroyan, *Minorities, Mullahs, and Modernity: Reshaping Community in the Former Soviet Union,* E. W. Walker (ed.), pp. 104–124. Research Series no. 95. Berkeley: University of California, International and Area Studies.

Sartori, P. 2006. When a Mufti Turned Islamism into Political Pragmatism: Sadreddin-Khan and The Struggle for an Independent Turkestan. *Cahiers d'Asie Centrale* 15–16: 118–139. Paris: Maisonneuve and Larose.

——. 2007. The Tashkent "Ulama" and the Soviet State (1920–1938): A Preliminary Research Note on NKVD documents. In P. Sartori, and T. Trevisani (eds.), *Patterns of Transformation in and around Uzbekistan,* pp. 162–184. Reggio Emilia, Italy: Diabasis.

Schiffauer, W. 1991. *Die Migranten aus Subay – Türken in Deutschland: Eine Ethnografie.* Stuttgart: Klett-Cotta.

——. 2000. *Die Gottesmänner: Türkische Islamisten in Deutschland.* Frankfurt am Main: Suhrkamp.

Schimmel, A. 1975. *Mystical Dimensions of Islam.* Chapel Hill: University of North Carolina Press.

——. 1994. *Deciphering the Signs of God: A Phenomenological Approach to Islam.* Albany: State University of New York Press.

Schoeberlein-Engel, J. 1994. *Identity in Central Asia: Construction and Contention in the Conceptions of "Özbek", "Tâjik", "Muslim", "Samarqandi" and other Groups.* PhD dissertation, Harvard University.

Schuyler, E. 1966. *Turkistan: Notes of a Journey in Russian Turkistan, Kokand, Bukhara, and Kuldja.* New York: Praeger.

Sengupta, A. 2003. *The Formation of the Uzbek Nation-State: A Study in Transition.* Lanham, Maryland: Lexington Books.

Shahrani, N. M. 1995. Islam and the Political Culture of "Scientific Atheism" in Post-Soviet Central Asia: Future Predicaments. In M. Bourdeaux (ed.), *The Politics of Religion in Russia and the New States of Eurasia,* pp. 273–292. Armonk, New York: M. E. Sharpe.

——. 2006. Reclaiming Islam in Uzbekistan: Soviet Legacies and Post-Soviet Realities. *Journal of Turkic Civilization Studies* 2: 77–103.

Shterin, M. 2003. Religion after Atheism. In J. A. Beckford, and J. T. Richardson (eds.), *Challenging Religion: Essays in Honour of Eileen Barker,* pp. 56–68. London: Routledge.

Simon, G. 1986. *Nationalismus und Nationalitätenpolitik in der Sowjetunion: Von der totalitären Diktatur zur nachstalinschen Gesellschaft.* Baden-Baden: NOMOS.

Smith, A. D. 1996. Chosen People. In J. Hutchinson, and A. D. Smith (eds.), *Ethnicity,* pp. 189–196. Oxford: Oxford University Press.

——. 2000. *Myths and Memories of the Nation.* Oxford: Oxford University Press.

Snezarev, G. P. 1963. Traditsia muzhskikh soyuzov v ee pozdneishem variante u narodov Srednei Azii. *Materialy Khoremzskoi expeditsii* 7 (2): 155–205.

——. 1969. *Relikty domusul'manskich verovanij i obrjadov u uzbekov Chorezma.* Moscow: Izd. Nauk.

——. 1974. On Some Causes of the Persistence of Religio-customary Survivals among the Khorezm Uzbeks. In S. P. Dunn, and E. Dunn (eds.), *Introduction to Soviet Ethnography,* pp. 215–238. Berkeley, California: Highgate Road Social Science Research Station.

——. 2003. *Remnants of Pre-Islamic Beliefs and Rituals among the Khorezm Uzbeks.* Berlin: Reinhold Schletzer Verlag.

Snow, D. A., and R. Machalek. 1983. The Convert as a Social Type. *Sociological Theory* 1: 259–289.

State Committee of Religious Affairs (ed.). 2004. *Interconfessional Bulletin of the State Committee of Religious Affairs.* Tashkent.

Stromberg, P. G. 1993. *Language and Self-transformation: A Study of the Christian Conversion Narrative.* Cambridge: Cambridge University Press.

Sultanova, R. 2005. Music and Identity in Central Asia: Introduction. *Ethnomusicology Forum* 14 (2): 131–142.

Swoboda, V. 1992. Was The Soviet Union Really Necessary? *Soviet Studies* 44 (5): 761–784.

Tabyshalieva, A. 1997. Women of Central Asia and the Fertility Cult. *Anthropology and Archaeology of Eurasia* 36 (2): 45–62.

Tapper, N. 1990. Ziyaret: Gender, Movement and Exchange in a Turkish Community. In D. F. Eickelman, and J. Piscatori (eds.), *Muslim Travellers: Pilgrimages, Migration, and the Religious Imagination,* pp. 236–255. London: Routledge.

Tapper, N., and R. Tapper. 1987. The Birth of the Prophet: Ritual and Gender in Turkish Islam. *Man* 22: 69–92.

Taylor, C. S. 1990. Sacred History and the Cult of Muslim Saints in Late Medieval Egypt. *Muslim World* 53: 72–80.

Taylor, P. 2004. *Goddess on the Rise: Pilgrimage and Popular Religion in Vietnam.* Honolulu: University of Hawaii Press.

Tett, G. 1995. Guardians of the Faith? Gender and Religion in an (ex) Soviet Tajik Village. In C. F. El-Solh, and J. Mabro (eds.), *Muslim Women's Choices: Religious Belief and Social Reality,* pp. 128-151. Oxford: Berg.

Tokhtakhodjaeva, M. 1995. *Between the Slogans of Communism and the Laws of Islam.* Lahore: Shirkat Gah Women's Resource Centre.

Tomlinson, J. 1999. *Globalization and Culture.* Cambridge: Polity Press.

Toulis, N. R. 1997. *Believing Identity: Pentecostalism and the Mediation of Jamaican Ethnicity and Gender in England.* Oxford: Berg.

Trimmingham, J. S. 1971. *The Sufi Orders in Islam.* Oxford: Clarendon Press.

Turner, V., and E. Turner. 1978. *Image and Pilgrimage in Christian Culture.* New York: Columbia University Press.

Tyson, D. 1997. Shrine Pilgrimage in Turkmenistan as a Means to Understand Islam among the Turkmen. *Central Asia Monitor* 1: 15–32.

Umbelino, J. 1999. *Lazer e território.* Lisbon: Centro de EstPlaneamento Regional.

UNDP (United Nations Development Programme). 2005. *Gender Equality in Uzbekistan: Facts and Figures 2000–2004. Statistical Bulletin.* Tashkent: State Committee of the Republic of Uzbekistan on Statistics.

van Bruinessen, M. 2004. Religious Practices in the Turco-Iranian World: Continuity and Change. *ISIM Newsletter* (International Institute for the Study of Islam in the Modern World) 14: 53.

Wanner, C. 1998. *Burden of Dreams: History and Identity in Post-Soviet Ukraine.* University Park: Pennsylvania State University Press.

——. 2003. Advocating New Moralities: Conversion to Evangelicalism in Ukraine. *Religion, State and Society* 31 (3): 273–287.

——. 2004. Missionaries of Faith and Culture: Evangelical Encounters in Ukraine. *Slavic Review* 63 (4): 732–755.

Waters, M. 1995. *Globalization.* London: Routledge.

Werner, C. 1997. *Household Networks, Ritual Exchange, and Economic Change in Rural Kazakhstan.* Bloomington: Indiana University Press.

Werth, L. 2002. Pakistan: A Critique of the Concept of Modernity. In J. Meuleman (ed.), *Islam in the Era of Globalization: Muslim Attitudes towards Modernity and Identity,* pp. 143–170. London: RoutledgeCurzon.

Werth, P. W. 2000. From "Pagan" Muslims to "Baptized" Communists: Religious Conversion and Ethnic Particularity in Russia's Eastern Provinces. *Comparative Studies in Russia's Eastern Provinces* 42 (3): 497–523.

Wilcke, C. A. 2001. Islam im Diskurs – Islam im Alltag: Zur Erneuerung religiöser Ausdrucksformen bei Frauen in Usbekistan. In D. Reetz (ed.), *Sendungsbewußtsein oder Eigennutz: Zu Motivation und Selbstverständnis islamischer Mobilisierung,* pp. 25–53. Berlin: Das Arabische Buch.

Wohlrab-Sahr, M., V. Krech, and H. Knoblauch. 1998. Religiöse Bekehrung in soziologischer Perspektive: Themen, Schwerpunkte und Fragestellungen der gegenwärtigen religionssoziologischen Konversionsforschung. In M. Wohlrab-Sahr, V. Krech, and H. Knoblauch (eds.), *Religiöse Konversion: Systematische und fallorientierte Studien in soziologischer Perspektive,* pp. 7–43. Konstanz: Universitätsverlag.

Yalçın-Heckman, L. 2001. The Political Economy of an Azeri Wedding. *Working Paper* 28. Halle/Saale: Max Planck Institute for Social Anthropology.

Zarcone, T. 1995. Sufi Movements: Search for Identity and Islamic Resurgence. In K. Warikoo (ed.), *Central Asia: Emerging New Order,* pp. 63–79. New Delhi: Har Anand Publications.

——. 2002. Le culte de saints au Xinjiang (de 1949 à nos jours). In T. Zarcone, and E. Isin (eds.), *Saints and Heroes on the Silk Road,* pp. 133–172. Paris: Jean Maisonneuve Successeur.

Zarcone, T., and E. Isin (eds.). 2002. *Saints and Heroes on the Silk Road.* Paris: Jean Maisonneuve Successeur.

Index